THE BEDFORDSHIRE
HISTORICAL RECORD
SOCIETY

THE PUBLICATIONS OF THE BEDFORDSHIRE
HISTORICAL RECORD SOCIETY
VOLUME 69

Hundreds, Manors, Parishes and the Church

A Selection of early documents for Bedfordshire

Edited by
John S. Thompson

PUBLISHED BY THE SOCIETY 1990

ISBN 0 85155 052 5

Cover picture: Harvest scene – said to be Higham Gobion with the Chiltern Hills in the background – by Sylvester Stannard (1870-1951).

Photo typeset, printed and bound by
Stanley L. Hunt (Printers) Ltd, Midland Road, Rushden, Northamptonshire

CONTENTS

ABBREVIATIONS

BCRO	Bedfordshire County Record Office
BHRS	Bedfordshire Historical Record Society
BPSHLA	Bedfordshire Parish Surveys Historic Landscape and Archaeology
LAO	Lincoln Archive Office

SYMBOLS USED IN TRANSCRIPTION

Cancellation	(^{c})
Insertion	(^{i})
Marginal note	(^{m})
Additions by the transcriber	[ ]
Omissions by the transcriber	. . .
Illegible or torn parts of MS	— — —

The transcript of the Eggington Manor Court Rolls needed a slightly more elaborate set of symbols, described in the introduction to the text.

John Stevenson Thompson

Most record offices profit from the work of volunteers, who come regularly to work on aids for readers which the staff would never have the time to provide. Some volunteers work on indexing newspapers, or transcribe from microfilm and then index the nineteenth century census returns. However, those who have Latin and enjoy a challenge, turn to transcribing and translating medieval manor court and account rolls and rentals, for very few readers at a local record office today could attempt to deal with the originals. Staff always try to help a researcher with a particular problem, but they will never have the time to translate the whole of a long document into English. The Bedfordshire County Record Office has been very fortunate in that since 1969 John S. Thompson has been coming in regularly two mornings a week, when free to do so, and has translated many medieval documents from the original Latin, and has also transcribed and typed out sixteenth and seventeenth century material written in English, where the hand is too difficult for the ordinary reader.

For some years before retirement gave John the time to use in this way, Isobel, his wife, had been coming to the Record Office with equal regularity, fitting her work there into a day that included running a house and caring for two children; part-time teaching; indexing and secretarial work; and (latterly) teaching in the children's ward of the local hospital. Her illness and death meant that since 1985 John has come alone.

Both John and Isobel were at Cambridge, John at Clare College where he gained a first in engineering, and Isobel at Newnham where she read French and history, though they first met later at Newcastle. John's career was in aeronautical research, first at Farnborough, and then at the RAE establishment at Thurleigh, which brought the family to live in Bedford. John has a mind that delights in solving puzzles – he was faithful to *The Listener* crossword for many years, not only solving but setting them – and his interest fails if a problem is too simple. However, with Latin learnt at Harrow, an old *Kennedy's* grammar, the *Medieval Latin Word List,* and occasionally a magnifying glass, he passed many happy mornings teasing out the meaning of some much-rubbed court or account roll. Account rolls gave him particular pleasure, for he could here test the arithmetic, and very seldom found an error. He was, naturally, among the first to own a word-processor, and he used it to store his transcripts.

Most of John's work ends as a typescript on the shelves in the Record Office searchroom. However, some of the documents are of such wide general interest as to merit publication, and so this volume was conceived as a tribute to the work done by John and Isobel Thompson over the years for all of Bedfordshire's local historians.

PLB

THE HUNDRED ROLLS
of 1274 and 1279

In 1800 George III appointed a Commission to consider 'The State of the Public Records of this Kingdom, and the Necessity of providing for the better Arrangement, Preservation, and more convenient Use of the same'. These records were 'in many Offices unarranged, undescribed, and unascertained', and were also exposed to the dangers of 'Erasure, Alteration, and Embezzlement' and destruction by damp or fire.

In 1812 this Commission printed and published a transcript of the Hundred Rolls of 1274, containing the evidence obtained by an Inquisition set up by Edward I in that year. The reasons for the inquisition are given in the introduction to the published volume as follows:

'During the turbulent Reign of King Henry the 3rd, the revenues of the Crown had been considerably diminished by Tenants in Capite alienating without Licence; and by Ecclesiastics, as well as Laymen, withholding from the Crown under various Pretexts its just Rights, and usurping the Right of holding Courts and other Jura Regalia. Numerous Exactions and Oppressions of the People had also been committed in this Reign, by the Nobility and Gentry claiming the Rights of free Chace, free Warren, and Fishery, and demanding unreasonable Tolls in Fairs and Markets; and again, by Sheriffs, Escheators, and other Officers and Ministers of the Crown, under Colour of Law.'

A second inquisition of 1279, with slightly different terms of reference, was printed in 1818. The 1274 Inquisition deals with the whole county; what survives of the 1279 Inquisition deals in considerably more detail with the Hundreds of Stodden (with Bucklow) and Willey in the north-west corner of the county.

The texts were printed in 'record type', which reproduces the original Latin manuscript, with special type for the conventional abbreviations. Today very few general readers can translate such a text, and so the English version below has been produced for the use of present-day local historians. The volumes and the pages relating to Bedfordshire are:

> *Rotuli Hundredorum* edited by W. Illingworth and J. Caley, 2 volumes: 1812 pp 1-8; 1818 pp 321-33.

In the translation, some freedom has been allowed when the meaning is quite clear, but when this is in any doubt, the original Latin has been followed as closely as possible. The arrangement of headings and paragraphs has been followed exactly, but additional punctuation is inserted occasionally. In the spelling of proper names, the modern English equivalent has been used for Christian names (as Geoffrey for Galfridus) and also for the Latin names of counties (as Cornwall for Cornubia), but for surnames and other place names, the original has usually been followed, with all its variations. Interpolations in square brackets denote notes, additions, or queries by the translator.

Surnames

In many cases in these documents surnames are not surnames in the modern sense of inherited family names, but second names for identifying individuals by their occupations (sometimes preceded by 'le') or their places of residence (often preceded by 'ad' or 'in'). To ensure consistency such names have not been translated, but the glossaries below give some of the common examples occurring in the text.

Place names

Bedfordshire place names are transcribed as spelt, and a list is appended showing a few of the less easily recognised variants of the modern spellings. Some of these seem to be misreadings of the original manuscript, which have no historical significance.

J.S. Thompson, 1979 and 1980

Glossary of names of occupations

Barker(e)	[?] tanner
Bareman	[?] tenant charged with carrying service
Bercarius	shepherd
Capellanus	chaplain
Carectarius	carter
Carneficus	butcher
Cissor	tailor
Clericus	clerk (cleric)
Cocus	cook
Colearus	[?] charcoal burner
Coterel	[?] mercenary soldier
Faber	smith
Lavendarius	washerman
Marchant	merchant
Marescal	farrier, marshall
Mazoun	[?] mason
Mercer	dealer in textiles
Messer	hayward
Molendarius	miller
Parmenter	tailor
Pester, Pestour	baker
Piscator	fisher
Pistor	baker
Plumer	plumber
Porc'	swineherd
Prepositus	reeve
Presbiter	priest
Sumpter	packhorse-man
Sutor	cobbler
Sutrix	semptress
Vacher	cowherd
Wodeward	woodward

Names from places of residence

in Angulo	in the corner
Bitheree	by the stream
ad Boscum, de Bosco	at the wood
de Cimiterio	from the churchyard
ad Crucem	at the cross
ad Ecclesiam	at the church
ad Fabrem	at the smith
de Fonte	from the well
de Forde	from the ford
de la Huse	by the Ouse
ad Laundres	at the lawn
de Montibus, de Monte	from the hills
de la More	from the moor
de Ponte	from the bridge
ad Pratum	at the meadow
ad Quarrerium	at the quarry
ad Scalam	at the ladder or steps
ad Scalar'	at the stile or footbridge
in Venella	in the lane
in Via	in the road
atte Welle	at the well
ad Wold	at the wold, forest

Variant spellings of some Bedfordshire place-names

Arlesey	Aylrich
Aspley Guise	Aspel
Barford Gt	Bereford
Battlesden	Badesdon
Biddenham	Bideham
Biggleswade	Bikleswade
Bletsoe	Blechesho
Bucklow	Botlone[?]
	Bukkelewe
Bushmead	Bissemede
Chawston	Chalmestern
	Chewketon[?]
Chellington	Chelvynton
Cowridge End	Karench[?]
Eaton Bray	Eyton(e)
Goldenlow	Goldringeshend[?]
Goodwick	Godewyk
Goswell End	Goldringeshend[?]
Herne	Hereu
Higham Gobion	Hetham
Houghton Regis	Houton(e)
Husborne Crawley	Husseborne-Crawel
Ickwell	Gikewell
Kempston	Kimston
Knotting	Gnotting
Manshead	Mannesheved
Marston Moretaine	Merston
Milton Ernest	Middletone
	Midelton
Moggerhanger	Metherhanger
Newnham	Neuham
Oakley	Akle
Odell	Wabull
	Wadhulle
	Wahull(e)
Ramridge End	Ram'dewyk
Riseley	Rise
Roxhill or Wroxhill	Wreschull
	Wrothath
	Wrothushull
Roxton	Rokisdon
Santon	Sun'ton
Shefford	Sepford
Shillington	Suthlingdon
Silsoe	Smellest
Southill	Suthgeinle
Stotfold	Stotfelt
Stoughton Lt	Stouton
Thurleigh	La Legh
Tilsworth	Talesworthe
Tingrith	Tyngri
Turvey	Thorney
Westoning	Weston
Willington	Wyburn[?]
Willey	Wilye
	Wylye
Wixamtree	Wyxconestre
Wootton	Witon
Wrest	Wrast
Wyboston	Wyboldiston

Unidentified place-names

Barwythe	in Studham
Chewketon	in Willey Hundred or Bucklow Half-Hundred
Cotes	in Wixamtree Hundred (?Eastcotts in Cardington) Caldecote in Northill)
Karench	in Flitt Hundred (?Kinwick in Biggleswade Hundred)

HUNDRED ROLLS
Time of Henry III and Edward I

BEDFORDSHIRE

Extracts of inquisitions made by order of the lord King in the counties of Lincs, Oxfordshire, Berks, Bucks, Beds, Cambs, Hunts, Devon and Cornwall, concerning the rights and privileges of the lord King, omissions and excesses of sheriffs, coroners, escheators, and other bailiffs of the lord King, of whatever other officers of whatever kind concerning the lord King, in the fourth year of the reign of King Edward son of King Henry. [1275-76]

Hundred of MANNESHEVED *and half-hundred of* STANBRIGG, *for the King in the county of Bedeford.*

Manors which used to be in the hands of Kings, &c.

They say that Houton was once a demesne of the lord King, and the lord King gave that manor to Hugh de Gurney, and the prior of Dunstaple holds from it one carucate of land from a gift of Hugh himself in alms. Also the same Prior has one piece of land which is called Kingesbyr from a gift of the King. Also they say that the vill of Dunstable was from a demesne of the King which the said Prior has from a gift of the same. Also they say that the heirs of William de Cantilupe hold the manor of Houton as mesne tenants from the heirs of Hugh de Gurney. Also they say Eyton was a demesne of the lord King by escheat, and the King gave the said manor to William de Cantilupe and it is held in chief by one knight's fee, except seven hides from the honour of Wendoure. Also they say that Stanbrigg was once a part of the demesne of Leyton and was held in his hand of the lord King, except half a service of Gilbert de Stambrugg; and he gave the said manor to 'Audusus' de Gatesden by giving four pounds to the monastery of Navenham as King's alms and for the care of two falcons, and it was changed to a 'falcon service' of sixty shillings a year to the Exchequer, and it is held in chief in serjeanty. Also they say that Weston was a demesne of the lord King, and the King gave the said manor to Roger de Sanford and his heirs, and it is held from the lord King in chief, but they do not know by what warrant. Also they say that fifteen acres of land were sold to the Prior of La Grave by John de Gatesden, which used to be from a demesne of the lord King at Stambrigg.

Of ancient suits and customs &c.

They say that 40d was taken away by Paul Peivre and his heirs from the tax liability of Hare. Also 6d was taken away by Geoffrey de Lucy for the same. Also whatever the lord King has at Holecote, except hidage, the Earl of Gloucester keeps, and they do not know by what warrant, and the father of the

Earl kept the same for four years, and that Earl has kept it up to now, but however it is from the fief of the Earl.

Those who claim rights of gallows, assize of bread and ale, &c.
They say that Dunstaple, Houton, Eyton, Totingedon, and other demesnes of the King have these, but they do not know by what warrant.

Of all purprestures [encroachments) &c.
They say that purpresture was made at Goldringeshend on the King's highway by the Prior of Dunstaple. Also Robert de la Mare made purpresture on a certain pond at Saleford, to the detriment of the whole vill.

Of sheriffs taking money for concealment &c.
They say that friends of Robert Travers were imprisoned on suspicion and could not be delivered [from gaol], although they had taken out a King's writ that they should be delivered, until they gave Thomas de Grey the sheriff 20s. Also Roger le Rider and Robert Trone took 5s for the same. Also John Florence was arrested on suspicion, and when he was delivered by a jury he could not be released from prison before he had given half a mark to the same sheriff and half a mark to Henry Trone. And Peter de Northewod took from the same one horse price 7s for the same and Roger le Rider 2s for the same. Also when John Bolte of Houton was released on bail he could not be heard unless he had first given the sheriff 10s.

Those who have received debts of the King or of debts and debtors &c.
They say that Adam de Horewod took from the vill of Holecote 5s for hidage and Ingram Sporun took 2s, and a certain Joppe, bailiff, levied the said 5s, and so the vill paid 12s for 5s. Also Hugh Seyl took 5s from the vill of Saleford and John de Sachenach 4s, and the said vill paid 9s for 4s. Also the same John took from the vill of Herlingdon 3s for head-silver which was formerly paid to Hugh Seyl, and he was not willing to discharge the said vill. Also they say that two thieves were taken at Holecote and kept in custody there for 6 weeks, and through the fault of the bailiffs, namely Randolph de Lechamstede, John de Seyntlburn, and Simon Clerk, they escaped. And nonetheless they distrained the vill for the escape and took 10s, and for respite of having the said money for one week the said John took 2s, and they took from Ralph de Westren 'langroso' [?wool merchant] 4s for the custody of the said thieves.

Of escheators and sub-escheators &c.
They say that master Richard de Clifford, escheator, took 20s from the vill of Eyton unlawfully. The same Richard took hunting rights in the park and fished in the fish-pond. Also Hugh de Eyncourt took 2s unlawfully from the same vill.

Hundred of WYLYE *and half-hundred of* BOTLONE

Of the fiefs of the lord King and his tenants &c.
They say that a certain tenement in Wynnington was at one time in the hand of the King, and William le Mercer and Isolde his wife now hold that tenement from the lord King for half a knight's fee, and they do not know by what warrant. Also they say that Roger de Nowers holds four and a half hides which used to give 9s for hidage, and 2s for view of frankpledge, and the aforesaid service is now withheld, but they do not know by what warrant. Also they say

that Robert de Tinyes holds in Stacheden a third part of one knight's fee from the lord King in chief, from which Robert de Kane holds 57 acres of land, Robert del Hind holds 8 acres of land from it. Also Robert le Rowe holds in Thorney a fifth part of one knight's fee from the lord King in chief, and from it the Prior of St Neot holds thirty acres of land, William de Hetot 40 acres of land, and Ralph de Normanville two acres of wood for a period of thirty years.

Of ancient suits &c.

They say that half of the vill of Thorneye, the vill of Bidenham, the vill of Chewketon, used to sue at the hundred, and [the right] was taken away by Richard Earl of Gloucester. Also they say that the Abbot of Wardon appropriated for himself 6d for a half-virgate of land in Stacheden from hidage belonging to the lord King, and they do not know by what warrant.

Those others who also from the King &c.

They say Baldwin Wake has gallows rights in Sun'ton, Ralph Moryn has gallows rights in Harewude, but they do not know by what warrant. Also John de Wabull has assize of bread and ale in Wahull by a charter of the lord King.

Of privileges allowed which hinder common justice.

They say that the lord King's bailiffs took a felon at Pabenham, and the bailiffs of the honour of Penbrok came and took him by force and held him in their prison for 12 weeks, and then they gave 40s to Thomas de Brey the sheriff to have him in Bedford prison.

Those who have also made new appropriations &c.

They say that John de Wahull, Reginald de Grey, and Ralph Moryn have right of warren by a charter of King Henry, father of the present King, for 30 years past.

Hundred of BEREFORD

Of customary ancient suits &c.

They say that Richard Earl of Gloucester, father of the present Earl, appropriated for himself suits and views of frankpledge belonging to the lord King, for four years before his death, from the vill of Rokisdon, that is, half a mark for view, four shillings for suit per year, from Chalmstern and Colisden 4s 2d for view and suit, and the present Earl has the same privileges, but they do not know by what warrant.

Others who claim from the King to have return &c.

They say that the Prior of Neweham has assize of bread and ale from all his tenants in the same hundred. Also the Abbot of Wardon has assize of bread and ale from his tenants in the same hundred. Walter de Treylley has assize of bread and ale and view of frankpledge in Ravenisden, but for all these they do not know by what warrant.

Those who have made new appropriations &c.

They say that John de Horebury and Beatrice de Bello Campo appropriated for themselves right of warren in Ronale, but they do not know by what warrant.

Of purprestures &c.

They say that in the vill of Wyboldiston in a hamlet called Godewyk a purpresture has been made on the King's highway by Roger Modele. Also they say that in the vill of Bereford John de Bordeleys has totally enclosed a certain road between his curtilage and the bank where all were accustomed to cross on foot and on horse. Also they say that Geoffrey the chaplain made purpresture in Colmworth on the King's highway. Also they say that in the same vill one road called Smithewellestrate is blocked so that nobody can cross there as they used to; first by Richard de Oyldebuf and afterwards by his heirs. Also they say that in the same vill, where all men used to cross, it has been blocked by John Oyldebuff, Ralph the reeve, Thomas Aldren, William le Neweman, and Avis de Cranele. Also they say that Henry Trewe, under-sheriff of Bedford, took 20s from Walter de Stepingle in respite for not having done knight's service.

Hundred of CLIFTON

The jury of that hundred say that the Abbot of Rameseye has view of frankpledge, gallows, assize of bread and ale, and warren, in his manor of Suthlingdon, but they do not know by what warrant. Also they say that the vill of Meperteshale is held in chief from the lord King in serjeanty, out of which the Prior of Chikesand holds four carucates of it, the Prior of Merton one carucate of land, the Prior Hospitaller of Jerusalem one carucate of land, master Roger de Raveningham ten acres of wood, the Abbot of Rameseye six acres of meadow and two acres of land. Alice de Insula holds four and a half acres of meadow and two acres of land. Those tenements aforesaid were held from the lord King in chief, but they do not know how they were transferred nor at what time. They say that Nicholas de Meperteshale holds the rest of the same vill, which is worth a hundred shillings a year, from the lord King in serjeanty from an ancient feoffment by service of one serjeanty in time of war at their own expense for 40 days within the boundaries of England. Also they say that John de Grenhull de Clifton holds half a virgate of land in the same. The Abbot of Wardon holds six acres of meadow and they do not know by what warrant. Also Ives la Zuche holds as mesne tenant one virgate of land from the King belonging to the barony of Eyton, and he has view of frankpledge and assize of bread and ale, but they do not know by what warrant. Also they say that the Abbot of Wardon holds in the vill of Henlawe two carucates of land and a fourth part of the same vill which was taxable to the lord King and now has been taken away by the same Abbot, they do not know by what warrant. Also they say that the Abbot of Wautham has return of writ in Aylrich but they do not know by what warrant. Also they say that Roger le Straunge holds the vill of Scotfeld in chief from the lord King belonging to the barony of Bedford [and] has tithing and has assize of bread and ale but they do not know by what warrant. Also they say that the Prior of Chilkesaund holds in Scotfeld two carucates of land from the barony of Bedford and they do not know by what warrant.

Of purprestures &c.

They say that the Prior of Chikesaund made purpresture by a certain wall built on the King's highway below his priory. Also they say that the same Prior built a certain pond otherwise than he ought by law, by which the King's highway was submerged so that nobody could cross where there was a common road. Also the same Prior blocked the common road in Staundon with a certain ditch, so that nobody could cross where there was a common road. Also they say that John de Breybrok made purpresture at Ram'dewyk by diverting the course of a certain stream, and he appropriated for himself certain ground of the King's highway from Bedfordshire to Hertfordshire so that nobody can hardly go there.

Hundred of WYXCONESTRE

Of customary ancient suits and others taken from the lord King &c.

They say that the Prior Hospitaller of Jerusalem holds half a fee in Gikewell from a gift of William de Holecote and used to make suit to the county and the hundred and now has taken away — — — by the said Prior. Also they say that Paul Peyvre had the custody of Cotes through the lord King H[enry] and before the entry of the said Paul the lord King — — — to have the fines of bread and ale, and now it is taken away and it is not known by what warrant.

Those who claim to have return &c.

They say that Edmund brother of the King has return of writs in Metherhanger. Also they say that Michael Picot and Beatrice de Bello Campo have view of frankpledge and assize of bread and ale in Kerdington. Roger le Straunge holds the regality in Wyburn, but it is not known by what warrant.

Of sheriffs taking gifts &c.

They say that Henry de Basing and Miles his servant took from several men of that hundred much money — — — in a sworn statement of that heading for removing them from the assize. Also Nicholas de Someshorp took from Stephen le Fraunkelyn 9d for the same.

Of coroners &c.

They say that Geoffrey Rodlaund, coroner, took 2s from the vill of Beston before he was willing to see one dead man, and he took 6s from the vill of Wardon for four dead men, and 4s from the vill of Suthgeinle for seeing two dead men, 2s from the vill of Beston for seeing a certain dead man.

Hundred of RADBURNESTOK

Of the fiefs of the lord King, his tenants &c.

They say that Armaric de St Amandus holds from the lord King in chief two knight's fees in Milebrok, and has [right of] gallows, warren, and market, and assize of bread and ale, but they do not know by what warrant.

Of customary ancient suits &c.

They say that William de Valence took away and appropriated for himself the suit of the King in Wrothath, and they do not know by what warrant. Also they say that Richard Earl of Gloucester [came] and threw out the aforesaid William and held [it] for four years and died in possession. And afterwards Alexander de Hamden, then sheriff, came and entered in the name of the lord King and took the rent of one whole year, and the arrears of four years were in arrear in the vill of Wrothushull, and then the present Earl of Gloucester came and threw out the aforesaid sheriff and appropriated [it] for himself, but they do not know by what warrant.

Of suit of hundred &c.

They say that Amaric de St Amandus took away suit of hundred of two circuits per year through Ralph de Merston his steward and appropriated them for his own demesne.

Of all purprestures &c.

They say that Ralph de Merston made purpresture in the vill of Merston between 'le hostierd' and the wood, and Dervorguilla de Balliol made purpresture in the vill of Kemston with a certain ditch.

Of sheriffs and bailiffs &c.

They say that the sheriff of Bedford, Thomas de Brey, was negligent in performing his duty because he did not arrest felons indicted by twelve jurors about a fish pond of Geoffrey Rodlaund. Also Roger le Ryder captured Joseph le Porc' and allowed him to escape for 2s.

Of sheriffs and bailiffs taking gifts for recognisances &c.

They say that Henry Tutprest, bailiff of the lord King, took two pence from Peter Astel to take him away from a certain assize, and so he received money from many others, and he took from the vill of Witon twice for the same.

Those who had imprisoned felons.

They say that John de Lene of Milebrok was indicted by a jury and imprisoned, and Thomas allowed him to go for money which he gave him, but they do not know how much.

Of gifts or money received by officers &c.

They say that Richard son of Richard de Sivelesho, coroner, took 2s from the vill of Milebrok before he was willing to see a certain man who had been killed. Also Geoffrey de Rodlaund, coroner, took 2s from the vill of Amthull for the same, and he took money from many others for performing his duty, as appears in a sworn statement of that county court. Also they say that Rither de Merston, servant of the lady de Wrexhull, Richard le Blount, Richard de Stewll', Alan Pynnak' and Robert Crond' took two mares of Andrew de Mannyngham worth 20s in Suthmade in the fief of the lady de Merston, and led them out of Bedfordshire into Buckinghamshire, and are keeping them up to now. Also they say that John de Schenkeburn, bailiff of the Earl of Gloucester, Henry le Blake & Joppe took five affers on the fief of the lady de Merston and took them on to the fief of the Earl of Gloucester at Wrexhull. Also they say that William, servant of the said bailiff, and Thomas Cotessone took three horses, and John Blanet raised a hue and cry and the men of Merston pursued the hue and cry and they fled and left the cattle and the said men came back with the cattle.

Hundred of STODDEN

Also manors which used to be in the hands of the King &c.

They say that the Prior of Huntingdon holds four hides of land in Den from a gift of William de Meschines who held them from the King in chief, but they do not know by what warrant. Also they say that the lord King Henry, father of the present King, gave the manor of Clopham to Richard Earl of Cornwall, and it belongs to the honour of Wallingford and has there royal prerogative in everything, in chief view of frankpledge, for ten years by the year, and it is not known by what warrant.

Of ancient suits &c.

They say that the Earl of Cornwall took away one mark from the service of the lord King for a period of 15 years, and they do not know by what warrant, and it is from the honour of St Wallerinus and takes return and view of frankpledge.

Of privileges allowed which hinder common justice &c.

They say that the Prior Hospitaller of Jerusalem holds rights at Melcheburn for the official taking of cattle, and they do not know by what warrant or from what time. Also they say that the Templars of Stouton in Melcheburn, Hugh Bossard in Gnotting, and Nicholas Peyvere in Pertenhale had warren and chase allowed to them by the lord King Henry, father of the present lord King, contrary to common liberty, for a period of 20 years.

Those also who are lords or their stewards &c.

They say that Thomas de Brey, sheriff of Bedford, was unwilling to release the cattle of Walter de Horley, taken by master de Melcheburn, although he had a writ of the lord King to release the said cattle, and up to now they have the aforesaid cattle, in default of justice.

Those who call others to military service &c.

They say that Thomas de Brey, sheriff, took 20s from James Grim in return for not having to do military service, and for half a mark which he demanded for the King's service, which as he said was in arrears.

Hundred of FLITTE

How many hundreds &c.

They say that the hundred of Flitt belongs to the manor of Buton [*sic,* probably Luton] and that the lord King Henry, father of the present King, gave that manor to William Earl Marshall the younger with Eleanor his [the King's] sister as a marriage portion, with all appurtenances, saving to the lord 60s per year for hidage, and the same Eleanor now holds it, and they say that she has return and right of prevention of distress, gallows, and assize of bread and ale.

Those who claim return &c.

They say that the Prior of Beaulieu has, in the name of the Abbot of St Alban, gallows and the assize of bread and ale. The Earl of Cornwall claims to have the same rights in Sonedon. Also Fulk Lovel and master Ralph de Emneth, a canon of London, claim to have the same rights in Cadindon, but they do not know by what warrant.

Those who have newly appropriated &c.

They say that Thomas de Scalar' claims warren in Wrast and Smellest' [Silsoe] but they do not know by what warrant.

Of sheriffs and bailiffs taking gifts &c.

They say that Thomas de Brey, sheriff of Bedford, took twenty shillings from

Richard son of William Presbiter who had been summoned for larceny. Also they say that he took half a mark from Nicholas son of Ralph de Martha who had been summoned. They say also that Bartholomew le Jovene took 1 mark from the aforesaid Richard for the same. Also Nicholas de la Penne took two shillings from the same. Also W. Clerk of Smelesh' took ten shillings from the same for having aid. Also the aforesaid Bartholomew took 20s from John de Everwiner because he harboured a certain felon; Nicholas his under-bailiff took half a mark for the same and Walter his servant 2s. Also they say that the aforesaid Bartholomew took 2s from Joan Rut who had been summoned for receiving of larceny.

Of coroners and their clerks &c.
They say that Geoffrey Rodland, coroner, sent Andrew his clerk to make a certain enquiry at Sonedon, and there he took 2s. Also from the vill of Barton half a mark for performing his duty and Andrew his clerk took 2s from the same vill when Richard le Folur gave up his office, and 18d from the vill of Hetham.

Of escheators &c.
They say that master Richard de Clifford took possession of the manor of Karench, in the hand of the lord King, about the feast of Blessed Andrew the Apostle in the first year of the reign of the present King [30 November 1272] and destroyed and partly took in a wood at Everton and fished a pond within the property of the lord King.

Those who by prayer or by price &c.[?]
They say that the same Richard has married two sisters who held from the King in chief, they do not know whether he had a licence from the King or not.

Hundred of BIKELESWADE

How many and what manors the King has &c.
They say that Walter de Huntercoumb' holds half a knight's fee in Wrestlingworth and he says he has a warrant from the lord King, but nevertheless they believe that he does not have a warrant.

Of the lord King's fiefs &c.
They say that Geoffrey Costintin holds half a knight's fee by serjeanty from the lord King in chief, and he has sold the said fee to Alexander de Somersham and Simon Sauvage who now hold it.

Those who have appropriated for themselves hunting rights &c.
They say that Henry de Braybrok has appropriated for himself right of warren in Sotton for 40 years past. William de Beauchamp in Ethon has appropriated for himself warren in Sondheye, Walter de Huntercoumb' at Wrestlingworth, but for all these they do not know by what warrant.

Of knight's fees given or sold &c.
They say that the Prioress of St Helena, London, in the vill of Eyworthe bought two virgates of land from John Gravenel which used to be held from the lord King in chief. Also the Earl of Gloucester came into the manors of Sutton and Potton after the death of Christiana Ledet and had entry through John de Breybrok, and the said Earl and his bailiffs did not allow the lord King's bailiffs to take possession of the said manors for the use of the lord King.

Of whatsoever sheriffs and bailiffs taking gifts for removing recognisances &c.

They say that all bailiffs, in the time of whatever sheriff, have taken gifts from men for removing them from assizes.

Those who deliver to extortionate bailiffs &c.

They say that Bikelswade hundred used to give 20s in the time of sheriff William de Holewell, and increased to 40s in the time of sheriff Alexander de Hamden', to 5 marks in the time of sheriff Bartholomew, and to six marks in the time of Thomas de Brey, and there was no reason for raising the charges except for plunder.

Of coroners &c.

They say that Geoffrey Rodlaund and Andrew his clerk took much money for performing their duty, as appears in a sworn statement under that head.

Vill of BEDEFORD

Manors which used to be in the King's hands, &c.

They say that the ancient borough of Bedeford was in the hands of the Kings of England, and the burghers of Bedford hold the aforesaid borough at a fixed yearly rent, namely for £40 paid to the Exchequer, and for that they have charters of Kings before the present King.

Of ancient suits &c.

They say that the Abbot of Wardon, the Prior of Chiksond', the Prior of Neweham, and the Prior of Caudewell ought to pay suit at the borough court of Bedford and tallage of the King with the burghers for their tenements which they hold in Bedford, and now they have taken away both for the suit and the tallage, to the prejudice of the lord King. Also they say that the tenants of Alexander de Balliol, Richard de Brus, Dervorguilla de Balliol in the suburbs of Bedford used to and ought to pay the lord King's tallage and assize of bread and ale breakage [i.e. loss through breakage of cask] to the burghers of Bedford, and other things belonging to the aforesaid borough which now they withhold and it is not known by what warrant.

Those who claim to have return or extract of writs &c.

They say that the burghers of Bedford claim to have return and extract of writs and pleas for prevention of distress, gallows, assize of bread and ale, and coroners, allowed by Kings of England from ancient custom.

Of purpresture &c.

They say that the Prior of Caudewell appropriated for himself a certain furlong which is within the borough of Bedford between the entrance of Caldewell and Barkedich, which used to be and ought to be common, and now the said Prior and convent make the said furlong private, to the prejudice of the lord King and his burghers.

Of knight's fees given or sold to religious [houses] &c.

They say that the Abbot of Wardon, the Prior of Chikesond, and the Prior of Neweham entered into possession of lands and tenements of the burghers of Bedford to obtain all services belonging to the said tenements except tallage and suit of court.

Those who have received the King's debts &c.

They say that Thomas de Bolton received from Abel Vinetar 100s from a debt of the King, and he has not yet cleared him, because up to now it has come into the Exchequer total. Also they say that two thieves had been taken with two bushels of barley by Ralph the reeve of Kemston William Sirlok' men [of] Dervorguilla de Balliol, who took them in a suburb of Bedford and led them to Kemston, outside the liberty of the burghers of Bedford, and took the said corn from them and made the said thieves escape, to the prejudice of the burghers. Also they say that the water which reaches from Bedford bridge up to the house of Neuham used in ancient times to be in the demesne of the lord King, and afterwards belonging to the borough of Bedford, from which Roger Extraneus [the stranger] holds part of that water, but it is not known by what warrant.

Vill of LUTON

The jurors of that town say that lord King Henry, father of the present King, gave the manor of Luton with the hundred of Flitte to William Earl Marshall with Eleanor his [the King's] sister as a marriage portion, which the said Eleanor now holds from the King in chief, saving to the lord King for the said hundred 60s per year. Also they say that Fareleye was once in the demesne of Luton and was given to the house of Suntinggefeld as free alms, but they do not know by what King, and the master of Suntingefeld' now holds it from the King.

Those who claim to have allowances &c.

They say that the aforesaid Eleanor claims to have return of writs and assize of bread and ale, pleas for prevention of distress, at the manor of Luton.

Roll of the hundred of MANNESHEVED *and half-hundred of* STANBRUGG

From an enquiry made by Peter de Tyngrye, John Poleyn, John de Seybroc, Geoffrey de Flitten, John son of Gilbert de Stanbrugge, Hugh son of John of the same, Steyn Wicum de Tulesworthe, Richard Sporon, Roger Pirot, Richard of the hunters de Eversolt, William atte Welle de Toternho, Peter Peverel de Eytone, Walter de Botesford, Nicholas Blaunfront, John de Cobelington, Robert de Linleye, William Underhill, William de Sevenhiden, Gilbert le lord of Talesworthe, on articles given to the same by lord John of Kirkeby. Who say on their oath as is contained below.

MIDELTON [MILTON BRYAN]

On the first article, that is of exchequer tallies and other tallies against various sheriffs, they say that they know nothing except of these which were given by the roll.

Also, of debts made two or three times &c. they know nothing.

Of vills &c. all things are written below.

Of knight's fees, there are two knight's fees there, one of the barony of Beuchamp which lord Roger le Estrange now holds from the heir of Robert Bryan, according to English law as though in tenure, which fee is held from the heirs of Beuchamp, and they from the lord King, and there is given 10s for hidage to the lord King, 5s for suit and ward, 3s for view, 2s for beaupleader [a fine for amendment of plea]. Also they say that Alexander de Hameldene, once sheriff of Bedford, first levied for beaupleader, and before nothing used to be given for beaupleader.

Also they say that there is there another fee, namely a fee of Rouecester, by which the Abbot of Woburn holds two hides of land from William de Optone. And the same William holds from the barony of Rouecester, and the barony from the lord King. Also John de Eversolt holds one hide of land in the same vill from the said barony and the barony from the lord King. Robert de Herlingedon holds one hide of land from the said barony and the barony from the lord King, and he pays annually to the lord King 8s for hidage, 2s for suit, nothing for ward, 12d for view, 2s for beaupleader, which beaupleader indeed Alexander de Hamelden the sheriff first levied. And each fee is taxable.

Also for sheriff's circuits they say that the sheriff makes his circuit as he should, and makes amends when corrections are needed at any time, except for brewers who ought to undergo statutory judgment for the same, and they certainly do not procure anything for money. Also they say that they give a fixed payment for view, namely 28s for hidage, suit, and view, besides the beaupleader which is 4s, but they do not appear in person.

Also, concerning proceeds of forfeitures they say that Gilbert de Lithegrave had been hanged, and his chattels had been delivered to the court in the last circuit, namely 5s, but how much the said court paid to the lord King is not known.

Of the county rents nothing certain can be known except what is presented and which vills, as appears in the rolls. Also from enquiries we have heard that the bailiff of the hundred of Manneshεved and the half-hundred of Stanbrugg used to give half a mark for the bailiwick, and this in the time of William de Holewell, then sheriff, and now William le Porter gives six marks for the bailiwick, and so did his predecessors, namely Roger le Rider and others afterwards from the time when Hugh de Stapelford was sheriff.

HERLINGTONE

The lord Ralph Pirot holds the aforesaid vill for one knight's fee from lord Almeric de Seint Amand, and lord Almaric from the barony of Caynho and the barony from the lord King, and he pays annually 10s for hidage, half a mark for suit and ward, half a mark for view, 10s for beaupleader, and Alexander de Hamelden levied beaupleader unlawfully as it is said, and it is taxable to the lord King in all things.

Also, concerning the sheriff's circuits and the rents of the hundred they say as next above. Also Roger Pirot paid Hugh de Stapelford, then sheriff, half a mark in equal parts and had two tallies for them. Also Walter Frebern had two tallies for having writs, and they were accidentally burnt.

TOTERNHO

They say that the lady Millicent of Mohaut holds the aforesaid vill. Roger de Weltone at one time held it for a fee and a half from the barony of Wodhull for homage in the time of King John, and then it was taxable and from it the lord

King received annually 20s for hidage, and all the free tenants paid two suits at the hundred of Mannesheved at the sheriff's circuit, and the lord King has all the amercements concerning his crown. Afterwards William de Cantelou was the old steward of the lord King and bought the said homage from the barony of Wodhull, which homage Roger de Weltone used to pay for the said vill of Toternho to the aforesaid barony of Wodhull; in fact the said William de Cantelou converted the said vill into a liberty, but it is not known in what way or by what warrant, and all his successors since then have held it in the same state up to now. Also John de Castretone, who is now the steward of the said lady Millicent, changed the customs of the aforesaid vill to bad practices by holding the aforesaid hundred from three weeks in three weeks. Also the men of the said vill used to elect for themselves a constable by common consent for making arrests where necessary, namely for hue and cry or bloodshed and for those [offences] which pertain to the crown. The same constable in the course of his duties sometimes places other offenders under pledge and with good sureties that they will come to answer at the next hundred; and if it happens that the said offender does not come, then the same steward of his own will and judgment may amerce the said constable and does not allow bail, and this is often exacted without lawful assessment. Also the said steward, when it happens that men of the said vill ought to be distrained, then he makes them drive their affers from one liberty to another, namely from the barony of Wodhull to the barony of Wendove. Also the said steward does other injuries, namely that whereas the tenants and men of the said vill used to be amerced at 6d before judgment and 12d after judgment, the same steward, by his own will and authority, amerces them at half a mark and sometimes more. Also he has increased the rent of the said vill beyond what it used to pay annually by half a mark, by converting that half mark to rent owed, by what law or for what reason is entirely unknown. Moreover the same steward amerces men without assessment, outside the court in camera, by his own will.

EVERSOLT

Of all tallies for debts made two or three times, and for sheriffs' circuits for view, they say as above at the beginning.

William de Leycestr' holds one virgate of land in the same vill from the lord King in chief, paying for it annually 4s to the lord King, which the sheriff received annually. The Abbot of Woburn holds in the same vill seven hides of land and three virgates from John de Horebury from the barony of Bedford for two marks to be paid to the aforesaid barony, and it is taxable. Also two hides of land are held in the same vill by many mesne tenants from the fief of Roucestr' and each fief pays 19s 6d for hidage, 9s for suit and ward, 7s for view, to the lord King, and 10s to the sheriff for beaupleader, which used not to be paid before the time of the abovesaid Alexander. Also they say that at one time Juliana, daughter of Roger Preston at Eversolt, was taken and kept in chains by J. de Chenee, sheriff, and he received from her twelve sureties up to the next county court, and before the day of the county court peace was made, but what she paid or how much is not known because the negotiation was done in secret, without the vill or the sureties, but she had never been delivered by a jury.

SALEFORD WITH HOLECOTE

They say that Saleford and Holecote used to be taxable to the lord King in all things, afterwards Richard de Clare Earl of Gloucester, through Walter de Bridentone his bailiff, separated Holecote from Saleford by appropriating the sheriff's circuit, for which the said vills paid annually 20s for hidage, 9s 8d for suit and ward, 6s 6d for view. Saleford for itself pays the sheriff 4s for beaupleader, and this through the abovesaid Alexander. John de Saleford holds one knight's fee in Saleford from John de Steyngreve and the said John from the lord King. Saleford for itself, for sheriff's circuit and view, presents the same as Middelton above at the beginning. Also the lady Mabel de Holecote holds one knight's fee in the same vill from Ralph de Beuchamp of Etone and the same Ralph from the lord King.

Chapel of WOBURN *with* BIRCHEMORE

For tallies of all kinds and for debts two or three times, they say as above in the beginning.

Also that the Abbot and convent of Woburn have the chapel and the aforesaid free vill from the lord King, confirmed with the same appurtenances, and they have a market on Friday and a fair on three days a year, with the liberties and appurtenances appertaining to the same, and they hold the abbey estate of Woburn with the chapel and all its appurtenances and privileges in pure and perpetual alms from the Earl of Oxford, the founder of the aforesaid Abbey, confirmed by the lord King. Also they say that the tenants of the lady Millicent de Mohaut hold three virgates of land in Birchemore and the lady Millicent holds from the lord King, and it is a liberty from time immemorial. Also they say that John de Chenee the sheriff took from Roger Brixy and Mabel his wife 20s in respect of their not having been in chains up to the day of gaol delivery, and since then they have found bail with sureties and they have been cleared afterwards by a jury.

HOCCLIVE

About tallies, all and singular, they say as at the beginning of the roll.

They say that the vill of Hocclive is held from the barony of Beuchamp de Bedeford, and that barony is held from the lord King, and it is held by one knight's fee and a quarter, and it lies with 11½ hides of land with Edwoldeswowe and pays 23s 6d for hidage. Also 4s for suit. Also 2s 8d for ward. Also 6s for view of frankpledge. Also 6s for beaupleader, and this unlawfully, because they never used to pay this except in the time of Alexander de Hamelden, and it is taxable to the King in all things, and the lord William de Monchensy holds the said vill now in keeping.

STANBRUGG

They say about tallies as above.

Also they say that lord John de Gatesdene holds the aforesaid vill from the lord King in serjeanty in chief, by paying £3 a year to the exchequer of the lord King and £3 to Neweham in alms of the lord King, nothing else to be paid to the lord King.

ASPEL

They say about tallies, all and singular, that they know nothing except about these which are given in the roll.

Also about debts two or three times &c. they know nothing.

Also they say that the vill of Aspel is a liberty by a charter of the lord King, acquired by lord Hubert de Burgo and confirmed by lord Henry the former King of England to Anselm de Gise, who now holds the same vill with appurtenances from the heirs of the aforesaid lord Hubert, and the said heirs from the barony of Bedeford and so from the lord King, and it is held for the twentieth part of a knight's fee.

About other articles or headings they know nothing, except that the vill has been a liberty from of old from time immemorial.

CHALGRAVE

They say about tallies as next above.

Also they say that lord Peter de Loreng holds the whole vill of Chalgrave with Humbrich for 7 hides of land from the barony of Bedeford, and the barony from the lord King in chief, and it is taxable. Also they say that the Prior of Dunstapel holds three virgates of land from the same hides and pays 14s hidage for the whole vill. He retains suit, it is not known by what warrant. The Abbot of Woburn holds one virgate of land from the same hides and used to pay external service and now pays none, it is not known for what reason. Also Thomas Ordwy and Ralph Ordwey hold one virgate of land in Chalgrave which used to be taxable before the time of Paul Peyvre, and at the time of the said P. it was changed to a liberty but it is not known in what way. Also William Glasney was a thief and a fugitive whose goods and chattels were valued at 17s 8d, and Richard Grocet received all the money. And the first[?] of the last justices, namely Roger de Seyton, Hugh de Stapelford sheriff, levied the said money from the said vill of Chalgrave, contrary to justice. Also it pays 18s for suit and ward, half a mark for view, and 4s to the sheriff for beaupleader contrary to justice, and this from the time of Alexander de Hamelden. Also they say that forty shillings was exacted unlawfully from John Poleyn, which a certain John Poleyn, who died before the aforesaid present John was in being, received as a loan from the lord King John over Berhamdoune, from which 40s a jury lawfully cleared and completely acquitted the present John and through four enquiries in the time of King Henry and also of the present King E.

WESTONE [WESTONING]

They say about tallies and other debts as above in the beginning of that roll.

Also Weston is held from the lord King, and a lesser bill of right is sued for there. Also they say that the lord King John conferred that manor on William de Boklond as a liberty paying no service at all to the lord King, no more than that the lord is to come before the itinerant justices on their first arrival and four men with the reeve. Also in the time of the said King John the aforesaid manor came to him. The same lord King conferred it on William de Boclond. Afterwards in the time of King Henry and the said John men used to work in the autumn for only three harvests, on which days they had to be supplied with food and drink at the lord's table, one day eating fish and the other two days eating meat. Afterwards William de Boclond increased the said service, and for it he provided for one day of harvest at the lord's table. Afterwards Hamon le Crevequer held the said on the same terms all the time. Also William de Averenge, who held the said manor, continued that service all his life, neither increasing nor reducing it. Also the said manor then came into the hands of John Tregoz, who increased the aforesaid service to such an extent that there are now 10 labour services made in autumn at his table. Also besides that labour service there was exacted from the aforesaid men one waterbedripe, and it was made and then they drank water, and this was first introduced by the aforesaid Hamon. In fact the aforesaid manor is now in the hands of Robert Burnel, who holds it on the aforesaid terms, that is to say as he found it. Also they say that the above-mentioned Hamon sought from the aforesaid men, when he had come from Wales, a subsidy of two marks which he had as a free gift of the same [men], which money indeed all the successors of the same H. have received up to now by coercion and extortion, and that money is recorded as if rent. Also they say that men who are sokemen and were in the time of the aforesaid Kings, when their sons and heirs ought to succeed them in inheritance, and used to do nothing else for their tenement except to enter the inheritance immediately by paying heriot, now they are not allowed to do so except completely at the lord's will, and this first by the said H. and then successively up to now. Also Robert de Worthinge, Matilda daughter of William, John Muriel, John son of Gilbert, Peter Pras, Robert Harding, John ad Gravam, say that they do a carrying service unlawfully, because in the time of the said King they used to do nothing at all, and this through the said Hamon and so successively at the will of the lords. Also Walter Sweyn says that he does a certain service unlawfully, that is by carrying capons, chickens, hens, and other things at the lord's will beyond thirty miles, also by driving the lord's cattle wherever the lord wants, and this through the said Hamon. Also they say that a boonwork used to have victuals in food and drink for four days of the year, that is Christmas, All Saints, Easter, and Whitsun, and in autumn for all the days of the harvest; the boonwork now indeed has nothing from it, and this through John Tregoz. Also they say that the sellers 'venditores' of wood who have been appointed by the lord, as long as they continue selling in this way, ought to be maintained by the lord in victuals; now they are kept neither in victuals nor in other allowances, and this unlawfully by the Bishop of Bath. Also they say that they used not to pay pannage unless the men's pigs were pastured in the lord's wood; now it is demanded from them by force and extortion to allow their pigs to remain at home, viz ½d for a yearling pig and ¼d for a pig of half a year, and this through William de Bocland. And the aforesaid sokemen can, however, plead a bill of right in the said manor to be freed, but only in the presence of the court when need shall arise for the sokemen, from time immemorial. Also they say that the sokemen paid for the default of the lord John Tregoz because he did not come nor appear before the court in circuit in Bedeford as he ought to do, 40s for an unlawful payment. They received a tally which Peter Bernard took away from them, for which they seek the said 40s to be returned to them. Also when all the said sokemen are obliged to pay two marks annually for tallage conjointly and not separately, one or two of them having been discharged by the lord of the manor from the aforesaid payment, nevertheless the whole entire sum is exacted from and levied on the remaining men. Also they say that the bailiff of the manor makes a circuit once a year as is right, and amendments are made for transgressions proved, except for brewers, who ought to undergo the judgement provided and ordained for such things, and they do not make that judgement, rather they sell it for a sum of money. Also they say together that the bailiffs of the manor amerce men at their will and not according to the assessment nor the amount allowed for the crime. The assessors are chosen for this, and this is done under cover and in camera unreasonably many times, and this through John Tregoz. Also they say that a view of frankpledge is held on Tuesday in Whitsun week, and then the holders of land will come in person and pay nothing in money, and absentees who do not hold land send money and are discharged. Also they say that the manor is held by charter, and as they believe from the lord King in liberty.

EYTONE [EATON BRAY]

They say that the lady Millicent de Mohaut holds Eytone for one knight's fee and a quarter, and it is held from the lord King in chief by a charter of the lord King J. and confirmed by the lord King H., for which nothing has to be paid to the lord King except one knight's service in war when it happens, and an exchange was made between the predecessors of the aforesaid lady M. and the lord King J. of England, and it is a liberty of which the status is not changed. Also they say that Thomas Hoxemere paid Bartholomew le Jevene, then sheriff, half a mark for a fine for one tally which he had from the same B. after [or 'afterwards'] the said tally had been lost, and this can be decided by a jury, and nevertheless the said Thomas paid the aforesaid half-mark to lord Ralph de Goldintone, now sheriff, for one and the same reason.

Of the sheriff's rents [corpus comitatum] they know nothing. Nor of the profit of the same.

Of the circuit: they make a circuit twice a year, and fines are made as fitting. Also men are amerced by assessment as the assessment is held.

Of other articles: nothing.

POTESGRAVE

They say that the vill of Potesgrave is held by one knight's fee and a quarter, and Robert Blanfront holds two parts of that fee and Edmund Everard holds a third part of that fee. Also Robert Savage and Ralph le Savage hold a fourth part of the said fee, and the whole fee is held from the heirs of lord Geoffrey de Lucy, and the heirs themselves hold from the Earl of Gloucester and the Earl from the lord King. And the Abbot of St Alban holds one hide of land and a half and a fourth part of a virgate of land in free alms from the said Earl and thus from the lord King. Also the Abbot of Woburne holds one hide of land in the same way from the said Earl in the same vill, and it is a liberty in everything except scutage when it occurs, and this from antiquity. They do not know if it was done by a charter of the King, and this from time immemorial. Also Edmund Everard holds one virgate of land which is from the fief of Beuchamp and he pays 6d for hidage for the same land to the lord King, and the heirs of the said G. de Lucy have all the privileges pertaining to the lord King, that is of view.

Of other things they know no more.

TALESWORTH

They say of tallies as in the first roll.

Also of debts twice or thrice &c. they say the same as before in the first roll.

They say that the vill of Talesworth is taxable and pays 20s a year for hidage. Also half a mark for suit and ward. Also 10s a year for beaupleader from the time of Alexander de Hameldene, sheriff of Bedford, and before his time they used to give nothing, and the said vill is held by one knight's fee, viz a portion of the lord John de Morteyn with two hides within-written, and the same John holds the said vill from lord William de Morteyn and he himself from the lord King. Also William Ambroys holds two hides of land from the aforesaid John and it is soccage. Also they say that the bailiff of the hundred used to give only two shillings for his bailiwick and now gives six marks, and this is through various sheriffs. Also that William Sprot received from the whole vill 13s 8d for hidage, view, suit, and ward in the time of John de Chene, then sheriff, and nevertheless Ralph de Coldington [sic] the present sheriff had the aforesaid money raised by William le Porter his bailiff and paid in full. Also they say that John de Stivenech, bailiff of Hugh de Stapelford, made a levy of 16s 8d from the aforesaid vill for a debt of the lord King, which money in fact Nicholas de Henescomp, bailiff of the same Hugh had received before and made a levy.

Of other things, nothing.

HUSSEBORNE-CRAWELEY

They say about tallies and debts as above.

Also they say that the whole vill contains one knight's fee and a half, of which Denise de Crawel holds one and a half hides from John de Northwode, Gilbert de Northwod and Henry his brother hold one and a half hides of land from the same J. and the same John holds from lord Robert son of Walter and lord Robert from the heirs of Pinkeney and they from the barony of Caynho. The Abbot of Thorney holds one hide of land from the abovesaid lord Robert, and the aforesaid R. in the way aforenamed, and it is taxable in everything and it is from the fief of Macy. Also John de Northwode holds in tenantry one hide of land from the same fief, and the same John from the Hospitaller of Herdewyk, and it is not known by what warrant they hold, and from it they have view, and the tenants of the said John are allowed in all markets and fairs by the privilege of the Hospitallers and they carry their signs. The Prior of Dunstapel holds in the same vill two and a half hides of land from the fief of Albemarl. Also Bartholomew de Flittewyk holds two and a half hides of land from the same fief, from which the Prior's part was owed for a privilege, that is of bread and ale and view, and the whole vill paid 18s for hidage, except that hide of land which is said to be the privilege of the Hospitallers, also from the fief of Macy 2s for suit and ward, also 6s a year for beaupleader from the time of Alexander de Hamelden and before they paid nothing, also 21d for view of frankpledge. They say also that the sheriff makes his circuit annually, and no fines are imposed for infringements of bread and ale presented to him.

Of other articles, nothing.

TYNGRI

They say that lord Robert son of Walter holds a moiety of one knight's fee from the heirs of Pinkeney, and the said heirs from the barony of Caynho and so from the lord King, and it is taxable in all things to the lord King. Also Peter de Tyngr' holds land from the Hospitallers in the said vill which is not assessed for hidage and is a liberty in all things. Also amends are made there for offences as in the county court. Also the fief of the lord Robert pays twice a year 43d for hidage and 2s for suit and ward. Also 4s for beaupleader in the aforenamed way, 2s for view. Also concerning circuits made, they are made twice a year as they should, but offences are not corrected; men are indeed heavily fined, but no amendment is made. Also they say that Adam Mansel and Peter Randulph have brewed, each of them once, and their goods had been burnt, and nonetheless Hugh de Stapelford the sheriff fined them 4s without assessment, and they only brewed three quarts. Also they say that William Est, on account of a certain allegation, was arrested and held in chains, and when he ought to be imprisoned at Bedford Hugh de Stapelford, then sheriff, on the pleas for intercession of certain people, dismissed and completely acquitted him for 2s. The same William was of good repute, but he had never been freed by a court.

Of other articles they know nothing.

STODHAM

They say about tallies and debts as above.

Also that the vill of Stodham was once held from John Mareschall in barony, and the same John held from the lord King, also after the death of the said John it was transferred to the hands of the lord King, and it is taxable. It used to pay only 4s a year for view at the 'great hundred' [sheriff's circuit] and for all other things of that kind, then Alexander de Hameldene the sheriff increased it to 6s beyond those four shillings, and all other sheriffs from that time up to now have taken those 6s with other four, whence 10s are paid altogether where only 4s used to be given. Also Walter de Botelesford now holds the vill of Stodham and Bareworthe as one vill, that is Stodham of Bedeford and Bareworth of Hertford, and they are held as two fiefs, except five virgates of land as scutage. Also the said Walter holds from the heirs of the said John Mareschall and they from the lord King. Also the bailiffs of Mannesheved used to give only half a mark for the bailiwick; now they give six marks for the same. Also the sheriff makes a circuit as he ought, above, and similarly for corrections as is noted above. Also the Prior of Dunstaple with his tenants has in the said vill of Stodham four virgates of land and a half and a quarter and a fourth part of a quarter, and from that they have view, but it is not known of what kind.

Of other headings they say that they know nothing.

TODINGEDONE

They say that the vill of Todingedon is an ancient liberty from time immemorial and they have 'infongenthef and outfongenthef' [the right to judge thieves within or without their territory] and John Peyvre holds the said vill from the Earl Marshall by paying to the same 100s annually for everything, and it is free soccage, and the Earl maintains against the King a share of the barony of Newebury.

HAREU [HERNE]

They say that there are there 5 hides of taxable land of the barony of Chaworthe and it used to give 10s a year externally, now it only gives half a mark for which the Abbot of Woburn is answerable. A third part remains in the hands of John Peyvre as a liberty, which liberty Paul Pevre acquired in the time of King Henry and it belongs to his manor of Todingedone. And the part of the Abbot of Woburn pays 2s for suit and ward, 2s for view, and 2s to the sheriff for beaupleader from the time of Alexander de Hameldon.

Of all other things, nothing.

And it should be known that in all the articles or headings given it was not possible to enquire carefully; it is allowed that some of the vills were investigated twice, but it is not implied to them that any of the said vills which had presented for one day in all denied for the greater part, led by what spirit or even frightened by fear is not known.

BADESDON [BATTLESDEN]

They say that the lord King Henry had the same vill and gave it to Warin son of Gerard. After the death indeed of the aforesaid Warin, William Talebot entered the said vill but it is not known by what right. Afterwards, William Talebot having died, the Earl of Gloucester came into possession of the same vill, and this before the time of war and it was then taxable. Now indeed it is changed into a liberty but they do not know by what warrant. Also they say that the said vill is held by one knight's fee, of which Nicholas Fermbaud holds in fief and inheritance three virgates and a quarter of land from the heirs of Ralph Passelewe, and for the term of his life four virgates of land from the same heirs, and the said heirs from the Earl of Gloucester and the Earl from the lord King. Thomas de Brikulle holds seven virgates of land in the same vill, of which he holds two and a quarter virgates for himself and his heirs and all the rest for the term of his life, and he holds from Baldewin de Belony, and the same B. from the heirs of Ralph Passelewe, and the said heirs from the Earl of Gloucester and the Earl from the lord King. Also the circuit is made there as is fitting, and offences which are proved are severely punished but are not amended, and amercements are made at will without assessment. Also they say that William Chamberleyn paid to Hugh de Stapelford the sheriff forty pence for which he had tallies, and nonetheless William Bicok clerk of the lord Ralph de Goldington the sheriff made a levy from the same of another 40d for the same reason. Also they say that it used to give four shillings for everything, now it gives 32d for beaupleader, contrary to justice. Also William Chamberleyn holds half a hide of land from the Abbot of St Alban in pure and perpetual alms.

Of other articles they know no more, except that they say that the vill used to give 4s for everything and the lord used to have all the rest. Also the Earl's bailiffs, where they have only one view, then hold all pleas there, transferring there suits begun at another court, namely Stivecle in Buckinghamshire.

HOUTONE NEAR DUNSTAPLE

They say that the said vill was once a manor of the lord King Henry the elder. The said King gave the whole of the said manor to lord Hugh de Gorney for his services and by his charter, as the lord King held that manor. The same Hugh held the whole manor from the said King in chief, and held the said manor with the barony of Gobney [sic] from the King for service of one knight's fee. The same Hugh gave a certain part of the said manor, worth £30 a year, as a dowry to Millicent his daughter who from a gift of the lord King John had been espoused to lord William Cantilupe as mesne tenant. Also the said Hugh gave to lord Richard de Weavile for his service the whole service and rent of 13 virgates of land 13 acres of meadow for a service of half a knight's fee, and it is worth £8 10d a year. And the lady Millicent de Mohaut now holds the aforesaid part of £30 from lord William Bardulf as the heir of the said William de Cantilupe, and Henry de Wevile holds the other part of £8 10d from the said William Bardulf as from the heir of the said Hugh de Gorney because he had espoused his daughter. And the said William Bardulf held them from the King as the said Hugh used to hold, nevertheless the said Millicent de Mohaut and her successors retained for themselves all the rule of the whole manor from the time when the wife of the said William Bardulf was a ward of the lord King Henry son of King John. Also they say that the customary tenants of Houtone before the time of lord William de Cantilupe were able to lease their lands to men of Dunstaple without objection and other interference, but on account of a certain contention aroused between the towns because the men of Dunstaple beat the men of Houton, therefore William de Cantilupe took and held the produce of the men of Dunstaple which they had rented from the men of Houton until each of them had paid 12d, and up to now that payment of the said 12d has remained and continued, to their great damage. They say also that the vill of Houton used to give on the day of the view in each year 10s for the chapter without having to appear and for absentees so that they should not be penalised while they were proved to be innocent, now the said 10s is recorded and registered as if rent, and they do not serve as deputies of the vill because John de Castreton, steward of the lady M. de Mohaut, nonetheless continued the causes and imposed heavy fines on tithingmen for being absentees, and wished that everyone should be present on the day of the view, or that they should come to the next court wherever they might be, in service or elsewhere, even if they were beyond the sea, or else be fined. They say also that a suit had been brought between the Prior of Dunstable at that time, who was the plaintiff, and Hugh de Gorney the younger, tenant of the whole manor of Houton, who had agreed in the court of the lord King that the said Hugh conceded to the said Prior one carucate of land of the said manor in pure and perpetual alms. After the said agreement the said Prior acquired for his house two hides of land and one half-virgate of land, that is one hide from William de Linleye and one hide and half a virgate from master Simon Robelyn, who for the whole time used to answer with the vill of Houton before the court in circuit in fines and all suits pertaining to the said vill, which the Prior and convent had made in the same way up to the court in circuit of master Roger de Seyton and his fellows, but from that time they have withdrawn themselves up to now, and they claim franchise through a charter of the lord King which they say they have for everything acquired in pure and perpetual alms, and the said town at the said time had been amerced before the aforesaid judges for evasion at 100s, and the money had been collected in parts and extents of lands, and the said Prior ought to have paid 10s for part of the said hides and he is not willing as he formerly used to be, and therefore they make the demand on the vill. Also they say that the vill of Houton was amerced before the aforesaid judges for evasion at 100s, of which the vill paid £4 10s, and there remain arrears of 10s which the Prior and convent of Dunstaple ought to pay for the portion of two hides of land and half a virgate newly acquired as stated above. Also, concerning John Spongebolle, 16s 8d was paid for a certain misfortune because a cart with two affers ran over a boy. Also 4s 6d was paid for the chattels of John de Westfeld, a felon. Also 6s 8½d for the chattels of John de Cimiterio [of the graveyard], a fugitive, and 48s 1¼d for the chattels of Joan wife of John Clarice. Also they say that John de Castreton, steward of lady Millicent de Mohaut, said that he wanted to hold the grand court on the day of St Matthew the Apostle [21 September] before the feast of Michaelmas in the 11th [sic] year of the reign of King Edward [1283], and the vill answering said that it was not usual to hold this before Michaelmas but after. And he said: I pray you, out of respect and love for the lady, that you may be willing to hold that court then without any objection, because I cannot make any delay in those parts, and when I am away I do not know when I shall come back. They indeed did not consent but disagreed, and this for the reason that the neighbours who owed suit had received no summons and thus could be fined. And he replied in this way: I shall not exercise the right to hold the court in such a way, nor do I wish that anyone should be punished on account of absence. Indeed the tenants who were present at the court in the aforesaid form had held the court because of respect. But the same steward fined all the absentees who owed suit after Michaelmas as if the said court were held after Michaelmas, hence John Manasse, Thomas Pictor, and many others were fined.

Of other articles they know nothing.

BAILIWICKS

All the vills of the hundred of Manneshevеd and the half-hundred of Stanbrugg were accustomed from of old to give as rent for the bailiwick only half a mark in the time of Simon de Holewell', and now they give 6 marks and they have no bailiff's headsilver nor courtesy of goods, hence the district is owed much and can hardly raise the lord King's money.

Memorandum which the bailiffs of the several hundreds of the county of Bedford answer concerning the sheriff's headsilver for their hundreds for raising which they have no headsilver, neither for perquisites nor for courtesies of various things such as sheaves, hay, and suchlike. Also the aforesaid bailiffs do not hold courts in their hundreds. That was found from the depositions of the several hundreds.

HUNDRED ROLLS
COUNTY OF BEDFORD

Inquisitions made on behalf of the lord King in the county of Bedeford in the seventh year of the reign of King Edward I [1278-79], both concerning the domains of the lord King and estates, fees, escheats, liberties and things concerned with the fees and holdings of the lord King, and also of any others whomsoever, and those who hold in demesne as in demesne, in villeins as in villeins, in serfs as in serfs, in cottars as in cottars, and also in free tenants as in free tenants, and in woods and in parks, in chases, and in warrens, in waters, in riparian rights, and in all privileges and fairs, markets, and other tenures of whatever kind and in whatever way, and from whom, whether from mesne tenants or from others, and from what fees and other tenures scutage is usually given and ought to be given, and how much from fees of honours of whatever kind, and who hold these fees, how much and in what way and from what time.

Of the hundred of STODDENE: *of privileges and tenures*

CLOPPAM John le Brun holds in the vill of Clopham in chief from the Earl of Cornwall and he from the King, from the honour of Walingford.

Of which he has in demesne one carucate of land which comprises 120 acres of land, 6 acres of meadow, 1 ancient park of 22 acres and 2 parts of a private fishery in his pond. In villeinage, 3½ virgates of land of which each is worth to him 16s a year or works to that value, and the tenants of these are serfs bound to redeem their tenure at the lord's will. The names of the tenants: Walter the reeve holds ½ virgate of land; Richard Liteman ½ virgate; William de Billinge, ½ virgate; Richard son of Adam, ½ virgate; Robert Gotyme, ½ virgate; William Neuman, ½ virgate; Henry Warin, ½ virgate.

In free tenants for fixed yearly services, namely: Henry Wygeyn holds 1 virgate of land for 12d; Gilbert Quadruns, ½ virgate for 6d; Richard le Espenser, ½ virgate for 2s; Geoffrey Pistor, ¾ virgate for 6s 5d; Ralph son of Robert, 1 quarter for 2s 8d; Walter de Monte, 1 quarter for 2s 6d; John le Ku of Clopham, 1 quarter for 2s 3½d; John Piscator, ½ quarter of land and common fishing from Middleton Mill as far as Halywell, except fishing in the pond, for 5s; Alice Scot, 3 acres of land for 11d; Sabina and Hawis Burgeys, 3 acres of land for 11d; William son of John, ½ acre for 4d; John Pout, ½ acre for 14d.

John de Burneby holds in the same vill in chief from the aforesaid Earl of Cornwall and the Earl from the King, from the aforesaid fee and honour. Of which the same John has in demesne ½ carucate of land which contains 40 acres of land, 3 acres of meadow, 1 wood of 15 acres. In villeinage, 2½ virgates of land, each of which is worth to him 16s a year or works to that value, and the tenants of these are serfs bound to redeem their tenure, whose names are:

Henry son of the reeve, ½ virgate; Richard Burnthard, ½ virgate; Adam West, ½ virgate; Walter Bertram, ½ virgate; Robert Pikel, ½ virgate; Alice Hoppere, ½ virgate.

In free tenants for fixed services per year: Gilbert le Ripere, 1 virgate of land, 1 wood of 1 acre, for 7s; John de Cissenerne, 1 messuage for 12d; Walter son of Walter de Monte, 1 messuage for 1¼d; Bertha de Rakelintone, 3 roods for ¾d.

Ralph de Wedone holds in the same village in chief from the aforesaid Earl and the Earl from the King for the said fee and honour.

Of which the same Ralph has in demesne ½ carucate of land which contains 40 acres of land, 3 acres of meadow, 1 wood of 15 acres. In villeinage: 2½ virgates of land, each of which owes him 16s a year or works to that value, and the tenants of these are serfs bound to redeem their tenure, whose names are: Richard Brese holds ½ virgate; Reginald Waryn ½ virgate; Walter Bretsel ½ virgate; Robert Brese ½ virgate; Robert Waryn ½ virgate.

In free tenants for fixed services per year: Emma le Bayhus holds ½ virgate of land for 3s; Henry le Bayhus ½ virgate for 3s; John de Eissenerne 1 messuage for 12d; William son of John a fourth part of 1 messuage for 2½d.

Walter Burdun holds in the same vill in chief from the said Earl and the Earl from the King, from the said fee and honour. Of which the same Walter has in demesne ½ carucate of land which contains 40 acres of land, 3 acres of meadow, 1 wood of 15 acres. In villeinage: 2½ virgates of land, each of which [owes] him 16s a year or works to that value, and the tenants of these are serfs bound to redeem their tenure at the will of the lord, whose names are: John West ½ virgate; Thomas Cotwaleys ½ virgate; Richard West ½ virgate; Simon Modi ½ virgate; Robert le Hoppere ½ virgate.

In free tenants for fixed services per year: John Piscator holds ½ virgate for 13d; Bartholomew de Raklintone 3 roods of land for ¾d; Juliana Peket 1 messuage for 2s; William son of John for part of one messuage 2½d.

Simon de Bayhus holds in the same vill in chief from the Countess of Aumarlye [Albemarle] and she from the Earl of Cornwall and the Earl from the King, from the honour of Walingford, half a knight's fee, and for so much it is assessed for scutage.

Of which the same Simon has in demesne 1 carucate of land which contains 120 acres of land, 8 acres of meadow, 1 wood of 40 acres, common fishing from Akle church to Oliver's ditch. In villeinage 6 virgates of land, each of which is worth to him 20s a year or works to that value, and the tenants of these are serfs bound to redeem their tenure at the will of the lord, whose names are: Henry Est holds ½ virgate of land; Simon Clay ½ virgate; John son of Richard ½ virgate; Roger son of Ralph ½ virgate; Roger West ½ virgate; Henry de Bereford ½ virgate; Roger of the same ½ virgate; Ralph of the same ½ virgate; Nicholas of the same ½ virgate; Henry de la Grene ½ virgate; Robert West ½ virgate; Richard Yngus ½ virgate.

In free tenants for fixed services per year: Ralph son of Robert holds 1 virgate of land except 4 acres for 9s; John de Bayhus 1½ virgates for 6d; John H'visius of Middleton 1 virgate for 1 lb of pepper; Gilbert le Ripere ½ virgate for 20d; Ralph Est ½ virgate for 5s; Henry Abel ½ virgate for 18d; Henry le Bayhus ¾ virgate of land, 1 wood of 10 acres, for 6d; John Cocus of Clopham 1 quarter 3 acres of land for 3s 4d & 1 lb of cummin; Wimecote Schatergod 1 quarter for 2s 6d; Richard Manypeny 1 quarter for 2s 6d.

And all the aforesaid tenants of the said honour give 4s a year for view of frankpledge.

AKLE Richard de Borard holds in the vill of Akle in chief from Robert le Ros and Robert himself from the King, from the honour of Beuver, 3 hides and a third part of a hide, and for so much it is assessed for scutage at ward of Beuver castle, 3s 4d a year to the sheriff for the use of the lord King, 8s a year for hidage, 3s for view of frankpledge. Of which he has in demesne 2 carucates of land which contain — — — acres, 8 acres of meadow, a wood of 16 acres, 1 watermill, a private fishery from Benerey to the aforesaid mill, common fishing from Middleton mill as far as Cothemannesholm. In villeinage 5¼ virgates of land, each virgate is worth to him 20s a year or works to that value, and the tenants of these are serfs bound to redeem their tenure at the will of the lord, whose names are: Roger de Canceler holds ½ virgate; John Marescall 1 quarter; Roger Fader 1 quarter; Hugh Caunceler 1 quarter; Richard de la Stile 1 quarter; Roger Ace 1 quarter; Henry Carectarius 1 quarter; Thomas Coterel 1 quarter; Henry Messer 1 quarter; Juliana Abbot 1 quarter; John Coterel 1 quarter; Simon Udeline 1 quarter; Richard en le Venel 1 quarter; Walter Bercarius 1 quarter; Gilbert Prepositus 1 quarter; Robert in Venell 1 quarter; Henry Brid 1 quarter; John Brid 1 quarter; Henry ad Fabrem 1 quarter.

In free tenants for fixed yearly services: Richard son of Ralph, Alice in Venella & Matilda hold ½ virgate for 2s; William Thurstans ½ quarter for 2s 4d; Alice Brok ½ quarter for 10d; Roger de Wilye ½ quarter for 2s.

MIDDELTONE John son of Roger Hervisius holds in the vill of Middeltone in chief from the Hospitallers of Jerusalem for 10s a year, and the Hospitallers from the King, 2½ hides and 1 virgate of land. The same John holds in the same vill in chief from Henry de Grey, and Henry himself from the Earl of Leicester, and the Earl himself from the King, from the honour of Leicester, 1½ hides and ½ virgate of land and for so much it is assessed for scutage. Of which he has in demesne: 1 carucate of land which contains — — — 13 acres of meadow, 2 woods of 12 acres, a third part of a fishery from Humberdale stream as far as the top of the pond at Middeltone mill.

In free tenants for fixed services per year: the Abbot of Wardone holds one mill for 7s and 'free toll'; also the same Abbot holds ¾ virgate of land in pure and perpetual alms; the Prior of Caudewelle ½ virgate of land, 6 roods of meadow, for 3 masses celebrated each week of the year for the souls of the ancestors of the said John; John Marescall 1 virgate of land, 3 acres of meadow, for 12d; William Babhe 3¼ virgates of land, 6½ acres 1 rood of meadow, a wood of 8 acres for — — —; William Rokle ½ virgate 2½ acres for 5s 2d; Robert de la Perere ½ virgate for 4s; Philip Canet ½ virgate for 2s 1d; William Frankeleyn ½ virgate for 12d; Robert de Camera 1 quarter for 2s; Robert Kuku 1 quarter for 2s; Thomas son of Richard 1 quarter for 2s; William son of Robert ½ virgate for 4s; Geoffrey Pistor ½ virgate for 2d; Roger de Wilye 1 quarter for 12d; William Bole 1 quarter for 3s; Robert Coleman 1 quarter of land for 2s; Robert Rolle and Mabel Rider 1 quarter for 2s.

Robert de Camera holds in the same vill in chief from Henry de Grey, and he from the Earl of Leicester and the Earl from the King, from the honour of Leicester 1½ hides and ½ virgate of land. Of which he has in demesne 1 carucate of land which contains — — — 10 acres of meadow. In free tenants for fixed services per year, namely: the Abbot of Wardone holds 3 quarters of land for

5s; John son of Roger Hervis' ¾ virgate of land for 12d; William Eschirmisur 1½ virgates of land for 5s; John son of Hugh Ribel ½ virgate for which nothing is paid except scutage.

William Basset holds in the same vill in chief from John de Stengrave, and John from the King, from the barony de Bello Campo of Bedford, 2 hides of land, and for so much it is assessed for scutage. To the sheriff for the lord King's use, 3s 9d a year for hidage, 2s for view. Of which he has in demesne 1 carucate of land which contains — — — 6 acres of meadow, a third part of the fishery from Humberdale to the pond at Middeltone mill. In villeinage: 3 virgates of land, each of which is worth to him 20s a year or works to that value, and the tenants of these are serfs bound to redeem their tenure at the will of the lord, whose names are: Simon Tot 1½ virgates; William Bok ½ virgate; William Mumpeyler ½ virgate; Simon Lenok ½ virgate; Walter Noreys ½ virgate; Richard Wrythere 1 quarter.

In free tenants for fixed yearly services: Robert Kincus 1 quarter for 18d and 2 capons; Richard Dreu 1 virgate for suit; Robert Rolle and Mabel Ridere 1 quarter for 2s.

Roger de Wilye holds in the vill of Middeltone in chief from the lord King ½ virgate of land in serjeanty.

William de Lega holds in the same vill in chief from John de Wahull, & John from the lord King 2 hides of land, and for so much it is assessed for ward of Rokingham castle, 2s 9¾d. Of which he has in demesne ½ carucate of land which contains 80 acres of land, 14 acres of meadow, a wood of 12 acres, and a third part of the fishing from Humberdale to the head of the pond at Middeltone mill. In villeinage, 1 quarter of land which is worth to him 5s a year or works to that value, and its tenant is a bondsman bound to redeem his tenure at the will of the lord, whose name is Adam Thurgis. In free tenants: the Prioress of Harewold holds 3 quarters of land for scutage given to her in the time of the last King Henry; Mauger de Northwode 1 virgate of land for which he pays no fixed annual rent; Mabel Riper 1 quarter; William son of Robert Gilbert 3 quarters; William Bole, Robert Kincus & Simon de Cayno hold 1 virgate of land for suit of court.

RISLE The Prior of St John of Jerusalem holds in the vill of Risle 1½ knight's fees in pure free and perpetual alms from the gift of a certain Alice de Clermund in the time of King John, and it is held in chief from the Earl of Gloucester, from the honour which is called de Gloucester, and the Earl himself holds that holding in chief from the King. He pays no service to the King yearly except foreign service, for which 1½ knight's fees the said Prior has the church of that vill of Risle, which is situated in that fee, for his own use, with 25 acres of land and one messuage from which that church is endowed, which the vicar of the same Prior of that church holds in demesne. Also the said Prior has from it in villeinage ½ virgate of land which John Espey, his bondsman and a serf bound to redeem his tenure at the will of the said Prior, holds for 10s a year or for various works to that value.

Also Walter son of Geoffrey de Risle holds thence from the said Prior 4 hides of land in which are contained 16 virgates of land for 16s 5d a year, suit of court of Melcheburne, for all services. Of which he has in demesne 10 virgates with 30 acres of wood. In free tenants for fixed yearly services: Ralph in Angulo with his tenants, 1 virgate for 3s, and he does fixed works to that value; also Mancerus de Pentelun ½ virgate from the same Walter for 18d; also William le Forester from the same Walter, ½ virgate for 5s; also Richard de Halm from the same Walter, ½ virgate for 3s and fixed works in ploughing, harrowing, scything and reaping to the value — — — per year and suit of court; also Joan le Neuman 1 quarter of land from the same Walter for 2s for everything; also John Cuntesse 1 quarter from the same Walter, with his lesser tenants, for 4s for everything; Reginald de Grange 1 quarter from the same Walter for 2s and fixed works to the value, 3 hens, 1 loaf, and 20 eggs a year; also Richard in Prato 1 quarter from the same W. for the same service; also Ralph Bareman 1 quarter from the same W. for the same services; also Randolph ad Scalam 1 quarter for 3s, hens, bread, and eggs, as the aforesaid Ralph Bareman; also Walter Gunnild 1 quarter of land from the same W. for 2s and other services like the aforesaid Ralph; also Nicholas Cocus 1 quarter free for 3s a year and suit of court for everything; also William Pati ½ virgate of land for 3s for everything; also Adam Hebert from the same Walter, ½ acre for 6d and suit of court; also Walter Fiz' 1 messuage for 12d, 2 hens, and fixed works to that value; also William in Prato, 1 cottage for the same service; also Elias Wnwyne 1 cottage for the same service; William Ry 1 cottage for 6d for everything; Wiliam Mori 1 cottage for the same service; William Bondi 1 cottage for 16d for everything; John Heyrun 1 cottage for 12d to the said Walter and suit of his court and [to] the Hospitallers of Melcheburne 1 lb of wax a year; Hugh de Monte 1 cottage for 12d and suit of court of the said Walter; John Ward 1 cottage for the same services and 6 [sic] to the aforesaid Hospitallers for fixed works; also William Halleberewe 1 cottage for 12d for everything; John Pese 1 messuage with a croft for — — — Faucus — — — for 1d and fixed works to that value — — — per year; Robert Mok 1 cottage.

Also in addition William Laurence holds in the same vill from the said Prior Hospitaller from the said fee 2½ virgates of land for 7s and suit of court of Melcheburne for everything. Of which he has in demesne a chief messuage — — — of land and 10 acres of wood. In free tenants for fixed annual services: John Sopbert with his lesser co-tenants, ½ virgate of land for 12d and fixed works to the value — — — per year; Walter son of Geoffrey with his tenants ½ virgate of land for 18d for everything; Also Mauncerus de Pentelun, 8 acres for 2d for everything; Thomas son of Hugh, 2 acres for 12d for everything; John de Tichemers, 1 cottage for 1 acre of wheat; Also Emma daughter of Walter Gorri, 1 cottage for 6d for everything; Randolph ad Scalam, 1½ acres for 1d; Walter Ace 1 messuage 4 acres of land for 2s for everything; Simon Mort and Robert de St Botolph, 1 cottage for 8d and 3 capons for everything; Walter Goderiche, 1 messuage and ½ acre of land for 2s a year for everything.

Also in addition William Babbe holds in the same vill from the said Prior from the said fee 1 messuage and 1 virgate of land for ½ mark a year for everything. Of this he has in demesne — — — . In free tenants for fixed annual services: Walter Trayly with his tenants ½ virgate; Reginald de Clopham 1 messuage 7 acres of land for 20d and other fixed services to the value - - - per year; Also John Humfrid' 1 messuage 3 acres of land for 2s and other fixed services to the value — — — per year; Also Walter Godriche 1 messuage 6 acres of land for 2s 6½d for everything; Also Hawis' Humfrey 1 messuage and 1 acre of land for 3s for everything; Also Henry Gundi 1 messuage for 14d for everything; Also John le Knit 1 messuage for 12d for everything; Geoffrey Murt 1 messuage for 14d for everything.

Also in addition Hervic de Risle holds in the same vill from the said Prior and from the said fee 1 virgate of land with appurtenances for 12d a year.

Also Roger Poynere in the same from the same Prior and the same fee ½ virgate with appurtenances for 15d.

Ralph Knyt in the same from the same Prior and the same fee 1 quarter — — — for — — — .

Thomas Rabi 1 virgate of land with his tenants for 2s 8d and suit of court of Melcheburne yearly and other services in ploughing and reaping in harvest to the value.

And it should be known that all the tenants of the said Walter son of Geoffrey, William Laurence, William Babbe, Hervic' de Risle, and other tenants of the said Prior and of their tenants owe various services, in ploughing and reaping corn and such, according to the portion of their holding, to the said Prior, for rights of common and for having free entry and exit in the woods and lands of the same Prior, except the term.

In the same vill of Rise, Simon de Pertesseye holds a certain holding in chief from William de Monte Canis through his wife from William de Bello Campo of Bedford and he from the King, on which holding he is assessed for 2 hides and to the sheriff for the use of the King 9s a year for hidage, 2s for view of frankpledge, and suit of court of the said William and his wife, of which the said Simon with — — — .

Of customary privileges in vills and holdings in the hundred of WILYE *and the half hundred of* BUKKELEWE

WAHULLE John de Wodhulle has a market on Thursday every week, right of warren, with other privileges at the aforesaid market according to a charter of King Henry son of King John, as it is said.

HAREWOLD John de Grey has in Harewold [trial by] fire and water, 'infongindethef' [right to arrest a thief on one's land], and all others which belong to the Crown, because the said vill is of the honour of Huntyngdone, with view of frankpledge and others belonging to it, and gallows, levied at most within 12 years last past &c.

HYNEWIC Walter de Trayly from the tenants of his fee which he holds from the Earl of Gloucester in the hamlet of Hynewik in Podintone, has view of frankpledge by permission of the said Earl. In the same hamlet of Hynewic the Prior of the Hospitallers of St John of Jerusalem has view of frankpledge and everything that pertains to the view from all the tenants of Simon de Bray, for 7 virgates of land, by what warrant it is not known.

WYMINTON The heirs of George de Cantelun have view of frankpledge and all others pertaining to it from Roger de Noers and his tenants of one knight's fee from the barony of Wahulle, which is taxable, by what warrant it is not known.

SULDROPE The prior of the Hospitallers of Jerusalem has in the same way view and all that pertains to it from all his tenants in Suldrope and elsewhere within the aforesaid hundred wherever they may be, by what warrant it is not known.

SARNEBROC The Master of the Temple of Jerusalem in the same way, in Sarnebroc and elsewhere, from all his tenants wherever they may be, has view and what pertains to it, like the aforesaid Hospitallers. In the same [vill] in the same way the Prior of Neuham has view from all his tenants, by what warrant it is not known, but the fee of the farm is from the honour of Buloyne.

LA LEYE [THURLEIGH] The Earl of Cornwall has view and all royal rights and all that pertains to them from the tenants of the fee of Walingford in La Leye.

STEVENTON & PABENHAM Baldwin Wake has in Steventon from all the tenants view of frankpledge and every royal right which pertains to fire and water and 'infongingethef' &c. by what warrant it is not known, since the whole vill is from the honour of Boluyne. Also he has gallows rights newly raised, that is within 12 years last past, and right of warren by a charter of King Edward. In the same vill of Pabenham the Earl of Gloucester has view and every royal right from John Daberun and all his tenants, by what warrant it is not known, but the fee is from the honour of Penbrok.

CHELENTON Walter Trayly has view and royal rights in Chelentone, which is from the Earl of Gloucester by a charter of the Earl of Gloucester within 24 years last past, from the lord King through the said Earl, the brother of Richard, father of Gilbert de Clare.

TURVEYE BIDENHAM Also the said Earl has view and every royal right from all the tenants of his fee which the said Walter Traly and his tenants hold in Turfeye and Bideham, occupied within the said time.

STACHEDEN William de Monte Canis holds view and every royal right from all his tenants in Stachedene, who are of the barony de Bello Campo of Bedford, and it used to be taxable, by what warrant it is not known.

These refused to answer and obey the precepts of the lord King and his ministers concerning their holdings and privileges, namely: William de Monte Canis de Edwardestone and all his tenants in Stachedene; also all the tenants of the fee of Gloucester in Turveye; also all the tenants of the Hospitallers in Suldrepe.

In the county of BEDFORDSHIRE. *Of the hundred of* WILYE *and the half-hundred of* BUKKELOWE

Of holdings and privileges

SHARNEBROC The Prior of Neuham holds in Scharnebroc a certain holding which is not assessed for hidage nor fee, from the honour of Buluyne in free, pure, and perpetual alms, from the gift of Baldwin Tryket and Simon his son and heir in the time of King John. Of which he has in demesne the chief messuage, 180 acres of land meadow and pasture, 10 acres of enclosed wood, a fishery in the river called Owse in common from Pinch mill to Stoke mill and from Sculteleye to the head pond of Pinch. In cottages: William Hegge holds 1 cottage at the will of the Prior for 2d a year. The aforesaid Prior has privilege, view of frankpledge, and pays nothing to the lord King because it is the honour of Buloyne.

The Abbot of Leicester holds the church of that vill for his own use with 20 acres of land, 4 acres of meadow, 4s 2d of annual rent for certain lands and tenements as below from the gift of the aforesaid Baldwin Triket in pure and perpetual alms given in the time of King John. The tenants of the same Abbot: John son of Alexander, ½ virgate of land with his tenants of it for 18d; Robert de

Alsey with his tenants, ½ virgate for 20d; Richard de Ripa 8 [sic] for 4d; Robert de Toft, 1 acre for 4d; Nicholas Clericus, 1 acre for 4d a year.

Peter Gregory holds from the aforesaid Prior of Neuham 1 quarter of land for 2s a year; John son of Alexander 1 quarter for 12d with John son of Peter who holds from the same John 5 acres for 6d; Robert de Alsey 1 quarter 1 rood from the same Prior for 20½d with his tenants who hold from the same, namely William Gery 1 plot for 6d, William son of Milo' 1 plot for 12d, Geoffrey Brutun 1 plot for 12d; John Manypeny 1 quarter from the aforesaid Prior for 5s, with his tenants; Bilehalt with his lesser tenants ½ quarter for 25d; Sybil Clevehog with her tenants 1 quarter for 5s; Robert Peytevyn 1 quarter for 18d; William Gery 1 messuage 4 acres of land for 3s 4½d; William Wrench 1 messuage 4 acres for 4s, with his lesser tenants; Robert de Toft 1 messuage 1½ acres for 6d; Nicholas Clericus and Isobel his wife 1 messuage for 8d; Nicholas Cok 1 messuage for 12d; Emma Smot 1 messuage for 4d; Ellen Pentyn 1 quarter for 10d; Robert Bacun 2 acres of land for 12d; William son of Henry 1 acre for 6d; Henry de Scarnebroc 2 acres of land 3 roods of meadow for 5d; The Templars of Jerusalem 1 messuage 9 acres of land for 2s; Walter de Chatur 5 acres for 9d; William Faber 1 messuage for 12d. The Templars of Jerusalem 10 acres in free alms given in the time of King Henry son of King John.

Peter de Loring holds 1 hide of land in the same vill, from the barony of Bedford, in chief from W. de Monte Canis through his wife, and W. himself from the King, for 1 hide at scutage to the sheriff annually, 2s for hidage, 2s for view. Of which he has in demesne 77 acres of land, 5 acres of meadow and separate pasture, 4 acres of enclosed wood. In villeinage 1 virgate & ½ quarter of which a virgate owes him [amount of money omitted] or works to the value, and the tenants of these are bondsmen, and serfs by blood bound to redeem their tenure at the will of the lord. These tenants are: Robert le Bonde who holds 1 quarter of land; Richard son of William the Reeve 1 quarter; Robert Warner 1 quarter; Thomas Renie 1 quarter; Matilda Wyot 1 quarter; John le Tenur 1 quarter.

In cottages on the same conditions: Robert Berard 1 cottage for 2s or services to that value; William Durant half a cottage for half a service.

In cottars who are not serfs but tenants at rent: Beatrice Burry 1 cottage for 20d; Matilda Warner 1 cottage for 18d.

In free tenants: John son of Alexander holds ½ virgate of land 2 acres for 2s and 1d for everything except foreign service, as much as belongs, with his tenants, namely Philip Spink 1 messuage for 12d, Robert de Alsey 1½ acres and ½ rood of meadow for 2d, with other lesser tenants of the said ½ virgate; William Pippin 1 messuage and ½ quarter from the said Peter for 9d; Robert de Toft from the same, 8 acres of land 1 acre of meadow for 12d; William son of Lyfyne 8 acres of land and ½ acre of meadow for 12d; Richard son of William with his lesser tenants 8 acres of land and ½ acre of meadow for 12d; Robert de Broc 1 messuage for 2d; William Gery 5 acres for 4d; John Manypeny ½ acre for 1d; Thomas Chepman 1 acre for 3d; Nicholas le Keu 1 acre for 3d; Walter Bars ½ acre for ¼d; John le Caracter 1½ acres for 3d; William Bory 1 rood for ½d; Robert Wyot 1 acre for ½d; Sarah de Stanburge 1 messuage 3 acres for 12d; Philip Spinc 1 acre for ½d; William le Taylur 1 acre for 1d; Agnes le Chatur 1 acre for — — — ; Robert de Stanbruge 1 acre in the same for 2d.

Helen de Pentyn holds in the same vill from the said barony of Bello Campo in chief from William son of Pagan, and W. himself from Roger de Mumbray.

And R. himself from the King, which he holds for one hide assessed to him for scutage and sheriff's fee, 2s a year for hidage, 2s for view. Of which she has in demesne 20 acres of land, 2 acres of meadow and pasture. In free tenants for annual service: William le Child with his tenants, 1 virgate for 6s; Richard de la Grene with his tenants, half a virgate for 4s 6d; Reginald Gobiun with his tenants, 1 virgate for foreign service, as much as belongs; William de Fulbek with his tenants, 3 quarters of land as a marriage portion, of which John Andreu with his tenants holds half a virgate from the same William for 8s; Simon Pope 1 quarter from the said Helen for 2s and 2 suits of court; Laurence Cole half a quarter for 12d and 2 suits of court.

In other lesser tenants: William Gery 6 acres for 12d; John Manipenyn, 1 messuage 2 acres for 15d; Richard Manipenyn, 1 messuage for 12d and 2 capons; John Clock, 1 messuage 2 acres for 14½d; Richard Stinkel, half a virgate for 6s and 2 suits of court; Nicholas le Ken, 2 acres of land and half an acre of meadow for 6d and 2 suits of court; Margaret Pipe, 1 messuage 4 acres for 27d and 2 suits of court; Robert Wiot, 1 messuage and ½ acre for 4d and 2 suits of court; William son of Michael, 1 messuage for 16d; Matilda Thorustan 1 messuage for 12d and 2 capons; William son of Henry, 5 roods of meadow for 8d; Robert de Ponte, 1 messuage for 16d and 2 capons; William Durant, 1 messuage with a croft for 1 pound of wax; Adam Hereberd', 2 acres of land for 1d; Robert le Chepman, 1 acre for 1d; William Clenehog, 1 acre for 1d; Richard de Ripa, 3 roods of meadow for ½d; John Neve, 1 rood for 2d; Thomas Chepman, [blank] and a half for 1d.

The Templars of Jerusalem hold from the same Helen from the said hide 22 acres of land 3 roods of meadow in free and perpetual alms given in the time of King Henry son of King John.

Henry de Bosco holds in the same vill from the said barony de Bello Campo of Bedford in chief from John de Pateshulle. And John himself on behalf of Roger de Mubray who holds in chief from the King, for part, that is, which Roger Lestrange holds through his wife a certain holding for half a hide at scutage and sheriff's fee, 12d a year for hidage, 12d for view. Of which he has in demesne 2 virgates of land. In free tenants: Richard le Neve, 1 quarter of land for 12d; Ralph de la More, 1 quarter for 12d; John son of Michael, 1 quarter for 6½d; John Manypeni, 1 quarter for 6s [sic]; John Gery and Walter de Baggenho, 1 quarter for 8½d; Thomas Greneslone, 1 messuage for 12d; Alice daughter of Michael, 3 roods for 3d.

Richard de Ripa holds in the same vill half a hide of land from the barony of Wahulle in chief from Reginald de Grey, and R[eginald] himself from John de Wahulle who holds the said barony in chief from the King and is assessed on scutage for half a hide and against the Sheriff 12d a year for hidage, 12d for suit, 12d for view, 3s for ward of Roginham Castle. Of which holding he has in demesne 1 virgate and half one quarter.

In free tenants: Laurence Cole, 1 quarter for 3s a year; Robert Sirecok, 1 messuage for 2s 8d; Nicholas Carpenter, 1 cottage for 18d; Nicholas son of Bele, 1 cottage for 8d.

The Templars of Jerusalem hold in the same vill a certain holding not subject to hidage or fee, from the fief and honour of Gloucester given by a certain Alice de Clermund in the time of the old King Henry the father of King John in free, pure, and perpetual alms, and pays no service to the lord King nor to another, and has free view of frankpledge from his tenants. Of which he has in demesne

60 acres of land. In villeinage 1½ virgates. In free tenants: John le Child with his tenants holds 1 virgate of land for 6s a year; William son of Henry with his tenants, 1 virgate for 18s; William Alexander, 1 virgate for 14s; William son of John, 1 quarter for 3s 6d; Richard Faber, 1 quarter for 9s; Robert Mercato, 1 messuage for 2s 5d.

Also the Templars hold in the same vill 26 acres of land and 6 acres of wood from the gift of a certain Richard Traysi in the time of King John, from the same fief of Gloucester.

Also the Templars hold in the same vill, in a furlong called Alfey, 27 acres of land and meadow; it is not possible to enquire by what tenure fief or barony. [footnote: 'to be investigated']

COLWORTHE hamlet John Druel holds in Colworth hamlet of Scarnebroc of the barony de Bello Campo of Bedford in chief from William Fruel through his wife and he himself from the King half a hide of land, and for so much he is assessed for scutage and sheriff's fee, 12d a year for hidage, 2s for view. Of which he has in demesne 300 acres of land, 3 acres of pasture, 8 acres of wood. In villeinage 2 virgates of which each owes him 20s a year or services to that value, and the tenants of these are bondsmen bound to redeem their tenure at the lord's will: Walter Mende, who holds half a virgate; Robert Bonde, half a virgate; William son of Adam, half a virgate; Richard Figel, half a virgate.

In cottars, bondsmen in the same condition, 3 who hold 3 cottages each of which owes him 18d a year or works to that value.

In free tenants: Simon de Toft, who holds ½ virgate and 4 acres for 11s, suit of court, and foreign service; Richard de Fonte with his tenants, ½ virgate for 10s & works worth 8d, suit of court and foreign service; Geoffrey de Gotesho, 1 quarter for 1 horse bridle, suit, & foreign service; Robert le Sotele with his tenants, 2 messuages, 6 acres, 1 hedge, for 2s 6d, 2 capons, ½ lb of pepper, suit of court and foreign service; John Canal, ½ quarter of land for ½ lb of pepper, suit of court and foreign service; William Canal with his tenants, 1 quarter for 4s 6d, suit, & foreign service.

BLECHESHO John de Pateshulle holds in Blechesho from the barony de Bello Campo of Bedford in chief from Roger le Estrange on behalf of Roger de Monte Canis who holds in chief from the King, a holding which is assessed for 1 knight's fee for scutage and sheriff's fee, 6s a year for hidage and 22s 8d for everything else. Of which he has in demesne 4 carucates of land which contain 320 acres of land, 10 acres of meadow, 5 acres of pasture, 20 acres of wood, 4 water mills, a private fishery in the river Owse from the head mill pond at Stoke to Humberdale, a fishery in the mill pond of Pinch to the pond of Stoke and from Humberdale to Pabenham lake. In villeinage, 6 virgates of land, each of which owes him 20s a year or works to that value, and the tenants of these are bondsmen bound to redeem their tenure at the lord's will, whose names are: William the reeve ½ virgate; John son of Faber ½ virgate; Simon son of the reeve ½ virgate; Ralph son of Simon ½ virgate; Hugh Craule ½ virgate; Simon Welsche ½ virgate; Ralph son of Robert ½ virgate; Hugh son of Peter ½ virgate; Hugh son of Elyenor ½ virgate; Ralph Tuneman ½ virgate; William son of Henry & Richard son of Hugh ½ virgate; Reginald Lestrange & Nicholas son of Ralph ½ virgate; Hugh son of Simon & Margery Cok ½ virgate.

In cottars, 8 in the same condition who hold cottages, one cottage each, and each owes the lord 28d a year or works to that value.

The same John is the patron of the church of the said vill, and the rector of the church holds 1½ quarters of land with which the church is endowed, and it has a tenant: Stephen Carneficus, who holds 1 messuage for one lamp burning in the aforesaid church. The same John has in free tenants: Nicholas Derebout with his tenants, who holds 2 virgates of land for 5s a year, suit of court and foreign service; Nicholas Friday, ½ virgate for 6s 6d, suit of court and foreign service; Hugh Pippard with his tenants, ½ virgate for 2s 5d, suit & foreign service; Michael Lestrange with his tenants, 3 quarters of land for 8s 7½d, suit of court and foreign service; William de Brunesfeld through his wife, 1 quarter for 3s 10d, suit and foreign service; Robert son of William with his tenants, ½ virgate for 4s ½d, suit of court and foreign service; Walter Gerenys with his tenants, ½ virgate for 7s, suit of court and foreign service; Richard Faber, ½ virgate for 2s, and he does the ironwork for 6 of the lord's ploughs per year; Nicholas Capellus, 1½ virgates for religious celebration for the souls of the lord's ancestors and descendants; Hugh Caru with his tenants, ½ virgate for 2s, suit & foreign service; Hugh de Pabeham, 1 quarter for 4s, suit and foreign service; Simon de Caynho, 1 quarter for 10d, suit and foreign service; Nicholas Spink with his tenants, ½ virgate for 1 lb of pepper; Stephen Spinc, 1 quarter for — — — ; Joan Tuneman with her tenants, ½ virgate for 5s, suit and foreign service; William Waryn with his tenants, 2 virgates for 5s, suit & foreign service, of which Nicholas de Bolnho holds ½ virgate for — — —, William de Bolnho with his tenants, ½ virgate for — — — , Michael de Bolnho and Duce de Bolnho, 1 quarter for — — — ; Hugh Trunket with his tenants, 1 virgate for 5s, suit & foreign service; Simon de St Edward with his tenants, 1 quarter for 2s 6d & foreign service; Michael de Bolnho, ½ quarter for 5s, suit and foreign service; Gilbert Blakeram, 2 virgates, of which 1 virgate and a quarter are now in the hands of the said lord John in demesne.

In free tenants: Duce de Bolnho, 1 quarter for — — — ; Michael de Bolnho, 1 quarter for — — — ; William de Bolnho, 1 quarter 3 acres of land — — — ; Stephen Alfred, 1 messuage 3 acres of land for — — — ; Robert Ruel, 1 messuage 1 acre of land for 12d; John Disaunt, 1 quarter of land from the said John for 12d, suit and foreign service; Adam Piscator, ½ virgate for 40d and foreign service; Alice la Lavander, 1 messuage 1 quarter of land for 6d; — — — Batewis and his sons, 1 quarter of land for 2s; Nicholas Spinc, 1 quarter which was Robert le Marescal's, for 3s, suit and foreign service; Jordan le Gros with his tenants, ½ virgate for 2s, suit and foreign service; Hugh son of Peter, 1 quarter of land for 3s; also Robert Pipard, 1 messuage for 18d; Miles le Messer, 1 messuage for 1 candle maintained in the chancel of the aforesaid church at the altar of Blessed Mary; Mabel Sutrix, 1 messuage for ½ mark; Robert Fader, 1 messuage for — — — ; Bateman le May, 1 messuage 1 acre of land for — — — ; The Prioress of Harewold, 1 messuage 1 acre in free and perpetual alms given in the time of King John.

LA LEYE for half a vill. Reginald de Grey the chief lord of the vill holds in chief from John de Wahulle from the barony of Wahulle, who holds the said barony in chief from the King, a certain tenement in the same vill for 3½ hides at scutage and sheriff's rent, 6s a year for hidage, 10s for suit, 5s for view, 8s 6d for ward of Rodingham. Of which he has in demesne 2 carucates of land which contain 200 acres of land, 1 ancient park of 12 acres, another enclosed wood of 12 acres, 1 windmill, a warren, by a charter of King Henry son of King John. In villeinage 3 virgates, each of which owes him 20s a year or works to that value, and the tenants of these are bondsmen bound to redeem their tenure at the lord's will: Geoffrey King, holds ½ virgate; Walter Plumer, ½ virgate; Adam le Messer, ½ virgate; Geoffrey Lilion, ½ virgate; Hamon son of Peter, ½ virgate; Stephen Aleyn, ½ virgate.

In cottars: 2 of the same condition are bondsmen, of whom each holds one cottage which is worth to him 12d a year or works to that value, whose names are: Richard le Spencer, Robert Wade.

The Prior of Esseby Canonicorum has the advowson of the church of La Leye with 1 virgate of land which is held from him in villeinage, which one of his bondsmen holds from the same Prior for service as above, another villein of the said Reginald does it and is in the same condition.

The Parson of the church holds ½ virgate and ½ quarter with which the church is endowed in pure and perpetual alms. Of which the Parson has in demesne 1½ quarters.

In free tenants: Henry Heyse holds 1 messuage 1 acre of land for 12d; Walter le Vacher, 1 messuage 5 acres of land for 18d; Gilbert son of Hugh, 1 quarter for 3s, and he gives foreign service to the said lord Reginald.

Free tenants of the said lord Reginald from the same fief: Geoffrey Eustace, for foreign service, as much as belongs; The Abbot of Ward', 3 acres for 3d.

William de La Leye holds in the same vill from the said John de Wahulle from the said barony of Wahulle held from the King a certain tenement for half a hide at scutage and ward of Rokingham and sheriff's fee 12d for hidage, 12d for suit, 2s for view, of which he has in demesne 1 carucate of land which contains 100 acres, 1 enclosed grove of 3 acres. In villeinage, ½ virgate which owes him 10s a year or works to that value, and his tenants are bondsmen as above, whose names are: Geoffrey Damernun holds 1 quarter; Richard Wicher, 1 quarter.

In free tenants: John son of John, 1 quarter for 6s, suit of court and foreign service; Rich. Malherbe, 1 quarter for 12d, suit and foreign service; Hugh le Parmenter, 1 quarter for 12d, suit & foreign service.

Reginald le Grey holds in the same vill a certain tenement from the honour of Walingford in chief from the Earl of Cornwall and he from the King, for ½ hide at scutage and no other service is due from it, of which he has in demesne 100 acres of land.

In free tenants: William de Lega with his tenant, who holds 1½ quarters for 2s 6d; the Prior of Caudewelle, who holds from him 1 quarter in free alms given to him in the time of King Henry son of King John; Nicholas Friday, 1 quarter of land for 2s 6d and foreign service; William de Druey, ½ virgate for 3s, suit and foreign service; Gilbert son of Hugh, 1 quarter for 3s, suit of court & foreign service; Hugh le Marchant, 1 quarter for 3d; & the Abbot of Wardone is a mesne tenant of it between the lord Reginald and the lord Hugh from the gift of the father of the aforesaid Hugh in the time of King Henry son of King John; the Prior of Caudewelle from the gift of the same, 1 quarter for 1 lb of pepper and foreign service; Payne Thurgar, ½ quarter for 2s and foreign service; Robert de Camera, ½ quarter for 8d and foreign service; Simon de Aspey, 1 quarter for 20d and foreign service; the Abbot of Wardone, 35 acres in free alms, & the Master of the Hospital of St John, Bedford with his tenants, 1 quarter 4 acres, given to the same Abbot and Master by Richard son of Hugh in the time of King Henry son of King John.

Richard de La Leye holds in the same vill ½ hide from the honour de Bello Campo of Bedford in chief from John de Pateshull, and John himself from Roger Lestrange on behalf of Roger de Munbry who holds in chief from the King, and is assessed for ½ hide at scutage and sheriff's fee, 12d a year for hidage, 2s for suit, 2s for view. Of this he has in demesne 100 acres of land. In villeinage, ½ virgate which is worth to him 10s a year or works to that value, and his tenants are bondsmen as above, of which: Robert le Carpenter, 1 quarter; Geoffrey Lete, 1 quarter; Stephen le Palmere, 1 cottage in villeinage in the same condition for 3s or works to that value.

In free tenants: Simon son of Stephen holds ½ virgate for suit at the hundred and county for the aforesaid Richard at the cost of the aforesaid Simon and outside at the cost of the lord, and both in common suits and in pleas he was proxy of the lord Richard; Nicholas Friday, 1 quarter for 2s and foreign service; Simon son of Robert, 1 quarter for 6d and foreign service.

In the same vill, Richard de Borard holds from the Castle of Beuper in chief from Robert de Ros through his wife, and R[obert] himself from the King, namely one virgate of land.

Of which: William de Lega with his tenants holds ½ virgate from the said Richard for 3s and foreign service; Simon le Charpenter, 1 quarter for — — — ; John Leysing, 1 quarter for — — — .

FELMERSHAM Nicholas de Pencurt & Almaric de Laundres of Felmersham hold 6½ hides of land in the vill of Felmersham from Nicholas de Mepershale. And Nicholas himself from the lord King in serjeanty. The church is from the same fief from which the ancestors of the said Nicholas de Mepershale gave the advowson to the Prior of Lentone in the time of King Henry father of John, and pays a yearly rent to the aforesaid Nicholas de Mepershale 38s, 1 mark a year for sheriff's fee, 4s a year for suit, 3s a year for tithe.

Nicholas and Almaric aforesaid hold half a knight's fee from the honour of Huntingdone in chief from Nicholas de Meperesh' and Nicholas himself from John de Hastingges and John himself from the King, and the lord King has from it no crown rent from fixed sheriff's dues annually. Of which hides and fiefs the said Nicholas de Pencurt has there in demesne 3 virgates of land, meadow and pasture, half a mill, his father gave to the Prior of Neuham a private fishery in the river Owse from Wahulle mill as far as the house of Richard de Ripa of Sarnebrok.

In free tenants: Robert de Herdwic with his tenants holds from the said N. 1½ virgates of land for 1 lb of pepper and ½d and foreign service per year; Walter Clericus with his tenants and other co-tenants, 1 virgate of land for 6d a year and foreign service; Gilbert Berenger with his tenants, 1½ virgates of land for 14d a year and foreign service; Roger Le Petyt, 1 quarter of land for — — — 10d a year & foreign service; Simon le Petyt, ½ virgate of land for 16d a year & foreign service; Master Robert Coffin, 1 virgate of land for — — — rent a year to the Abbess of Heunestoue from a gift of the father of the said Nicholas de Pencurt in the time of King Henry father of King Edward; also Master Robert holds ½ virgate from the said N. for 16½d a year and foreign service; John Lupus with his tenants, 1 virgate of land for 14d a year and foreign service; Hugh de Herdwic with his tenants, 2 virgates for 2s a year and foreign service; Dametta with her tenants, 1 virgate for foreign service; Walter Bele with his tenants, ½ virgate of land for 4 [sic] a year rent to the Prior of Caudewell from the gift of

Eileen le Pencurt in the time of King John, and for foreign service; also Dametta with her tenants, 2 virgates of land for foreign service; Walter Molendinarius and Agnes Burgeys with other lesser tenants, 1 quarter of land for 6d a year and foreign service; Ralph son of Adam, ½ virgate of land for 16 [sic] rent to the Prior of Caudewell for 1 quarter of the aforesaid ½ virgate from the gift of Eileen de Pencurt in the time of King John and for foreign service and for 2s a year rent; Roger de Wilye for another quarter and foreign service; Agnes la Chatur, ½ virgate for 2s 6d a year rent to the Abbess of Haunestowe from the gift of the said Eileen in the time of King Henry father of John and foreign service.

In cottars: Matilda Est holds 1 cottage for 12d a year; Robert Est, 1 cottage for 12d a year; Walter Canun, 1 cottage for 6d a year; William le Petyt, 1 cottage for 12d a year; Margery de Ecclesia, 1 cottage for 8d a year; Thomas Witte, 1 cottage for 1½d and 2 capons a year; William le Mercer, 1 cottage for ½ lb of wax a year; Robert de Laundres, 1 cottage for 10d a year; Robert le Webbe, 1 cottage for the term of his life for 20d; Roger de Pencurt, 1 cottage for 4d a year; Alice Bernard, 1 cottage for 12d a year; Robert Dreu, 1 cottage for 4d a year.

Almaric de Laundres aforesaid holds in the same vill a half part of the said vill as aforesaid with the aforesaid Nicholas de Pencurt. Of which he has there in demesne 3 virgates of land, half a mill. A fishery in the deep water of the Owse was given by his father to Walter de Wadhulle, the lord of Wadhulle, namely from the top head of the mill pond of Felmersham as far as the whole mill of Wadhulle, save to the said Almaric and his heirs the fishing with 'wade and botur', paying the same W. de Wadhulle for the said fishing 6d a year, and a private fishery from Felmersham mill as far as Pinch mill, which the father of the said Almaric gave to Dametta for 2s a year, half of Pinch mill which his father gave to Roger de Wilye for 1d a year. In villeinage, ½ virgate of land which William de Ropere holds for ½ mark a year or works to that value, and the same William is as a serf because he cannot marry his daughters nor sell chickens or caponised cocks without the lord's permission.

In free tenants: Master Robert Coffin holds from the said Almaric ½ virgate and a quarter of land for 3s 3d a year and foreign service; Alexander Buzim with his tenants, 4 virgates of land and a meadow for foreign service; John le Waleys with his tenants, 3 virgates of land for foreign service; Robert de Laundres 1 virgate of land for 12d a year and foreign service; Walter le Packer, 1 quarter of land for 2s and for foreign service; Gilbert de Laundres with his tenants, ½ virgate of land for 12d and foreign service; Reginald de Fonte, ½ virgate for 3s a year and foreign service; Ralph son of Roger, ½ virgate and a quarter of land for 5s a year and foreign service; the Rector of the church of Felmersham, 1 virgate of land for 4s a year; Roger le Freman with his tenants, 1 virgate for 2s a year and foreign service; Henry Faber, 1 quarter for 2s a year and foreign service; William Frankeleyn with his tenants, ½ virgate of land for 3s and foreign service; Adam le Careter & Henry Cullebulloc with their tenants, ½ virgate of land for 2s 6d a year rent to Robert le Parentyn & for foreign service.

In cottars: Isolde Cortenhale holds 1 cottage from the same Amaric for 16d and foreign service; Alice daughter of Gisselot, 1 cottage for 12d a year; Richard Clergis, 1 cottage for 3d a year; Walter Clergis, 1 cottage for 6d a year and foreign service; Simon son of the reeve, 1 cottage for 2s a year; Nigel de Pabenham, 1 cottage for 2s a year; Reginald de Fonte, 1 cottage for 6d a year and 1 lb of cummin; Henry Balde, 1 cottage for 12d a year; Robert Bernard, 1 cottage for 12d a year.

RADEWELLE Robert de Radewelle the lord of the vill holds in the same 7½ hides, that is for 1 fief at scutage, in chief from Ralph Perot. And Ralph himself from Almaric de St Edmund of the barony of Cayho. And Almaric himself from the King, and sheriff's fee per year 15s for hidage, 3s for view, 2s for suit. Of which hides he has there in demesne 2½ hides and ½ virgate, one watermill, a private fishery in the river Owse from Humberdale as far as Pabenham fence in common with other lords. In villeinage 3 virgates of land, each owes him 8s a year or works to that value, and the tenants of these are as serfs because they cannot give their daughters in marriage without the lord's permission, nor sell chickens or caponised cocks.

Of these: Simon the reeve holds ½ virgate; Robert Balle, ½ virgate; Richard Neubonde, ½ virgate; Robert Heyloy, ½ virgate; Simon Sprot, ½ virgate; William Pollard, 1 quarter; Robert de la More, 1 quarter.

In cottagers, two, each of which owes 12d a year and 3 hens: Hugh Benne, 1 cottage, and Richard the miller, 1 cottage.

In free tenants: Richard le Clergis holds from the same Robert ½ virgate of land for 2s a year, suit and foreign service; William Frense, ½ virgate for 2s a year, suit and foreign service; Robert son of Richard with his tenants, ½ virgate for 2s, suit and foreign service; Robert Martel, ½ virgate and 2 parts ½ virgate and 3 acres and 1 rood for 3s a year and foreign service; Robert de Herdwic with his tenants, 1 virgate for 4s, suit and foreign service; William Godanter, ½ virgate for 2s, suit and foreign service; Richard de Ripa with his tenants, 1 virgate for foreign service; Gilbert le Marescal with his tenants, 1 virgate and 1 quarter for 1d, suit and foreign service; William le Bray, ½ quarter for 14d and foreign service; Richard de la More, 1 quarter for 12d and foreign service; the Parson of Felmersham, 1 virgate of land and 3 acres of meadow belonging to Felmersham Church, for finding a chaplain to celebrate mass in Radewelle three times a week.

In cottagers: Walter Benet holds from the said Robert 1 cottage for 2d a year; Walter de la Grene, 1 cottage for 12d and suit; William de Thindene, 1 cottage for 12d a year.

John le Wolf holds in the same vill from the said fief of the said Robert 9 virgates of land, of which he has in demesne with John his son 3 virgates.

In free tenants: Henry le Ku, ½ virgate of land for ½ lb of pepper a year & foreign service; John le Gaylur, ½ virgate of land for ½ lb of pepper a year and foreign service; John de Radewelle, 1 virgate for a penny and foreign service; Agnes de la More, 1½ quarters for 4d and foreign service; Richard de Cusyn, ½ virgate for 6d and foreign service; Richard Burnhard, ½ virgate of land for 6d and foreign service; Adam le Sumpter, ½ virgate for 2s and foreign service; William le Franceys, ½ virgate for foreign service; Richard de Ponte with his tenants, ½ virgate for foreign service; Alice le Wolf & Agnes her sister, ½ virgate for 2s and foreign service; Ralph de Thindene, ½ virgate for 1 acre [sic] and foreign service; Adam le Sumpter & Geoffrey Brok, ½ virgate of land from the Hospitallers of Melcheburne for 12d a year, given in the time of King John; William le Monek, 1 cottage for 4½d a year.

John de Pateshulle holds in Radewelle 2½ hides and ½ virgate from the barony de Bello Campo in chief on behalf of Roger de Mubray paying sheriff's fee yearly 5s for hidage, 12d for suit, 12d for 'virg.' [?a virgate], of which he has in demesne of meadow — — — .

In free tenants: William le Broy, 7 virgates of land for 16s a year, 1 lb of pepper, suit and foreign service, and the same William has tenants, that is to say, Walter de la Grene holds from the same William 1 quarter of land for 12d and foreign service; William Godanter, 1 quarter of land for 12d a year and foreign service; Emma le Wolf, 1 quarter of land for 6d a year and foreign service; Ralph le Brey, 1 quarter of land for 4d a year and foreign service. In cottagers: William le Cusyn holds from the same William le Broy 1 cottage for 4d a year; Richard son of Simon, 1 cottage for 8d a year.

Nicholas del Grene holds from the said John de Pateshulle 1½ virgates of land for 6s 2d a year and foreign service; Walter Tappe, 1 virgate of land for 4s, suit and foreign service; John de Middelho, ½ virgate for 3s a year and foreign service; Richard Piscator, ½ virgate of land for 2s, suit and foreign service; Robert Clergis, 1 cottage and 3 acres of land for 6d a year.

STACHEDENE William de Monte Canis holds in chief through his wife from the barony de Bello Campo of Bedford from the King 3 hides of land from which the sheriff has 6s a year for the use of the King; he has in demesne in the vill of Stachedene the chief messuage, 3 carucates of land containing 360 acres of land, meadow and pasture, 1 ancient park containing 180 acres, 1 windmill; he is the patron of the church and the Prior of Neuham has the church for his own use and the land belongs to the church, and the said church was endowed to the Prior of Neuham by Rois de Bello Campo in the time of King Henry grandfather of the last Henry. In villeinage, 5½ virgates and 1 quarter, each of which owes him 1 mark per year or works to that value, and foreign service, and the tenants of these are: Robert Ace, ½ virgate; Richard Ace, ½ virgate; Richard Aleyn, ½ virgate; Henry Prepositus, ½ virgate; William de Caysho, ½ virgate; Richard Faber, 1 virgate; Robert le Coupere, ½ virgate; Robert Hanfort, ½ virgate; William Laurence, 1 quarter; Cecil Camp, 1 quarter; Robert de Beydene, 1 quarter; Almaric Burgoyne, 1 quarter; Thomas Neel, 1 quarter; William Alewy, 1 quarter; William Neuman, 1 quarter.

In cottars, there are 2, and they are serfs as the others, each of them gives him 12d a year or works to that value.

In free tenants: William le Heyr holds from the same 1 virgate of land for 6d as hidage, foreign service and suit; Hugh Goldston, 1 quarter for foreign service; Robert Goldston, ½ virgate for foreign service; the Prior of Neuham, 1 quarter for foreign service and he has tenants, that is to say Robert Arnold, who holds from the same 1 messuage 2 acres of land for 12d a year, Robert Sampson 2 messuages with crofts for 5s a year, Richard Molendinarius 1 acre with a messuage for 12d, Hugh Goldston 1 messuage for 8d a year; and the whole of the aforesaid holding is assessed for 3 hides and gives 6s a year as hidage.

The Abbot of Wardon holds in the same vill 1 hide 3 virgates and ½ quarter of land from a gift of Robert le Broy in the time of King John from the said barony of Bedford in free and perpetual alms. He has nothing in demesne, but in free tenants: John de Burdeleys holds from the same Abbot 1 hide for 1 lb of cummin and foreign service with his tenants in it, that is to say the Prior of Bissemede holds from the same John 2 virgates for 12d and foreign service, Ralph Goldston 1 messuage for 2s, Thomas Downe 1 messuage for 2s, Adam Goyz 1 messuage for 9d.

Also from the said Abbot: John Cocus, 1 virgate for 5s 2d a year and foreign service; Michael Goldston, 1 virgate for 12d and foreign service; Robert Perteseil, ½ virgate for 6d and foreign service; Henry le Poleter, ½ virgate for 12d; Nicholas le Dylewic, ½ quarter for foreign service.

Robert de Stachedene holds in the same vill one virgate of land in chief from J. de Steingr' and J. himself from the King, from the said barony for foreign service and suit of the twentieth part of one knight's fee and sheriff's fee for hidage 6d.

Hugh le Blund holds in the same vill through his wife one virgate of land in chief from John de Holebur and he himself from the King, from the said barony for suit and foreign service for the twentieth part of 1 knight's fee and 6d as hidage. H. himself has free tenants: Bertram le Blund holds from him 1 quarter for 2d & foreign service; Hugh de Hull, 1 quarter for foreign service; Cecil de Newntone, 1 quarter for foreign service; John le Wyte, 1 messuage and ½ quarter of land for 4d and foreign service; Nicholas le Rous, ½ quarter for 6d and foreign service; John de la Wykhend, ½ quarter for 12d and foreign service; Robert Cok, 1 quarter for 8s; the Prior of Bissemede, ½ quarter for foreign service; the Prior of Neuham, 9 acres in free and perpetual alms, from a gift of the ancestors of the said Hugh in the time of King Henry son of King John.

Peter de Goudintone with his tenants holds 1½ virgates of land in the same vill through his wife, in chief from John de Stengr' and he himself from the King, from the said barony for foreign service, a fortieth part of one knight's fee, and he gives 3d as hidage.

Henry de Dylewik with his tenants holds in chief from Ralph Painel. And he himself from the King from the aforesaid barony for foreign service and 6d as hidage.

Richard Koc holds ½ virgate of land from the aforesaid Ralph from the aforesaid barony for foreign service and 6d as hidage.

Adam Harlew holds ½ virgate of land from the said Ralph Paynel from the said barony for foreign service.

Alexander Buzun holds 1 hide of land in the same vill in chief from John de Steingr' and he himself from the King, from the said barony for foreign service, and he has the whole in demesne except one messuage which Nicholas Edward holds from him for 25d a year, and ½ quarter of land which Roger de Champ' holds for foreign service.

John de Burdeleys with his tenants holds in the same vill in chief from Roger Lestrange from the aforesaid barony, 3 quarters of land for foreign service.

Robert de Gemys holds in the same vill in chief from the King a third part of one knight's fee, 3s 6d a year for scutage and hidage, ½ mark for suit, and 5s for view. Of which he has in demesne one carucate of land which contains 120 acres of land, 4 acres of meadow and pasture. In villeinage, 5½ virgates, each of which owes him 10s a year or works to that value, and the tenants of these are as serfs and bondsmen because they cannot give their daughters in marriage without the permission of the lord. Their names are: Michael Losse holds ½ virgate; Nicholas son of Lete, ½ virgate; Richard West, 1 quarter; Walter Prudfot, ½ virgate; Gous [or Goet] de Hyrand, ½ virgate; Thomas Prepositus, ½ virgate; Nicholas Losse, ½ virgate; Robert Brond, ½ virgate; John Sipwif, ½ virgate; Agaus [or Agaet] Sipwif, 1 quarter; Adam Walseg, 1 quarter; Jordan Hudelin, 1 quarter; Nicholas Brond, ½ virgate.

In free tenants: Agnes le Knit holds from the same R. 3 quarters for 2s a year and foreign service; Robert de Conintone, 1 quarter for 3s and foreign service; Henry de Dylewic, ½ virgate for 6d and foreign service; Robert Valet and William Parseyl, 1 quarter for 3s 6d and foreign service; Robert le Conintone, John son of Richard, and Sampson le Cunerer, 1 quarter for foreign service; Hugh Wake with his tenant William son of Richard, 1 quarter for foreign service; Robert Goldston, 1 quarter for 1 lb of cummin and foreign service; Sybil Virly, 80 acres of land for 15d and foreign service; Hugh Goldston, ½ virgate & foreign service [sic].

BIDENHAM Ralph Passelewe holds in Bidenham 1 knight's fee in chief from Ralph de Bello Campo and Ralph himself from Walter Traly, and Walter de Traly himself from the Earl of Gloucester, from the honour of Gloucester, and the Earl himself from the King, and he pays the sheriff 9s 9½d as hidage for the use of the King, and 2s 6d to the Earl of Gloucester for view. The church of that vill is in that fee, and the advowson with 1 quarter of land belongs to John de Kerkeby, which quarter of land Gilbert Goze holds in villeinage from the said John for 5s or works to that value, and he is a serf bound to redeem his tenure at the lord's will. The aforesaid church is endowed with ½ virgate of land of that fee, which the rector of the church holds in demesne. Indeed the said Ralph Passelewe of the said fee has in demesne one carucate of land which contains 60 acres, 6 acres of meadow and pasture. In villeinage, 2 virgates of land each of which owes him 25s a year or works to that value, and they are serfs and bondsmen bound to redeem their tenure. Of which: Nicholas Prepositus holds ½ virgate; William Aldith, ½ virgate; Nicholas Herbert, ½ virgate; Nicholas Denys, ½ virgate.

In free tenants, Nicholas Passelewe holds from the same Ralph and is assessed at half a knight's fee according to his share. The same Nicholas has in demesne 100 acres of land, 6 acres of meadow and pasture, one watermill, a fishery in the river Owse from the head of the pond of the said N. as far as Reyford.

And in free tenants: Ralph Passelewe holds from the same Nicholas ½ virgate of land for 3d [sic] & foreign service; Robert Astell, ½ virgate for 3s and foreign service; Richard son of Thomas, ½ virgate for 3s and foreign service; John Elys, ½ virgate for 3s and foreign service; Robert Passelewele, ½ virgate for 2s and foreign service; Paganus de Forde, 1 messuage for 12d and foreign service; Peter de Clopham, ½ virgate for 6d; Robert de Crokeshale, 1 messuage for 12d and 1 lb of cummin & foreign service; Reginald Faber, 1 messuage for 18d; Stephen de Scheltone, 1 messuage for 12d; Benedict Clericus & Robert Burnard, 1 quarter for 1 lb of cummin and foreign service; the Prior of Neuham, 1 messuage, 1 acre of land, 3 acres of meadow for 22d; the Abbot of Wardon in free alms, 6 acres of meadow from the gift of Thomas Passelewe in the time of King Henry.

Also from the said Ralph Passelewe's tenants, namely: Nicholas Blankoste with his tenants, ½ virgate for 2d and foreign service; William Bonde, [no amount given] for 2s 4d and foreign service; Nicholas Freelove, ½ virgate for 40d and foreign service; William Red, ½ virgate for 10s and foreign service; Richard Faber, ½ virgate for 15s and foreign service; Roger Malyn, 1 quarter for 4d and foreign service; Richard son of William, 1 quarter for 1 lb pepper and foreign service; Robert Passelewe, ½ virgate for 2s 6d; Thomas Halyday with his tenants, 1 virgate of land, 7 acres of meadow, for 1 lb of pepper and 12d;

John Clericus with his tenants, ½ virgate for 9d a year; Richard de Forde with his tenants, 1 messuage, 3 acres of land for 2s; Robert Burnard, 1 quarter for 2s 2¾d; Robert Hayword, 1 messuage for 2s; Robert Croft, 1 messuage for 2s; the Prior of Neuham, 2 virgates 1 quarter for 3s and foreign service; the Prior of Caudewell, ½ virgate for foreign service; the Prioress of Harewold with her tenants, 1 virgate in pure and perpetual alms from the gift of William Passelewe in the time of King Henry son of King John; the Master of the Hospital of St John Bedford, 1½ virgates in free alms from a gift from the ancestors of the said R. Passelewe in the time of King John, of which he has in demesne 1 quarter, and free tenants who hold from him are William son of Nicholas 1 virgate for 4s and foreign service, and Sarah daughter of Adam, Beatrice Mabel & Lucy her sisters, 1 quarter for 40d and foreign service.

In the same vill, Hamund son of William has a holding on which he is assessed for scutage for 3 virgates and sheriff's fee annually for the use of the King, for hidage and other – – – . Of which he has in demesne 60 acres.

In free tenants: – – – .

In the same vill the Prior of Neuham holds from the prebend of St Paul Bedford from the gift of King William the Bastard 3½ virgates of land in pure and perpetual alms, of which he has in demesne 2 virgates. In free tenants: Isolde Blancoste, ½ virgate for 5s, 3 hens, 40 eggs; William David, 1 quarter for 14d; Ralph Passelewe & William Bed', 3 quarters for 3s 4d.

In the same vill the Mother Church of Lincoln has in prebend in free and perpetual alms free tenants of 5 virgates of land from the gift of the said King William the Bastard, namely: Nicholas Blankoste with his lesser tenants, 1 virgate for 5s 3d; Richard de Forde with his tenants, 1 virgate for 4s; William son of Henry, 1 virgate for 4s; Simon Piscator, Paganus de Ford & Matilda Halbot with their tenants, 1 virgate for 3s; Simon de Rochewelle with his tenants, 1 virgate for 2s 6d.

In the same vill the Prior of Dunestaple has free tenants of 3 virgates of land from the gift of the said King William the Bastard for foreign service, as much as belongs for the term of the tenancy, and sheriff's fee annually for the use of the King, 18d for hidage and other things, of which: William Mile with his tenants has 1 virgate for 4s; Roger Mile with his tenants, ½ virgate for 2s; the Prior of Neuham, ½ virgate for 2s and foreign service; Nicholas Frelove, the Prior of Neuham & Robert Passelewe, 1 virgate for 4s and foreign service.

In the same vill the Abbot of Wardon has from the gift of the said King W. the Bastard, in a meadow which is called Kingesmede, 25 acres of meadow. Also the Abbess of Hannestowe in the same place from the gift of the said King W., 13 acres of meadow which John de Pateshulle holds from the same for 10s a year. Also the Prior of Caudewelle, in the same way in the same place, 5 acres of meadow, and all these hold in free and perpetual alms.

In the same vill there is a certain holding which is called Bromham Hyde.

SULDROPE half-vill The Prior of the Hospitallers of Jerusalem holds in Suldrope 6 virgates of land from the gift of a certain Alice de Clermund' in pure and perpetual alms in the time of King William the Bastard; it must be enquired from which barony. [footnote: 'to be enquired']. Of which the Prior of the said Hospital has in demesne the advowson of Suldrope church with 40 acres of land which Roger de la Despense and Joan his wife hold freely from the said Prior for 28s a year for everything. He has other free tenants for annual service, namely: William son of Roger holds ½ virgate for 8d; Michael in la Venele, 1 virgate of land for 13s a year; Thomas le Duk, 2 parts 1 virgate of land for 2s and suit and works worth 12d; Richard le Peer with his tenants, ½ virgate for 20d and suit and works worth 8d; Alice Baret with her tenants, ½ virgate for 32d and works worth 8d; Richard son of Hugh, 1 virgate for 4s 4d and suit in the same vill and works worth 16d; John le Taylur, ½ virgate for 25d and suit in the same vill and works worth 8d; Reginald le Clerk, 1 quarter of land for 6d a year and 4d for the aforesaid works; William Faber, 1 quarter for 1d and works worth 4d; William le Kyng, 1 quarter for 17d and suit at Melcheburne & works worth 4d; Michael de Schrintone, 1 quarter for 2s and works worth 4d; Geoffrey ad le Pond, 1 quarter for 2s and works worth 4d and suit in the same vill; William de Lond' with his tenants, [no area given] for 3s 11d and works worth 8d and suit at Melcheburne; Robert Bacun, 1 messuage for 8½d and works as others for his share; Ralph son of Stephen, 2½ acres for 3½d and suit in the same vill; Juliana de Pond' with her lesser tenants, 1 acre for 16d and suit in the same vill; Wariner Wrench, 1 messuage for 1d and works worth 4d.

WAHULLE John de Wahulle, lord of the vill and patron of the church and of the benefice, holds in chief from the lord King through the barony, and that vill Wahulle is a barony, and the whole of that vill of Wahulle is assessed on behalf of that barony for 1 knight's fee for scutage and ward of Rokingham for 3s 3d a year and sheriff's fee, 9s 3d for hidage and 11½d for suit. Of which fee the lord John holds in demesne 180 acres of land, meadow and pasture, one ancient enclosed park of 100 acres, two watermills, a private fishery in the river Owse from the top head of the pond of the said mills as far as the top head of the pond of Felmersham mill, also he has the Thursday market by a charter of the last King Henry. He holds 4½ virgates of land in villeinage, each of which owes him 20s a year or works to that value, and the tenants of these are villeins and serfs not able to give their daughters in marriage nor to sell hens or caponised cocks without the lord's licence. Of which: Walter de Newbonde holds 1 virgate; Richard le Wolf, 1 virgate; Walter Wolf, 1 virgate; Richard Gerold, 1 virgate; Henry Kane, one ½ virgate.

The church of Wahulle is endowed with 1½ virgates in pure and perpetual alms, which the rector of the church holds in demesne.

Also he has free tenants. William de St John holds from the said lord J. land which used to be Robert Pentyn's from the same barony for a quarter of a knight's fee, namely 1 carucate which contains 100 acres, of which he has in demesne the chief messuage and 2 acres of land, and he has many tenants under him: Simon Lakelove holds 6 acres for 1d; Robert Hayrun, 12 acres for 1d a year; Roger de Wyly – – – ; Robert la Norice, 7½ acres for 8d a year; Alice Denet, 16 acres for 1 lb of cummin a year and ½d; Samson de Batesforde, 13 acres for ½d a year; Joan Maykot, 6 acres for – – – a year; Selade, 3 acres for 1d a year; Hugh Mariot, 1 messuage and 3 acres of land for 2½d a year; Walter le Serjant, 2½ acres – – – a year; Agnes de Pottone, 18 acres of land and meadow for – – – ; Hugh Godard, 2 acres for 1d a year, and other small and – – – [te]nants of lesser holding for a small rent.

Also Roger de Wylye holds from the said J. from the said fee and barony.

Geoffrey de Hingham with his tenants of lesser holdings holds from the same John 1 virgate for 1d a year; Gilbert Bene with his [tenan]ts, 1 virgate for 1d a year; Isabel la Franceys with her lesser tenants, 1 virgate for 12d a year;

Richard de Sivelesho, 1 virgate for — — — year; Gilbert de Pottone with his tenants of lesser holdings, 2 virgates of land for 4d a year; Alice Beneyt with her — — — 1½ virgates for 1d a year; Alice Caperun with her lesser tenants, ½ virgate for foreign service, as much as belongs, and suit of court; Sybil Caperun with her tenants, ½ virgate for 1d service; Joan Faber with her lesser tenants, ¾ virgate for 3s and suit of court per year; Hugh de Akle, ½ virgate and 1 piece of meadow for 16½d, 6 capons per year; Robert Heyrun, ½ virgate with his tenants John Heyrun and Hugh his brother ½ virgate and 2 cottages for 4s 7d a year; Robert Clericus, ½ virgate for 2s a year; William de Hale, 1 messuage 6 acres of land for 1 arrow per year; Simon Likelove, ½ virgate 2 acres of land for 5s 4 capons per year; Matilda de Pentym with her tenants, ½ virgate 1 quarter 2 acres for one rose flower per year; Robert Finegod, 1 messuage 7 acres of land and meadow with his tenants Robert Hayrun, Robert le Clerk & Selade, for one lamp burning in the church for the said lord John; Joan Maykoc, 1 messuage 3 acres of land for 2 lb of wax at the 'cum' of Blessed Mary in the aforesaid church per year; Walter le Serjant, ½ virgate of land for keeping the park of the said John; Henry Page, ½ virgate of land for 1 lb of wax at the 'cum' of the Blessed Mary; Henry King with his tenant Hugh Hayrun, 1 messuage and 1 acre of land for 1d a year; John le Marescal, 1 messuage 3½ acres of land and meadow for 1 pair of gloves; Ralph Parentin, 1 messuage with a croft for his service and so much foreign service; the Prior of the Hospital of Jerusalem, in free alms from the gift of Simon de Wodhulle in the time of King John, with his tenants, 1 virgate 1 quarter 1 cottage in perpetual alms.

Cottars who hold from the said J. for fixed annual service: William le Webbe, 1 cottage for 6d; Roger Petyt, 1 cottage for 6d; Robert Brid, 1 cottage for 18d; William Galun, 1 cottage with ½ acre for 16d; Rose Belle, 1 cottage for 3s ½d; William Mariot, 1 cottage for 2s; William Baril, 1 cottage for 25d; Walter le Serjant, 1 cottage for 12 arrows; Joan Maykoc and Hugh Godard her tenant, 1 cottage for 6d; Hugh Maykoc, 1 cottage for 25d; Matilda le Plumer, 1 cottage for 18d; John Hayrun, 1 cottage for 12d; William le Webbe with John le Parmenter his tenant, 1 cottage for 6d; Robert Maheu, 1 cottage for 28d; Amar' Finegod, 1 cottage for 12d; Robert Crow, 1 cottage for 8d; Roger de Wylye — — — ; Walter Herdebi, 1 cottage and 1 acre of land for ½d; Geoffrey Pistor, 1 cottage and 1 acre of land for 4s and 2 suits of court; Robert Brid, 1 cottage for 12d; Hugh Piscator, 1 cottage for 12d; William Prikeavant, 1 cottage for 1 falcon's hood; Gilbert Bene, 1 cottage for 2s; Selade with Richard Pach his tenant, 1 cottage for 3s 3d; Margaret Seer, 1 cottage for 2s; John le Parmenter with Stephen his brother, tenant, 1 cottage with a croft for 18d and suit of court and 3 capons; Geoffrey le Plumer with Richard le Barke his tenant, 1 cottage for 2s; Walter Sturpot, 1 cottage for 6d.

LITTLE WAHULLE hamlet. The said John de Wahulle holds Little Wahulle in chief from Badewin Wake, and B. himself from the Earl of Boham [of Hereford] and the Earl himself from the King for half a knight's fee at scutage and no other service, which is from the honour of Bolonie, of which the said John has in demesne 1 carucate of land which contains 200 acres of land meadow and pasture, an ancient park of 20 acres, 20 acres of common woodland, a fishery in common with Walter Traly as the other party in the river Owse from Harewold bridge as far as the pond of his mill at Great Wahulle. He has in villeinage 12¼ virgates of land, of which each virgate of land is worth to him 20s a year or works to that value. And the tenants of these are as serfs, like the aforesaid villeins of Great Wahulle, and they hold by the same service. Of which: William Danger holds 1 virgate; Robert Legeman, 1 virgate; Robert le Coliere, 1 virgate; Geoffrey Harding, 1 virgate; Walter Legeman, 1 virgate; William Lovent, ½ virgate; William Bonetone, ½ virgate; Robert Wolf, ½ virgate; William Gille, ½ virgate; Richard Hayward, ½ virgate; Stephen Danger, ½ virgate; Walter Hunting, ½ virgate; John Godhine, ½ virgate; John Haddy, ½ virgate; William de Cestre, ½ virgate; Henry de la Barre, 1 quarter; William Mose, ½ virgate; Alexander de Patteshulle, ½ virgate; Alan le Long, ½ virgate; William son of the reeve, ½ virgate.

Cottars: Robert son of Peter, a serf like the others, holds in villeinage a cottage for 12d or works to that value; Walter Wicher, in the same condition, 1 cottage for 20d or works.

Free tenants: Hugh cum barba [with the beard] with his tenant Geoffrey Wodeward, 1 virgate of land for 3d a year; Simon de Hynevik, ½ virgate and 4 acres of land for 5s 1d a year and 2 suits of court; Walter le Plumer, ½ virgate and 1 acre in fee for 11s and suit of court, and the same holds 1 quarter for the term of his life for 5s a year for everything; Hugh de Wilye holds from the same lord John one villein by name Henry Legeman with 1 virgate of land for one rose garland a year; William de St John with his tenants of lesser holdings, ½ virgate for foreign service, as much as belongs.

Roger de Wilye with his tenants Thomas de Hinewik and others; Henry le Clerk, 7 acres for ½d, one root of ginger; Alan Danger, 1 messuage 1 acre for 2s; Matilda de la Ho, 1 messuage for 11d; William Bolle, 1 messuage & ½ acre for 19d a year; the Prioress of Harewold holds 3 virgates in free and pure perpetual alms, that is 1 virgate from the gift of William son of Warin, and 2 virgates from the gift of Walter de Wahulle in the time of King Henry son of King John.

PODINTONE Reginald de Grey holds in Podintone 1½ knight's fees in chief from John de Wahulle from the said barony of Wahulle, and John himself from the King, and he pays 11s a year to ward of Bukingham Castle, sheriff's fee 8s for hidage, ½ mark for suit, 4s for view with 'lega'. Of this he has in demesne 3 carucates of land which contain 180 acres of land and 2 acres of meadow and pasture, 8 acres of enclosed wood, one windmill. He has in villeinage 11¼ virgates of land, each of which owes him 1 mark a year or works to that value, and the tenants of these are as serfs, because they cannot marry their daughters except by the lord's will. Of which virgates the tenant villeins are: Nicholas Prepositus, ½ virgate; William Prepositus, ½ virgate; Roger Bole, ½ virgate; Nicholas atte Grene, ½ virgate; Simon Gerard, ½ virgate; Henry le Taylur, ½ virgate; John Carectar, ½ virgate; Emma Raynold, ½ virgate; Simon le Vacher, ½ virgate; Bateman Prepositus, ½ virgate; Geoffrey le Messer, ½ virgate; Agnes wife of Robert, ½ virgate; William de Bonetun, ½ virgate; Richard son of Simon, ½ virgate; Simon Kene, ½ virgate; Michael le Careter, ½ virgate; Robert Cope, ½ virgate; William Kent, ½ virgate; William son of Roger, ½ virgate; William son of Richard, ½ virgate; Geoffrey Carectar, ½ virgate; William le Wodeward, 1 quarter.

He has 2 [sic] cottars who hold in villeinage; they are serfs in the same condition as the others: Richard son of William, 1 cottage for 12d or works to that value; Robert Viol, 1 cottage for the same service; Robert Reg', 1 cottage for the same service.

And he is the patron of the church of Potingdone which an ancestor of the said Reginald de Grey gave to the Priory of Esseby Canons with one virgate of land in the time of King John, and it is thus there in his own use. Also he has free tenants who hold from the same fee: the Prior of Esseby holds 1 virgate for foreign service and suit; Hugh Glenie with his tenants, 2 virgates for suit and foreign service; Robert son of William, 1½ virgates for suit of court and foreign service, as much as belongs to an eighth part of one knight's fee; Robert le Heyr with his tenants, 2 cottars, 1 virgate for suit of court and foreign service; Peter de Delve, 1 virgate for the same service; Nicholas le Sauvage with Hugh le Sauvage his son and with William Bikere, 3½ virgates, suit and foreign service and 1 mark annual rent paid to the Prior of Hundingdon from an endowment to the said Prior in the time of King John, and the said Hugh owes that service and the said William Bikere holds by frank-marriage ½ virgate of the said land of the said Nicholas; William son of Isabel, 1¼ virgates for 21s annual rent and foreign service; Simon son of Richard, ½ virgate for suit and foreign service and 2s rent to the Hospital of Jerusalem, given to the same Hospital in the time of King John; John Cocus, ½ virgate for suit and foreign service and 2s annually.

The Abbot of Sybeton, ½ virgate in pure and perpetual alms given to him in the time of King John, and Walter de Piwelle holds that from the same Abbot freely for 8s annually.

William Botevilein also holds from the said Reginald de Grey half a knight's fee in the same town. Of which he has in demesne 1 carucate of land which comprises 60 acres. In villeinage 2 virgates, each of which owes him 1 mark per year or works to that value. Of which: Robert le Carpenter, ½ virgate; Simon son of Henry, ½ virgate; Henry Hunwine, ½ virgate; William Meksop, ½ virgate; and those villeins are as serfs because they cannot marry their daughters except by the lord's will.

In cottars in the same condition of serfs: Reginald son of Ralph, 1 cottage for 12d or works to that value; Agnes wife of Henry, 1 cottage for the same service.

In free tenants: Henry son of Nicholas holds ½ virgate for foreign service and suit and 17d annual rent; the Prioress of Harewold, ½ virgate in pure and perpetual alms given to her in the time of King John.

John de Pabeham holds in the same vill 7 virgates of land from the barony of Bello Campo in Bedford in chief from William de Monte Canis and his wife from the inheritance of the same wife, and she herself in chief from the King for the third part of one knight's fee and pays the sheriff 26½d a year for hidage. Of which he has in demesne 5½ virgates. In villeinage, ½ virgate which Michael Baynel holds as a serf as others abovementioned, for ½ mark or works to that value. In free tenants: William Heyr, 1 virgate of land for 1 pound [probably pepper or cummin] and suit and foreign service as much as belongs.

Nicholas le Cruse holds in the same vill 7 virgates from the fee and honour of Gloucester for half a knight's fee at scutage. He holds in chief from Walter de Traley, and W. himself from the Earl of Gloucester and the Earl himself from the King. Of which he has in demesne 5 virgates, in free tenants 2 virgates, of which: John de Pabeham holds 1 virgate which 2 villeins of the said John hold from him as serfs aforesaid, namely Alan Parson & Michael Baynel; Henry Cruse holds from the said N. 1 quarter for — — — ; William Sayer, 1 quarter for — — — ; Robert Creuse, 1 quarter for — — — ; John son of Thomas, 1 quarter for — — — ; Thomas le Dekhe, 1 messuage for 6d a year and foreign service; Henry Carectar, 1 messuage for 6d and foreign service; Matilda Croyse & Alice her sister, 1 messuage for 26d; William Creyste, 1 messuage for 1d; Nicholas le Bray, 1 messuage for 6d.

Simon de Bray holds in the same vill 7 virgates of land from the Prior Hospitaller of Jerusalem, namely from his house of Herdwic in the county of Bedford, for 3s a year and suit of court and no other service, and it is not possible to find out from what fief or honour or barony nor in what way the said Prior has come by that fee, nor through whom. [footnote: 'to be enquired']. Of which the said Simon holds in demesne 2½ virgates. In free tenants for an annual rent: John son of Robert, 1 virgate for 8s; Henry son of Nicholas, ½ virgate for 4s; Elias le Freman, ½ virgate for 6d; Robert Trippe, ½ virgate for 6d; Peter le Dekne, 1 virgate for 5d; Nicholas le Cruse, 1 virgate for 1 lb of pepper.

Simon Harlewine holds in the same vill ½ virgate of land from the lord King in chief in petty serjeanty for 2s. Robert Bagge and William Cows, another ½ virgate from the lord King in chief for the same service and for making sure that the Sheriff of Bedford receives annually the aforesaid rent.

HAREWOLD John de Grey, the lord of the vill and patron of the church, and the Priory of Monks [Monacorum] in the same vill who have the church for their own use given to them in the time of the old King Henry from the gift of a certain Sampson le Fort. And the said John holds in the same vill 2 knight's fees in chief from John the heir of Henry de Hastinge. And John himself from the King from the honour of Huntingdone, and he has the privilege belonging to the said honour and warren by a charter of the last King Henry. Of which fee he has there in demesne 3 carucates of land comprising 240 acres of land, 10 acres of meadow, 3 acres of pasture, 1 ancient park of 120 acres, 2 water mills, a fishery in Owse water in common with Ralph Perot and Ralph Morin from Budewelle as far as Harewold bridge. In villeinage, ½ virgate of land which Simon Hunting' holds as a serf, so that he cannot marry his daughters nor sell chickens or cockerels without the lord's leave, for ½ mark a year or works to that value.

In cottagers, 7 who are also serfs as the other above, and each of them holds 1 cottage for 2s a year or works to that value. Their names: William Ward, Bartelot, William Pekkebene, William Leman, Roger Wylk, Robert Raven, William Ho.

The aforesaid Priory holds with the church from which it is endowed in pure alms, 1 virgate of land, 20 acres of wood, and from one part 1 carucate of land which contains 120 acres in free alms acquired in the time of King John, and from another part 3 virgates of land which it holds in pure and free alms from the Abbey of Butlesdene, which Ralph Morin gave to the same Abbey in the time of King Henry son of King John in free alms for 1 lb of pepper a year and foreign service.

The Temple of Jerusalem holds from the aforesaid John from the aforesaid fee and honour, in free and perpetual alms from a gift of Flaundrina Mauduyt in the time of King Henry son of King John, 200 acres of land, 2 acres of meadow, and 3 virgates of land. In demesne it has 3 virgates of land and 4 cottages in villeinage, in free tenants — — — for 2s a year and foreign service as much as belongs and each virgate in villeinage as aforesaid owes 1 mark a year or works to that value, and they are serfs like others — — — to redeem their tenure. Of which: William Barkur, ½ virgate; William Ode, ½ virgate; Hilary, ½ virgate; William in le Hurne, ½ virgate; Robert — — — , ½ virgate; Roger de Cakebroc, ½ virgate.

And the aforesaid cottars are in the same condition as serfs, and the tenants are: William Howel, 1 cottage for — — — ; Adam Parsun, 1 for 1d and service; Henry Ketel, 1 cottage for 1d service; Reginald le Mercer, 1 cottage for 1d and service.

From the aforesaid free tenants: Richard Leman, — — — 1 cottage for 12d a year; Waltere le Barkere, 1 messuage for 18d; Hamon de Circestre, 1 messuage for 6d a year.

Ralph Morin holds in Harewold from the said honour of Huntingdone from the said lord John de Grey 3 hides of land. Of which he has in demesne — — — acres of land, 3 acres of meadow, 10 acres of enclosed wood, a third part of the said 2 water mills of the said John, a fishery in the said water in common with the said John. In — — — 1½ virgates of which [each] owes him 1 mark a year or works to that value. And they are serfs and villeins bound to redeem their tenure. And the tenants of the same are: — — — Richard the reeve holds 1 virgate; Robert le Poter, ½ virgate.

In cottagers, 5 in the same condition as serfs: William Gydun holds 1 cottage for 12d — — — or works to that value; William — — — 1 cottage for the same service; and another 3 for the same tenure for the same service.

In free tenants: Robert le Caunceler, ½ — — — of land for foreign service and suit; Robert Amory, 1 virgate of land in frank-marriage; William son of Stephen, 1 virgate for 3s a year and suit; John Morin, 2 — — — for 1d and foreign service; Isabel Ingelard, 1 messuage for 12d a year; Simon le Neue, 1 messuage for 12d a year; Richard Faber, 1 messuage for 14d a year.

Richard de Pabenham holds from the said John de Grey from the same fief and honour 4 virgates and 4 acres of land, 20 acres of enclosed wood. Of which he has there in demesne 4 acres of land, 20 acres of wood. In villeinage 2 virgates and each owes him 1 mark a year or works to that value. And the tenants of these are serfs like the others as above, and their names are: Henry de Brocstrate holds ½ virgate; John de Brocstrate, ½ virgate; William Bidun, ½ virgate; — — — at will of which each owes him 12d a year.

In free tenants: Nicholas Engayne holds from the same 1 virgate for foreign service & suit; Robert le Champiun, 1 virgate for 1 lb of pepper a year and 1 lb of wax each year.

Richard de Esseby holds in the same vill from the said John from the said honour 3 virgates of land for 1 lb of cummin a year and he holds it all in demesne — — — 1 cottage which Richard Leman holds as a bondsman tenant for 12d a year or works to that value. Robert Amary, 1 virgate of land from the same John in frank-marriage; Roger de Boyner, 2 virgates for 1d; Reginald son of Reginald, 3 quarters of land — — — for 6s 9d, suit and foreign service; Henry son of Hilary, 1 virgate of land for suit of court & foreign service; Richard Curtevalur, 1 virgate for 6d a year and foreign service and suit of court; Henry de Brocstrate, 1 virgate for suit of court & foreign service and 6d a year; William le Flemyng, 1 virgate for 7s 2d a year & suit & foreign service; Gilbert son of Matthew, 1 virgate for ½ mark and foreign service; William Romay, ½ virgate for ½ mark, suit and foreign service; Robert le Champiun, ½ virgate for 2s, suit, and foreign service; William de Habinton, 1 quarter for 4d rent to the said John, and 25d to the said Ralph Morin and to the said J. suit of court & foreign service; John de Montibus, 1 quarter for 2 capons a year, suit of court, and foreign service; Ralph Ravenleg, 1 messuage for 2s a year; Hugh Cudding, 1 messuage for 1d a year; Isabel daughter of Geoffrey, 1 messuage for 6d and suit of court; 'Eletnys', 1 messuage for 7d a year; Richard de Brocstrate, 1 messuage for ½d a year; Robert Megge & John son of Walter, 1 messuage for 6d and suit; Richard Druye, 1 messuage for 1d and foreign service; Robert le Marescal, 1 messuage for 6d; The Master of Bedford Hospital, 1 messuage in free and perpetual alms, given to him in the time of King John, and William son of Stephen holds that from the same Master for 2s a year.

FARNEDYS Geoffrey de la Huse holds in Farnedys 3 hides of land with the advowson of the church from the barony of Wardon in the county of Bedford in chief from Hugh le Boys. And he himself from the King, and he pays as scutage, when it happens, for 3 hides to the sheriff 6s a year for hidage, ½ mark for suit, 16d for view. Of which he has in demesne 2½ hides and 1 virgate. In villeinage, 5 virgates of land, each of which owes him 5s a year or works to that value. And the tenants of these are as serfs like those above-mentioned, bound to redeem their tenure. Of whom: John Sparue holds ½ virgate; William Sparue ½ virgate; Walter son of Gunild, ½ virgate; Henry Bole, ½ virgate; 'Geze' the reeve, ½ virgate; Richard the reeve, ½ virgate; Robert son of Agnes, ½ virgate; Roger ad Ecclesiam, ½ virgate; Agnes Godwyne, ½ virgate; Richard le Pester, ½ virgate.

Ralph Basset holds in the same vill 1 hide of land in serjeanty in chief from the King for ½ mark a year paid to the sheriff. To the same sheriff 2s for hidage and 2s for suit and 2s 8d for view. From this in villeinage 2¾ virgates each of which owes him 10s a year or works to that value. And the tenants of these are serfs like the others above-mentioned, bound to redeem their tenure in the same way. Of whom: Roger son of Simon holds ½ virgate of land; Roger Benethetun, ½ virgate; John Tebald, ½ virgate; Henry le Mercer, ½ virgate; Richard le Mercer, ½ virgate.

In free tenants: John de Deneford, 1½ virgates for 40d a year and foreign service as much as belongs.

WYMINGTONE Roger de Nowers holds in Wymygtone 1 knight's fee from the barony of Wodhulle in chief from Robert Burnel and R. himself from the heir of Cantulun and the heir himself from John de Wodhulle who holds that barony in chief from the King, and is assessed at scutage for 1 knight's fee annually, 6s as ward for Roginham, 9s to the sheriff for hidage. Also he has privilege and warren by a charter of King Henry son of King John. Of which fee he has in demesne 2 virgates of land, 1 windmill. In villeinage, 4 virgates, each of which owes him 14s a year or works to that value. And the tenants of these are bondsmen and serfs bound to redeem their tenure in the same way, whose names are: William le Careter, ½ virgate; William Gollay, ½ virgate; Hugh son of Henry, ½ virgate; John Hardekyn, ½ virgate; Nicholas Giffard, ½ virgate; Simon atte Allegate, ½ virgate; Hilda Hopesort, ½ virgate; Mabel Godard, ½ virgate.

In free tenants: Henry Dine holds from the same 2 virgates of land for 1d & foreign service; Stephen de Weltone, 1 virgate for 6d and foreign service; William Russynoke, 1 virgate for 6d, foreign service & suit of court; Nicholas le Cerjant, 1½ virgates for 12½d, 1 lamp burning in the church, and foreign service; John de Bergeveny, 1 virgate for 12d and foreign service; Walter son of Fulc' 1 virgate for 10d, foreign service and suit; Letitia de Rowelle, 1 virgate for

1d and foreign service; Ralph Punteny, 1 virgate for 1d and foreign service; Geoffrey de Gotesle, 1 virgate for 12s, foreign service & suit of court; Adam Kneu, ½ virgate for 12d, foreign service and suit of court; Geoffrey de la Huse, ½ virgate for ½d and foreign service, and Stephen son of James holds that from the same G. for 15s; the Parson of Wahulle, 1 virgate belonging to his church of Wahulle, from which the church is endowed, for keeping one lamp always burning in the chancel of Wahulle. Everything else in pure and perpetual alms.

Isolde Cardun, Philip Burnel, and William de Monteforti hold in the same vill 3 hides of land in chief from the King at scutage for 3 hides, to the sheriff 6s a year for hidage, ½ mark for ward and suit, 2s for view, and they have the advowson of the church of that vill which is endowed with 2 virgates of land in free alms, foreign service excepted, which the rector of the church holds in demesne. And the said Philip has two parts of the advowson of the said church with half a virgate of land for glebe through Isolde de Cardun who gave it to the same Philip, and William de Munfort has the third part of the said advowson from the gift of the ancestors of the said Isolde Cardun. The said Isolde has in demesne from the said hides 2 parts, 2 virgates of land. In villeinage, 2 virgates, each of which owes her 1 mark a year or works to that value. And the tenants of these are serfs and bondsmen like others aforesaid: John Hulle, who holds ½ virgate; Aspelon son of Nicholas, ½ virgate; Reynfrey, ½ virgate; Sarah Jacob, ½ virgate.

In free tenants: Isabel de Nouhers, ½ virgate for 7s a year; John de Sceltone, ½ virgate for 21s, foreign service and suit of court; Hugh Flemyng, ½ virgate for 2s a year, foreign service and suit; Walter Bonde, ½ virgate for 2s, suit, and foreign service; Richard son of Alexander, 2 parts [sic] ½ virgate for 3s, suit of court and foreign service; Geoffrey de Gotesho, 1 quarter for 12d, suit, and foreign service.

The said William de Monteforti holds from the said Isolde 3 virgates and 2 parts ½ virgate for foreign service. Of which he has in demesne 1 virgate and 3 parts 2 virgates.

In free tenants: Stephen de Thoternho holds 1 virgate of land for 1 lb of cummin, suit, and foreign service; John de Monfort, ½ virgate for 1d and foreign service; Roger Cocus, a third part of ½ virgate for foreign service; the Prior of Bissemede, 1 messuage in pure and perpetual alms given to him in the time of King John; Roger de Novers through his wife, 6 acres for 6d.

Isabel Quarrel holds in the same vill 1 hide of land in chief from John Latimer and his wife who hold from the King from the barony of Wardone for 6d or 1 pair of golden spurs for all services. Of which he has in demesne 3½ virgates.

In free tenants: Richard de Irencester, Henry de Wenlingbur', Margaret la Mazun & Emma de Lay hold ½ virgate for 3s 6d, suit, and foreign service.

In cottagers: Walter King who holds 1 cottage for 12d or works to that value, and he is a bondsman like others aforesaid.

Henry Bissop holds in the same vill 3 virgates of land in chief from William le Enneyse, and he himself from the Abbess of Hewnestone for 5s and 1 lb of pepper for everything; no rent to the King nor the Sheriff, nor foreign service. It is not possible to enquire from what barony or honour or in what way the Abbess has lordship of these virgates. [footnote: 'to be investigated']. Of which the said Henry has in demesne the whole except 1 messuage and 4 acres of land, of which Richard de Irencester and Stephen de Weltone hold the 4 acres of land aforesaid, John Spere and Emma Lay the said messuage for 2s a year.

CARLTON Ralph Perot has in Karlton a holding which answers for 1 knight's fee for scutage and sheriff's fee and annual hidage. He holds in chief from Almaric de St Amandus and he from the King, and it is from the barony of Carnho in the county of Bedford. Of which he has in demesne 1 carucate of land which contains 80 acres of land, 6 acres of meadow and pasture, 15 acres of wood, the site of a watermill, a common fishery in the water called Ouse from Bedewell against Neunton as far as Hachenewell in Chelvynton. In villeinage, 1 virgate of land which is worth to him 1 mark in money and works. The tenants of this are bondsmen and serfs bound to redeem their tenure at the lord's will, whose names are: Walter Cade, who holds 1 quarter; William Cade, 1 quarter; Simon the reeve, 1 quarter; 'Gerinus' Wyting, 1 quarter.

He has the advowson of the church of that vill which is endowed from 1 virgate of land which the parson of that church holds in demesne in pure and perpetual alms. Also the said Ralph has in free tenants: Robert Amari with his tenants, who holds 5½ virgates of land for 20s a year and suit of court, of which he has in demesne 1 virgate.

In free tenants: John de Pabeham, 3 quarters of land for 2s a year; Roger le Serjaunt, ½ virgate for 6d; Richard Curtefaloun with his tenants, ½ virgate for 2s 6d; John Ate with his lesser tenants, 3 quarters of land for 4s 6d; Walter de Neuho, 1 quarter of land for 15d; Henry Herbert, 1 quarter for 15d; John son of William, ½ virgate for foreign service, as much as belongs; Richard son of Robert, 1 quarter for 14d; the Prioress of Harewold, 1 messuage and 2 acres for 4d; Richard le Champioun, 12 acres for – – – ; Roger le Charpenter, 2 acres for 8d; Walter Trayli, 4 acres for 8d; and many other lesser tenants of acres, half-acres, roods, for a small rent.

Also the said Ralph Perot has many other free tenants for annual rent: Hubert Gerin with his own tenants, 1 virgate for 2s and suit of court and foreign service; Brithelin, ½ virgate for 5s, suit of court, foreign service; Philip son of Ralph, ½ virgate for 12d, suit, foreign service; the Abbot of St James North[ampton], ½ [virgate] for 12d; Agnes Wymund, 1½ virgates for 2s; Roger le Serjaunt, 1½ virgates of land for 3d; Roger Albot, 1 quarter of land for 6d; Henry de la Leye with his tenant John Hareng and others, 1 quarter of land & 40 acres, 2 acres of meadow and pasture, for foreign service. The said John Hareng with his tenants holds the said quarter of land from the said Henry for 5s a year.

Also from the said Ralph the tenants: Simon le Mazoun, 1 messuage for 12d; Robert le Neuman, 1 messuage for 3s; William de Eston, 1 messuage for 1d; Nicholas le Palmere, 1 cottage for 1d; and he has many other lesser tenants of the same kind from the said knight's fee.

Baldwin Wake has a fief in that vill aforesaid from the honour of Boloyne, held in chief from the Earl of Bovan, and he himself from the King, belonging - - - to the said Baldwin de Grenenton in the next vill, that is 120 acres of land of which Ralph Perot holds two parts of those acres from the said Baldwin for ½ mark a year and foreign service, and Henry de Lega a third part of those acres for 40d and foreign service.

In the same vill, John de Pabenham holds in chief from the lord King by a knight's fee for foreign service, as much as belongs, that is 5 virgates of which he has in demesne 3½ virgates, 1 enclosed wood of 20 acres. In villeinage 1½ virgates of which [each] virgate owes him 1 mark a year or works to that value, and the tenants of these are serfs and bondsmen bound to redeem their tenure at the lord's will: Jordan Crane, who holds 1½ quarters; Alan son of Philip, 1 quarter; Robert Reyner, 1 quarter; – – – de Kaldecote, 1 quarter; William de Caldecote, 1 quarter; Avis, ½ quarter.

Also he has Henry Herbert, a free tenant of 1 messuage for 9d and 2 capons a year.

In the same vill John Malerbe has free tenants who hold 3½ virgates of land from the barony de Bello Campo of Bedford, which the said John holds in chief from William de Montecanisio through his wife and she herself from the King, and the whole holding is assessed for ½ hide at scutage and against sheriff's fee for 3s 2d a year for hidage, suit, and view of frankpledge, of which: Geoffrey de Karlton with his tenants, 2½ virgates for 7½d a year and foreign service; Robert de Efforde, 1 virgate for 8s and foreign service.

In the same vill, Henry de Scarnebrok holds in chief from John de Pateshull and he himself from Roger le Estraunge on behalf of Roger de Mounbray from the said barony of Bedford, and R. himself from the King, and it is assessed for – – – at scutage and sheriff's fee per year – – – of which the said Henry has in demesne the chief messuage and ½ virgate of land.

In free tenants: the Prior of Caldewell, 1 virgate of land in free alms from the gift of Henry his grandfather in the time of King Henry son of King John, which virgate John Hareng with his tenants holds from the said Prior for 12d a year rent; also Geoffrey de Karlton holds from the said Henry ½ virgate for foreign service; Geoffrey, ½ virgate from the same Henry for 1 mark a year; William le Champioun, 1 virgate for 2s 6d a year; Richard le Moun, 1 messuage 4 acres for – – – ; Robert Godefrey, 1 messuage.

In the same vill, John de Montibus holds from the said barony ½ hide for foreign service in chief from Ralph Paynel, who holds from the King through his wife and pays annually sheriff's fee for foreign service, that is 2s for hidage, suit, and view. Of which he has in demesne 3 quarters of land.

In free tenants: Nicholas de Montibus, 1 quarter for 2d and foreign service; Gilbert de la More with his tenants, 1 virgate for 6d and foreign service, and from that virgate Henry Herberd holds ½ virgate from the said Gilbert for 6d and foreign service.

CHELVYNTON hamlet. Walter de Trayli holds in Chelvynton hamlet of the said vill of Karlton half of one knight's fee in chief from the Earl of Gloucester of his county and honour of Gloucester, and the Earl himself from the King. He pays the King no sheriff's fee nor anything else except the scutage appropriate to one knight's fee when it occurs. Of this the said Walter has nothing in demesne, but in villeins and free tenants who are in the hand of Philip Burnel for the term of his life and in the hands of other free tenants as below, except that the advowson of the church of that vill is in his hand, to which church there belongs 1 messuage with a croft and 3 roods of land which the parson of that church holds in demesne, and the said Philip Burnel holds for the term of his life 5 virgates, that is in villeinage from that holding, each of which owes him 20s a year for everything, and the tenants of these are serfs because they cannot marry their daughters without the lord's leave.

Of which tenants: William de Ponte, ½ virgate; William de Rysle, ½ virgate; Richard Hand, ½ virgate; John de Beyden, 1 quarter; Richard de Beyden, 1 quarter; William Grote, ½ quarter; Geoffrey Godwyne, ½ quarter; Roger Waker, 1 quarter; Roger le Hayward, ½ quarter; Hugh in Via, 1 quarter; John Waker, 1 quarter; William son of Hugh, ½ quarter; William son of Emma, 1 quarter; John le Messer, ½ quarter; Geoffrey Bonde, 1 quarter; William de Gynelden, 1 quarter; Gregory de — — — , 1 quarter; Ralph de Derecroft, 1 quarter.

In cottars of the same condition and service: Ralph son of William, 1 cottage for 12d; Richard son of Emma, 1 cottage for the same service; Sarah, 1 cottage for 5d; Mary Bernard, 1 cottage for 16d.

In free tenants: Norman son of Walter, 1 virgate of land for 4s a year, payment for maintaining a lamp in the same church in the chancel. Also John de Cowe who holds from the said Walter 1½ virgates and half a quarter for 1d a year, of which he has in demesne the chief messuage with a fishery in the water called Ouse, namely half the fishing from Harewold bridge as far as Wahull pond.

In villeinage 1½ virgates and half a quarter: the wife of Arnulf Hady, ½ virgate; John Hode, 1 quarter; Geoffrey son of William, 1 quarter; John son of William, 1 quarter; Walter Denys, 1 quarter; Roger de Wotton, ½ quarter, and it is worth to the same John 20s each virgate each year.

In cottages: Roger son of William, 1 cottage for 5d; Thomas Piscator, 1 cottage for 5d; Roger Kyn, 1 cottage for 5d.

Also Geoffrey de Carlton with his tenants holds from the said Walter ½ virgate for 2s.

Richard de Ponte holds from the said Walter ½ virgate for 2s. Roger Abbot, 1 messuage for 1d.

STEVENTON In Steventon, Baldwin Wake holds through Hawisa de Quency his wife, the daughter of Robert de Quency, a certain holding in chief from the Earl of Bowan and he himself from the King, namely from the honour of Boloyne, for two knight's fees at scutage when it occurs, with Little Wodhull which answers for it by the same for half a knight's fee as elsewhere in Wodhull, and for one mark per year paid to the Sheriff of Bedford for the use of the King, for everything. From which holding the said Baldwin has in demesne 7 virgates 1 quarter of land, 1 ancient park which contains 40 acres, 1 other wood, a grove of 5 acres, 1 watermill, a fishery in the river called Ouse in common from Radewell hedge as far as the mere between Steventon and Bromham. In villeinage, 24 virgates of land of which each owes the same B. 17s a year in works and other services. In fact the tenants of these are serfs bound to redeem their tenure at the lord's will, whose names and tenures are: John ad Pratum, ½ virgate; Roger Mile, ½ virgate; Stephen Parker, ½ virgate; Robert the reeve, ½ virgate; Roger Abraam, ½ virgate; William le Fader, ½ virgate; Roger Brid', ½ virgate; John Clay, ½ virgate; William the reeve, ½ virgate; Matthew de Freyuse, ½ virgate; Robert le Lavender, ½ virgate; John Abraam, ½ virgate; Alice la Mazoun, ½ virgate; Nicholas de Polescroft, ½ virgate; Robert Faber, ½ virgate; William Brid',½ virgate; William Aumary, ½ virgate; Florence Abraam, ½ virgate; Simon Fulcon, ½ virgate; Alice Thurgod, ½ virgate; John Gentilman, ½ virgate; William Crisp, ½ virgate; Nicholas the reeve & William his son, ½ virgate; Simon son of Robert, ½ virgate; William Fraunkeleyn, ½ virgate; Stephen Fraunkeleyn, ½ virgate; Robert le Loung, ½ virgate; William Burgeys, ½ virgate; Juliana in Trewes, ½ virgate; John Hurlefreyus and Hugh le Vaus, ½ virgate; Richard le Careter and Roger David, ½ virgate and ½ quarter; Rose the miller and John son of Geoffrey, ½ virgate; Richard Fox and Adam son of Adam, ½ virgate; Reginald de Coventre and William Frampe, ½ virgate; William Wyte and Richard Pake, ½ virgate; Emma daughter of Adam and Lettice ad Grene, ½ virgate less ½ quarter; John ad Wold and Emma his wife, ½ virgate; Isabell de Polescroft and John le Wyte, ½ virgate; Richard le Glovere and Matthew de Pixhull, ½ virgate; Gervase de Pixhull and Roger Cok, ½ virgate; Roger Ammary and Simon Child, ½ virgate; Richard Ammary and Roger Brid, ½ virgate; Mabel Brid and Thomas Fraunkeleyn, ½ virgate; Nicholas Gentilman Strumpe, ½ virgate; Reginald ad Ston and William le Parker, ½ virgate; Hugh son of Matilda, 1 quarter; Alice le Falour, Gilbert Fraunkeleyn, and Thomas Faber, 1 quarter; Nicholas Ammar and Geoffrey le Clerk, ½ virgate; ; Hugh son of William, 1 quarter; Simon son of Adam and John Lutewyne, 1 quarter; Gilbert Fraunkeleyn, 1 quarter; John Trigh, 1½ quarters; Robert Benjamin and Richard le Pestour, ½ virgate; William Edrich and Ralph Faber, 1 quarter.

In cottars in the same condition of serfs, 21 cottages whose tenants are: Simon le Careter, 1 cottage; Robert son of William, 1 cottage; Nicholas le Palmer, 1 cottage; John le Taylur, 1 cottage; Geoffrey de Kemeston, 1 cottage; Robert son of the reeve, 1 cottage; John Baroilf, 1 cottage; Wymark Crisp, 1 cottage; Robert Careter, Richard son of Thomas, 1 cottage; John Cissor, 1 cottage; Reginald de Vinour, 1 cottage; Nicholas le Webbe, 1 cottage; Ada [Adam?] ad Crucem, 1 cottage; Alice la Careter, 1 cottage; Agnes Pake, 1 cottage; Reginald son of Eve, 1 cottage; Agnes ad Ecclesiam, 1 cottage; Agnes Piscator, 1 cottage; John le Taylur, 1 cottage; and John Piscator, 1 cottage.

Each of the aforesaid cottars owes his lord of aforesaid 9d or works to that value.

Also: James Carpenter, 1 cottage with 3 acres of land for 2s; Thomas le Mouner, 1 cottage for 8d; Juliana Piscator, 1 cottage for 6d; Mabel ad Crucem, 1 cottage for 6d.

Each of those owes works to that value if the lord wishes, and they are in the condition of serfs like the others.

In free tenants for fixed annual service as below and for foreign service and suit of court: Henry de Polescroft with his tenants, 1½ virgates for 21s; also Lucy de Burdeleys and John Alulf with their tenants, ¾ virgate for 10s 2d; also Ada Alulf, ¾ virgate for 10s 6d; Roger le Fleming and John de Gynes with their tenants, ¾ virgate for 20s 4d; Philip Barculf with his tenants, ¾ virgate for 5s 6d; Roger de Wylie, ½ virgate for foreign service, and so much suit of court; Ralph Passelewe & Nicholas Passelewe, 48 acres for 48d a year for everything; the Prioress of Harewold, in pure and perpetual alms through the gift of Roger de Quency in the time of King Henry son of King J., 10 acres; Reginald le Clerk, 1 messuage for 2d for everything.

Also the said Baldwin Wake is the patron of the church of the said vill of Steventon, which the said Prioress of Harewold has for her own use with 4 acres of land and 1½ acres of meadow from which the church is endowed in pure alms, which the said Prioress holds in demesne. That church had been given to the said Prioress in the time of King John.

PABENHAM In the vill of Pabenham the said Baldwin Wake has from the said tenure 6 virgates of land in villeinage, which are from the same fiefs as were named above in Steventon and from the same honour, and they belong to his manor of Steventon and are held like the other virgates of Steventon in works and services, and their tenants are in the same serfdom as the others aforementioned of Steventon, and the tenants' names are: John Randulf, ½ virgate; Edith de Pabenham; Robert her son, 1 quarter; William Wyth, ½ virgate; Mary Fleming, ½ virgate; Philip ad Ree, ½ virgate; William Broun, ½ virgate; Aline, ½ virgate; John le Pounter, ½ virgate; Hugh Druye, 1 quarter 1 quarter; [sic]; Walter Richeree [?Bitheree], 1 quarter; William Est, 1 quarter; Beatrice Shyrlok, 1 quarter; Richard Utlawe, 1 quarter; Lefeke Daffe, 1 quarter; William Finch, 1 quarter; Ralph Eustace, ½ quarter.

Cottars of the same condition and serfdom in the same: Thomas Dore, 1 cottage for 5d or works; Richard le Clerk, for 17d or works to that value; Agnes Druye, 1 cottage for 9d or works to that value; William Abraam, freely, ½ virgate for 8s 1d & suit & foreign service.

In the same vill of Pabeham, John de Abernoun holds half a knight's fee in chief from the Earl of Gloucester and the Earl himself from the King, and it is from the barony or county of Penbrok. The lord King has no service from it, but the Earl of Gloucester has there all the royal service and scutage when it occurs, as much as belongs to half a knight's fee. Also 4s annually for view of frankpledge. The church of that fief and vill is a chapel belonging to the church of Felmersham, that chapel is endowed from 1 virgate of land. From which half fee aforesaid the said John has in demesne 1 carucate of land in which is contained 100 acres of land, 12 acres of meadow and pasture, a fishery in the river called Ouse from Radewell hedge as far as Pabeham mill, in common with other lords of various fiefs of that vill. In villeinage, 12 virgates each of which [owes] him ½ mark a year or works to that value. The tenants indeed of these are serfs bound to redeem their tenure at the lord's will. The tenants are: William Est, 1 virgate; William de Colmorth, 1 virgate; Richard the reeve, 1 virgate; Henry le Tippe; William Toni, 1 virgate; Simon Est & Margery Est, 1 virgate; Simon Knew & Henry ad Quarrer, 1 virgate; Sarah Knew, Benedict de Hul, 1 virgate; Richard Mareys, Michael de Overende, 1 virgate; Geoffrey Wyth and Hugh ad Grene, 1 virgate; Simon Cok and Simon Godefr', 1 virgate; John Scot and William the reeve 1 virgate; John Fosun and Gilbert Purs', 1 virgate.

In cottars in the same condition and serfdom: Wymare Broun, 1 cottage for 2s or works; John Est, 1 cottage for the same service.

In free tenants: William de Edelond with his lesser tenants, 3 virgates for 10s and foreign service; John Champioun, 1 virgate for 5s and foreign service; Katherine le Champioun, for 2s and foreign service; Benedict Daur', ½ virgate for 2s 6d and foreign service; Simon son of Emma, 1 messuage for 12d; Phision, 1 free cottage for 6d; Gilbert Dare, 1 cottage for 6d, and 1 virgate of land, from which the aforesaid chapel of Pabeham aforesaid, as David de Mazoun, holds freely from the rector of Felmersham ½ virgate of land for 4s for everything; John Trese, 1 quarter for 3s in the same way; William Fraunkeleyn, 1 quarter for 3s in the same way.

In the same vill of Pabeham John de Pabeham holds from the barony de Bello Campo of Bedford in chief from William de Monte Canis and he from the King a holding which is assessed for 2 hides at scutage and annual sheriff's fee at the court of the lord King for homage, suit, and at – – –. Of this he has in demesne 5 virgates with a fishery in the said river Ouse in common with other lords of that vill from Radewell hedge as far as Pabeham mill. In villeinage, 5 virgates, each of which is worth 10s a year or works to that value, and the tenants of these are serfs bound to redeem their tenure at the lord's will. The tenants are: Ralph de Huntvil & Walter Beneyt, 1 virgate; William Terry & William de Stacheden, 1 virgate; William de Overende & Ralph son of Rose, 1 virgate; Isabel la Repe, 1 virgate; John Kneuc, 1 virgate.

In free tenants: John West, 1 virgate for 6s and suit and foreign service; John son of Robert Cerne with his tenants, William West, Simon West, William Reyn' and others, 1 virgate for 5s and suit of court.

In the vill of TURVEY The Prior of St Neots has the advowson of the church of that vill from the gift of William le Heyr in the time of King Richard with 3 messuages and ½ virgate of land from which that church is endowed in pure &c, and it is from the barony de Bello Campo of Bedford, of which church the Prior holds half for his own use; the other half he always gives when it is vacant. The tenants of the aforesaid holding of that church are: Hugh le Moyne, 1 messuage and ½ virgate of land for 5s a year for everything; Ralph le Moyne, 1 messuage for 2s; Gunild Piscator, 1 messuage for 12d for everything.

In the same vill, William de Montecanisio of——— delton holds through his wife from the aforesaid barony of Bedford 1 hide of land in chief from the King and pays annual sheriff's fee of 2s for hidage, 2s for suit, 2s for view. He has none of it in demesne, but in free tenants for suit of court and foreign service: Joan de Northo 1 virgate and 1 quarter, with her tenants, Roger le Serjaunt, who holds from it ½ virgate for 1d, Ralph Perot & Henry de Leya, 1 quarter for 6d, and Nicholas le Champion, 1 quarter for 1d. Also Adam son of Robert, who holds from the said W. de Montecanisio 1¼ virgates for suit and foreign service, and Adam himself has many lesser tenants for small annual services. Also Roger de Wilie with his tenants holds in the same vill 1½ virgates for so much foreign service. Roger's tenants, who all hold for as much foreign service as belongs, are: Henry Capellus, 1 quarter; William Henry & Walter le Carpenter, 1 quarter; William de Hotot & Hugh le Proude, 1 quarter; Roger son of Matilda, Adam le Wyse & William de Hotot, ½ quarter; Sarah de Holewell, ½ quarter; William Cuggel & Nicholas Faber, 1 quarter.

In the same vill——— heir of John le Reve holds in chief from the lord King 4 virgates of land for 1 hide at scutage in serjeanty, for which he has in rent 8s a year for hidage, suit and view. Of this he has in demesne 1 messuage and 1 quarter of land.

In free tenants: William de Hotot, 2 virgates and 1 windmill for so much foreign service; Philip son of Roger, ½ virgate for foreign service; Geoffrey ad Boscum, 1 quarter for foreign service; the Prior of St Neots, 1 virgate in pure &c, from a gift of an ancestor of the said John le Reve in the time of King Henry son of King John.

In the same vill the Prior of Neunham outside Bedford has a hide of land from a gift of the aforesaid King Henry in pure &c, which had been held in chief from the King, in what way it is not known. The said Prior has none of it in demesne, but from free tenants 10s a year: from Gilbert de Lavenden for ½ virgate, 2s 6d; from Simon son of Ellis for ½ virgate, 2s 6d; John son of Elye, ½ virgate for 2s 6d; from Ralph Faber, William Hamelyn, Robert Carpenter & Adam Kuggel for ½ virgate, 2s 6d for everything.

In the same vill the heirs of Richard de Ardres & William Mordaunt hold a certain tenement for 1 fee at scutage in chief from Walter de Trayli and Walter himself from the Earl of Gloucester and the Earl himself from the King, from his county of Gloucester, and the Sheriff of Bedford has from it yearly for the use of the lord King 8s for hidage, and the said Earl has a fixed payment for 3s a year for view of frankpledge and whatever belongs to the view.

From the said fee indeed the heir of the said Richard de Ardres has in lordship 2 carucates of land which comprise 200 acres of land, 10 acres of meadow and pasture, 1 ancient park of 40 acres enclosed. In free tenants for annual foreign service: John Bruel, 40 acres for — — — ; John de Burdeleys, 7 acres for 7½d; Roger le Serjaunt, 3 quarters of land for 1 lb of cummin; William Kuggel, ½ virgate for 5s; Robert le Mordaunt, ½ virgate for 2s; Hugh le Serjaunt, ½ virgate for 2s; Thomas le Walys & John King, ½ virgate for 11s; William de Hotot, 1½ virgates for 1 mark and 1 lb of cummin; Hugh le Proud, 1 quarter for 5s paid to the Hospital, a payment for the assignment and donation of an ancestor of the said Richard de Ardres in the time of King John; Also Robert le Proud, 1 quarter for 6s rent to the said Richard.

In free cottages: Walter le Proude, 1 cottage for 12d; William le Comerur, 1 messuage for 12d; Matilda Pynchoun, 3 acres for 12d; Michael Burre, ½ messuage 1½ acres for 12d; Peter le Carpenter, 1 messuage and 2 acres for 2s; Hubert Gerin, 1 cottage for 2s; Robert Kuggel, 1 cottage for summoning the lord's courts yearly.

Also the said William de Mordaunt who holds from the same fief has in demesne 180 acres of land, 12 acres of meadow & pasture, 2 watermills, a fishery in the river called Ouse in common from Landimareswell as far as Budewell, 40 acres of enclosed wood. In villeinage 3 virgates and ½ quarter, each of which owes him 10s a year or works to that value at his will, and the tenants of these are like his serfs, bound to redeem their tenure at his will.

The tenants of which are: Robert the reeve ½ virgate; Reginald de Monte, ½ virgate; Nicholas Neubonde, ½ virgate; Robert de Karlton, ½ virgate; Beatrice de Wykes, ½ virgate; Robert Aleyn, ½ virgate; Geoffrey Choppere & Richard Pice, ½ virgate.

In cottars in the same condition and serfdom: Reginald King, 1 cottage for 16d or works; Adam Stokke, 1 cottage for 2s or works; Richard le Taylur, 1 cottage for 12d; Michael Burre, Henry Duretelle, & Geoffrey le Moun, each of them 1 cottage for 6d or works.

In free tenants for annual service: Simon de Norho with his tenants, ½ virgate for 1 lb of pepper; Roger son of Roger le Serjaunt, ½ virgate and 6 acres for 10s; the Prior of St Neots with his tenants, ½ virgate in pure & perpetual alms; Robert ad Crucem, 1 quarter for 6d; Henry le Rous, 1 messuage for 18d; Hugh le Noble, 1 messuage for 12d, 4 hens; Walter le Covertur, 1 messuage for court service.

In the same vill William son of Sampson le Maunsel holds half a knight's fee from the barony of Wahull in chief from Reginald de Grey, and R. himself from John de Wodhull and John himself from the King, and for half a knight's fee he is assessed at scutage and annually 3s for ward of Rokingham castle, and sheriff's fee for the use of the lord King, 2s 4d for hidage, suit and view, of which half fee the said William has in demesne 2 virgates.

In free tenants for annual service & foreign service: Hugh le Wyte, 1 virgate for 2s 6d and foreign service; Hubert Mauduyt, ½ virgate for foreign service; Henry le Dylewyk, ½ virgate as marriage portion and for 8d a year; Walter de

Estwode, 1 messuage 3 acres for 2s; Roger le Ken', 1 messuage for 12d; 'Cons', 1 messuage for 2s.

In the same, William de Hotot holds a tenement which is assessed for 1½ hides at scutage per year, ward of Belver castle of the barony of Belveor, in chief from Richard de Bochard, and R. himself from Robert de Ros and Robert himself from the King. [footnote: 'He gives no other service to the lord King']. Of this he has in demesne 20 acres of land and meadow.

In free tenants: Alexander Besoun through his wife, 1 wood of 8 acres for — — — ; Sarah de Holewell, 40 acres for 14d a year and foreign service; Roger son of Hugh de Wylie, 40 acres for the same service and from the same Roger Geoffrey de Bosco holds ½ virgate for 10s, and Roger le Serjaunt with his tenant John Kneu, holds 1 quarter for foreign service; also from the said William, Walter Mannalet holds 1 quarter for 12d a year; also from the same William, Simon Heroun, 1 quarter for 2s a year.

In the same vill the Prior of St Neots holds 100 acres of land; it is in no way possible to enquire from what fief, barony, or honour, nor how the said Prior holds them except by intrusion. [footnote: 'To be investigated']. Also in the same way in the same vill John de Burdeleys holds 16 acres. Also in the same vill Alexander Besoun holds 20 acres through his wife.

BROMHAM William Malherbe has in Bromham 4 hides of land from the barony de Bello Campo of Bedford. He holds in chief from the heirs of the said barony and they themselves from the King, and that holding is assessed at 3 hides for scutage and sheriff's fee, 15s a year for hidage, suit, and ward, from each hide. He has in demesne 160 acres of land, 18 acres of meadow, 14 acres of enclosed wood, a fishery in the river called Ouse from a place called Holm as far as Brochiseved in common with Ralph Passelewe. In villeinage, 3¾ virgates, each of which owes him 20s a year or works to that value at his will. The tenants of these are serfs bound to redeem their tenure at his will, and the tenants are: Robert Neuman, ½ virgate; Roger de Wylden and William Berngate, 3 quarters; Thomas le Juvene and William Sutor, 3 quarters; Nicholas Frend, John Perenhale, William Sutor and William Osebern, 1 virgate; Henry Kip, Alex & Mary Scot, 3 quarters.

The ancestors of the said William gave the church of that vill to the Prior of Caldewell in the time of King Richard with 30 acres of land from which the same church is endowed, which the said Prior holds with the said church for his own use.

The said William also has in free tenants for annual service and foreign service: Richard Marlerbe with his tenants, who holds 2½ virgates of it for 2s, suit of court, and foreign service, of whom Thomas de Faccon holds from the same Richard ½ virgate for 2s, William de Bosco, 5 acres for 10½ d, and the heirs de Bello Campo, 7 acres for one root of ginger. Also from the said William, Roger Grant, ½ virgate for 10s & foreign service; Richard Bonum, ½ virgate for 2d, suit, and foreign service; William ad Boscum, ½ quarter for 2s, suit, and foreign service; Henry Godiman, William Ros & William Sweyn, ½ virgate for 2s, suit, and foreign service; Walter le Plumer, 1 quarter for the same service.

In the same vill Ralph Passelewe holds from the said barony in chief from W. de Montecanis through his wife and he himself from the King a holding which is assessed for 2½ hides at scutage and sheriff's fee for the use of the lord King 9s 2d a year for hidage, suit and ward. Of this he has in demesne ½ quarter, 2 watermills, a private fishery in the river called Ouse from Holewell as far as his curtilage and in common from his curtilage as far as Bideham bridge, 1 enclosed wood of 10 acres. In villeinage, 1½ quarters which pay him 7s 6d a year or works to that value, which Walter Hachet and William Denys hold, and they are as serfs bound to redeem their tenure at the lord's will.

In free tenants: Robert son of James ½ virgate for 10s and foreign service; Geoffrey le Ros, ½ virgate for 10s, suit, and foreign service; Thomas Warde, ½ virgate for 18d, suit, and foreign service; Roger Grant, Geoffrey de Aspele, Nicholas Freman, and John le Ros, 1½ virgates for 1 lb of pepper, suit, and foreign service; Nicholas Knel and Richard Nenon, 3 quarters for ½ mark; Nicholas le Clerk, 3 quarters for 1 lb of pepper & suit & foreign service; Henry Coterel, ½ virgate for 10s and foreign service; James Patoun, ½ virgate for 2s 6d, suit and foreign service; Gilbert le Freyuse, ½ virgate for 7s 4d, suit, and foreign service; William Bonde, 1 quarter for 18d, suit, and foreign service; Peter de Northende, ½ quarter for 8d, suit, and foreign service; William de Bosco, ½ quarter for 2s, suit, and foreign service; Juliana Wycher and Walter Est, ½ virgate for 2s 6d, suit, and foreign service; Agnes Swon, Ralph Scharp, and William Scharp, ½ virgate for 3s, suit, and foreign service; William son of Reginald with his tenant John Kane, ½ virgate for 12d; Richard Haliday, 1 quarter for 3s and foreign service; Nicholas Passelewe with his tenant N. de Brazour, ½ virgate for 4s and foreign service; the same Nicholas Passelewe with his tenant William Alulf, 1½ virgates for 1 lb of pepper and foreign service; the Prior of Caldewell, 1¼ virgates for foreign service.

In the same vill William Passelewe holds from the said barony in chief from Alexander Bosoun and A. himself from John de Steyngr' and J. himself from the King a holding which is assessed for 2 hides at scutage and sheriff's fee for the use of the King 11s 8d a year for hidage, suit, and ward. Of this he has in demesne 1 hide, that is 4 virgates. In villeinage ½ virgate which is worth to him 10s a year or works to that value. Nicholas de Bideham and Richard Bouregate hold that and they are serfs like others as above.

In free tenants: Geoffrey ad Hokes with his tenants, 1 virgate for 9s, suit and foreign service; James son of Richard, 1 quarter for 18d, suit, foreign service; Gilbert le Clerk and Nicholas le Clerk, 1 quarter for 6s, 4 capons a year, and foreign service; Gilbert Freyuse, 1 quarter for 5s and foreign service; Peter Hamby, 1 quarter for 18d, suit, foreign service; Nicholas Bonde, 1 quarter for 2s, suit, and foreign service; William Bonde, 4 acres for 18d, suit, foreign service; William le Ros, 1 acre for 12d, suit, and foreign service.

In the same vill of Bruham Bartholomew le Blound holds ½ hide of land in chief in petty serjeanty for 18d a year rent to the Sheriff of Bedford for the use of the King. Of this he has in demesne 16 acres.

In free tenants: Thomas le Warde, 8 acres for 6d; Nicholas Knok, 10 acres for 2s, and other lesser tenants of acres and such from the same holding are James son of Richard, 2 acres for 1d, William le Ros, 2 acres for 2d, William le Freman, 2½ acres for 2½d, Ralph Leecke, 1 acre for 1d, Letitia wife of Nicholas, 1 acre for 4d.

In the same vill of Bromham, William Passelewe holds in chief from Baldwin Wake, through his wife, from the honour of Bolon, and the same B. from the Earl of Bovan, and the Earl himself from the King, a holding which is assessed at 1 hide for scutage and to the said Baldwin 10s a year and suit of court and foreign service. Of this he has in demesne 3 virgates. In villeinage: Nicholas de

Bydeham, who holds 1 quarter for 5s or works to that value, and he is a serf bound to redeem his tenure &c.

In free tenants: John Hardi, 1 quarter for 18d, suit, and foreign service; Gilbert le Clerk, 1 quarter for 5s, suit, and foreign service; Richard Haliday, 1 quarter through a mesne tenant, Ralph Passelewe, for 3s for everything.

ACCOUNT ROLL FOR HIGHAM GOBION AND STREATLEY, 1379-1382

This account roll [BCRO cat. no. BS 1175] contains accounts for the manor and grange of Higham Gobion, and also accounts dealing with Streatley, for the years 1379-1382. It was deposited at the Bedfordshire County Record Office in March 1940 by the London solicitors, Messrs Farrer & Co., as part of an archive of about 110 deeds and documents relating to Higham Gobion manor and rectory and Streatley manor dating from 1379 to 1595.

The parish of Higham Gobion originally lay in three detached parts, of which the largest, containing the church, the present manor farm house, and the old rectory house, was bounded south and west by Barton in the Clay, north by Silsoe and Gravenhurst, and east by Shillington and by Hexton in Hertfordshire. To the west lay two smaller areas: the first, containing the site of a deserted hamlet, and also Faldo Farm, presumably the site of the manor of Westhey and Faldo, is bounded south and east by Barton, west by Pulloxhill and north by Silsoe; further west is the second detached area, containing Higham Bury, and bounded north-west by Flitton, south-west by Westoning, south by Harlington and east by Pulloxhill. This contained also Gubbins (for Gobions) Wood.

The manor of Higham was by 1158 in the hands of the Gobion family, from whom the parish derives its name. This family had acquired also by 1158 the nearby manor of Streatley with Sharpenhoe. Richard Gobion died in 1300, and his heirs were his two daughters of whom Hawisa, the elder, was the wife of Ralph Butler, and to her and her descendants came these two main manors. Ralph Butler died in 1342 leaving a son, Sir John Butler, but it would appear that both Higham Gobion and Streatley with Sharpenhoe continued in the hands of Hawisa until her death in 1360. By then the son, Sir John, had predeceased her, as had Sir John's own elder son, Ralph, and so the two manors came to a second grandson, Ralph's younger brother, Sir Edward. Sir Edward eventually died without issue in 1412, and it was, therefore, for Sir Edward Butler that these accounts were made. On his death without a direct heir the manors passed to an uncle's grandson. Sir Philip Butler of Woodhall in Watton, Herts, and from that time onwards the family's main seat was in Hertfordshire. Though the account roll is headed 'Hegham', it is clear that it dealt also with the administration of land in Streatley with Sharpenhoe.

Higham Gobion was sold from the Butler family in 1638 by the guardian of Jane Butler, daughter of a Sir Robert Butler, who had died in 1622, but on Sir Robert's death Streatley with Sharpenhoe went to his brother, John Butler, and so this manor remained with the Butler family for a few more years.

The *Inquisition post Mortem* on the death of Richard Gobion in 1300 describes the manor of Higham as consisting of a capital messuage with garden worth 3s p.a.; two dove cotes; 360 acres in demesne at 6d an acre, worth £9; 24 acres of meadow at 1s an acre, 24s; 6 acres of pasture, 3s; a watermill, 13s 4d; a vineyard, 12d; and 21 acres of wood with underwood which in 2 years would be worth 6d an acre, 10s 6d. Then are listed 8 free tenants and their houses and land, and an indeterminate number of villeins, the document at this point being defective. The total yearly value is £19 14s 2¼d.[1] The vineyard is not mentioned in these accounts, but the accounts can only be partial, and so it might still have been in operation. The present manor farm by the church in Higham Gobion is, presumably, in the area of the ancient manor house. The curious triangular earthworks in the north-east corner of the parish are now considered to have been an extensive fish-pond and water-fowl preserve, but there is no evidence for this in the accounts. In the same *Inquisition post Mortem* of 1300 Streatley manor consisted of a capital messuage and garden, 3s per annum; 140 acres of arable; 2 acres of meadow; a windmill worth 6s 8d a year; 10 acres of woodland, 6d; the rents of customary tenants worth 22s, and 2 virgates in villeinage, 28s 1d, total £6 14s 1½d.

It is not easy to discover the area of the manor of Higham Gobion at the time of the accounts. Certainly it included Wrestmede of about ten acres in Silsoe in the parish of Flitton, and a small piece of arable in Gravenhurst. There is some evidence that the two manors were run together under one court. There was an order to the escheator in 1342 not to intermeddle further with the manor of Higham Gobion with Stratele,[2] and an eighteenth century translation of court rolls for the manor of Higham Gobion for 1525 and 1547, shows that most of the business done concerned property in Streatley and Sharpenhoe.[3]

The Ralph FitzRichard, to whom the profits of the warren were granted, and who appears elsewhere in the accounts, held the manor of Newbury in Flitton, and so was a near neighbour. Also, in the mid-fourteenth century, he held by right of his wife Alice, two parts of the manor of Westhay and Faldo, presumably based on the old manor house in the nearer of the two detached parts of the parish of Higham Gobion, and so this would have been a convenient place for holding Higham manor courts, as in 1381. It has been shown that the earthworks on Sharpenhoe Clappers in Streatley were constructed as part of a medieval rabbit warren – one of the definitions of the name 'Clappers' is 'rabbit warren'.[4] Presumably this was the warren granted every year to Ralph FitzRichard.

The accounts deal with certain aspects only of the administration of the manor. Besides the rent received and paid for both Higham and Streatley, there is the sale of wood in both places, and the income from customary services. The Higham water-mill is kept in repair. The accounts deal with all things necessary for working the arable, as ploughs, seed baskets, crow scaring equipment, carts, forks for the harvesters, dung carts and dung forks; and the inventory of livestock covers all draught beasts, as horses, affers and oxen. Grain and pulses (beans and peas) were harvested, ricks thatched, then the sheaves threshed and the grain winnowed. Malt was made from barley, and sold, with the wheat, in London. Besides the draught animals, the list of livestock includes fowls, as geese, hens and eggs, capons and pigeons, perhaps as consumers of grain.

However, though the shepherd had his wages and tar and hurdles for the folds, there are no sheep; no pigs; a dairyman is mentioned making malt and the pottage for the servants, but there are no milk cows, except one hired for the harvest workers. Of particular interest is that, from the amount of seed used on a given number of acres, and, in the following year, the crop harvested, it is possible to calculate the yield per acre of the arable at this time.

Patricia L. Bell

Abbreviations are:

£	s	d	pounds, shillings and pence;
ac	rd	p	acres, roods and perches;
qu	bu	pk	quarters, bushells and pecks.

1 Chan. Inq. p.m. 29 Edw I, no. 49.
2 *Cal. of Close Rolls, 1341-43,* p 441.
3 BCRO cat. no. X95/392.
4 *BPSHLA no. 7, Streatley with Sharpenhoe,* p 19.

[1r]

HEGHAM

Account of John Hened, bailiff there, of all his receipts, expenditure, and allowances made there, from the day after Michaelmas in the third year of the reign of Richard the second after the conquest, up to the day after the same festival in the fourth year of the same king, that is for one whole year [1379-1380].

	£	s	d
Arrears			
None			
Fixed rents			
Hegham cum Faldho for St Andrew's term [30 Nov]	1	6	1½
Strattele cum Scharpenho for the same term	2	5	5
Hegham for Christmas term [25 Dec]	—	—	1½
A certain rent called "wodesilver", for the same term		3	4
Strattle for the same term	—	—	1½
Hegham for Lady Day term [25 Mar]	1	6	3
Strattele cum Scharpenho for the same term	2	7	10½
Hegham for Midsummer term [24 Jun]	1	6	1½
Strattle cum Scharpenho for the same term	2	5	5
Hegham for Michaelmas term [29 Sep]	2	7	3½
A certain rent called "langavel" coming from the lord's customary tenants for the same term		6	3
Strattel cum Scharpenho for the same term	2	7	10½
Concerning 4s from Walter Aleyn for 1 ac 1 rd of land for the year, nothing here because it was leased to Robert Hened at rent, as appears in the titles of rented land in the court roll, on account of the incapacity of the said Walter	—	—	—
From Henry Longe for one croft of land called Horoldescroft leased to him at rent for the year	—	4	

	£	s	d
From Simon Newman for 3 sellions of land, thus leased to him at rent for the year	–	2	
From Richard Aleyn for 3 acres of land, leased to him in Southfeld and Oxfoldefeld for the year	–	7	
Total	16	15	2½

	£	s	d
From John atte Brooke for a croft of land of the holding once John Aleyn's and which John Holewell held, so leased to him this year	–	2	–
From John Thurland for 1 ac 3 rd of the said holding in le Hammen, so leased to him this year	–	2	–
Concerning the house of the said holding, nothing here this year because it remained in the lord's hand, taken in default	–	–	–
From John atte Brooke, for herbage sold to him in the garden of the said holding this year	–	–	8
Concerning the rest of the land of the said holding, nothing here because it was taken for the lord's cultivation	–	–	–
From Robert Helder and Agnes his wife, for a house with a croft of land, once held by Smyth, leased to them this year and no more money received because the rest of the said land was taken for the lord's cultivation	–	8	–
From William atte Ston, for a house and a croft of land and one acre of land once held by John Wilgod senior, thus leased to him this year	–	8	–
and no more because the rest of the said holding was taken for the lord's cultivation			
Concerning 8s from Walter Aleyn, for 3 acres lately leased to him at rent, nothing here because it was leased to Robert Hened, as in the court roll, on account of the incapacity of the said Walter, as appears below	–	–	–
From Thomas Totegos for a cottage once Cripses, leased to him at rent for a term of 40 years, this year being the 8th	–	2	–
Concerning 3s from Walter Aleyn, for one acre of land lying on Wouwefurlong, lately leased to him at rent, nothing here because it was leased to Robert Hened, as in the court roll, on account of the incapacity of the said Walter	–	–	–
From Robert Hened, for 5 ac 1 rd of land which Walter Aleyn once held, leased to him at rent for the year	–	5	–

	£	s	d
Hegham rents			
From William Aleyn, for a croft and 3 roods of land of Thomas Neweman's holding, thus leased to him at rent this year	–	6	8
From Israel Spynner, for a house with garden in the said holding, thus leased to him this year	–	2	–
Concerning the rest of the said holding, nothing here because it was taken for the lord's cultivation	–	–	–
From 16 customary tenants for 80 acres of demesne land, leased to them at rent at the lord's will at 12d per acre and no more because 20 acres of demesne land, which John Holewell, Thomas Newman, John Smyth, and Walter Aleyn lately held was taken for the lord's cultivation	4	–	–
From John Priour for 1 rood of demesne land leased to him at rent at Littlewell this year	–	–	6
From Richard Aleyn, for a holding once John Hened's, leased to him at rent for the year	1	8	4
From Henry Longe, for a holding once Richard Hened's, leased to him at rent for the year	1	8	4
Concerning 28s 4d from Geoffrey Whether, for a holding once Walter Aleyn's, nothing this year because the said Geoffrey gave back the said holding into the lord's hand, as appears in the court roll	–	–	–
From Thomas Hened, for John Hened's holding, leased to him at rent for the year	1	8	4
From William Elis, for a holding once Robert Bonde's, leased to him at rent for the year	1	8	4
From John Wilgod, for a holding once John Wilgod junior's, leased to him at rent for the year	1	8	4
From Alexander Jekes, for a cottage with 1½ acres, called "le Mulnehous", leased to him at rent this year	–	5	–
From John Thurland, for a cottage which Walter Wildemor once held, thus leased to him at rent this year	–	3	–
For a house with a small croft of land, once Walter Aleyn's, which Geoffrey Whether held, being in the lord's hand and thus leased at rent this year	–	2	–
Concerning the rest of the land of the said holding, nothing here because it was taken for the lord's cultivation	–	–	–
Total	13	8	6

	£	s	d
Strattle rents			
From various tenants in Strattel, for rents of the lord's meadows and land at Strattle, and no more this year because one meadow called Fanmede was leased this year for 10s	7	6	10
Total	7	6	10
Perquisites of court			
For perquisites of 3 courts for the year	–	13	1
Total	–	13	1
Sale of underwood			
For 3 acres of underwood sold in Strattelewode this year	2	–	–
For bushes sold in Berdecoumbe this year		6	8
From Nicholas Ber for half a rood of underwood sold to him in Oxefold this year		1	3
From Richard Cook for half a rood of underwood sold to him in the same place		1	3
From Hugh Makehayt and John Whitbred for one rood of underwood sold to them in the same place		2	6
From Thomas Totegos for one rood of underwood sold to him in the same place		2	6
For 3 acres of underwood sold in Pullokeshullewode this year	1	10	–
Total	4	4	2
Sale of pasture and herbage			
For pasture sold at Eyebrook this year	–	2	–
Concerning pasture sold at Madefurlong, nothing this year because it lay fallow	–	–	–
For pasture sold at Hulheg this year	–	–	8
For pasture sold at Estheg this year	–	–	6
Concerning 6d for pasture sold at Hammenheneden, nothing this year because it lay fallow	–	–	–
Concerning 6d for pasture sold round the garden ditch, nothing this year because it lay fallow	–	–	–
For pasture sold at le Flete this year	–	3	–
Concerning 8d for half an acre of meadow sold at Colverhousmed, nothing here because it was leased with other meadows to customary tenants of the lord, as appears below	–	–	–

	£	s	d
Concerning 20s for herbage sold in Wrastmede, nothing here this year because the lord allowed the herbage from it this year to Lady de Grey, as a courtesy to her because Lord de Grey had pardoned him a debt of money for his board of 25s 6d	—	—	—
Concerning 12d for pasture sold at Hexstounbrook, nothing here because it was leased to customary tenants of the lord at rent as appears below	—	—	—
Concerning pasture sold at Longelonde, nothing here for the aforesaid reason	—	—	—
Concerning 6d for pasture sold at Mersfurlong, nothing here because the headland was ploughed this year	—	—	—
For pasture sold at Colverhousponde this year	—	1	8
For grazing 18 animals going on the meadows called Estmede and Newemede and in half an acre of meadow at Colverhousemade for which the customary tenants usually pay 26s 8d per year	—	15	—
and no more this year because the sheep remaining in the lord's fold depastured it this year	—	—	—
From Robert Hened for a cottage lately Baldewynes, leased to him at rent, as in the court roll, for which the usual rent is 14d per year	—	—	4
Total	1	3	2

Proceeds of the manor

	£	s	d
Concerning 8d for mustard seed, nothing this year because none was grown	—	—	—
Concerning 12d for garden fruit, nothing here because there were no apples in the lord's garden	—	—	—
From nettles and herbage sold in the lord's garden this year	—	1	—
From the hire of 3 geese for the year at 12d a head	—	3	—
From the hire of 12 hens for the year at 6d a head	—	6	—
From 24 capons sold at 4d a head	—	8	—
From 44 hens coming as rent, sold at 2½d a head	—	9	2
From 110 eggs sold at 1d a score	—	—	5½
From 144 young pigeons sold at ½d a head	—	6	—
From one hide of a worn out ox, sold	—	1	4
From another ox hide sold	—	1	10
From Walter Wildemore for straw "stramen" sold to him	—	3	—
Total	1	19	9½

	£	s	d
Sale of corn and malt			
From 20 qr of wheat sold at 4s 8d a quarter	4	13	4
From 15 qr of wheat sold in London at 7s 4d a quarter	5	10	–
From 22 qr ½ bu of beans and peas sold at 3s a quarter	3	6	2¼
From 29 qr of malt sold in London at 4s 4d a quarter	6	5	8
From 80 qr of malt sold at 3s 4d a quarter	13	6	8
From 43 qr of malt sold at 3s 6d a quarter	7	10	6
Total	40	12	4¼
Sale of livestock			
From 2 aged oxen sold at 11s a head	1	2	–
From one worn-out affer sold	–	2	9
From one gander sold	–	–	4
Total	1	5	1
Sale of services			
From 11 loaves coming from the proceeds of 11 customary tenants, sold at 5d per loaf	–	4	7
From 220 small services sold to the aforesaid 11 customary tenants at ¾d per service, viz 20 services to each tenant	–	13	9
From 33 harvest services sold to the said 11 tenants, viz 3 services to each tenant at 3d per service	–	8	3
From 44 carrying services sold to the said 11 tenants, viz 4 services to each tenant at 6d per service	1	2	–
From 11 customary tenants for 2 days boonwork at harvest, sold to them, viz each of them comes each day for the said boonwork with 2 men	–	11	–
Total	2	19	7
Above the account			
From various items put on the dorse and sold above the account	–	–	8¼
Total	–	–	[1]8¼
Sum total of receipts	90	8	5½

1 Presumably the 11 small services sold at ¾d each

EXPENSES

Rents paid, with various allowances for holdings in the lord's hand and at rent

	£	s	d
Rent paid to the manor of Wraste, for the year	–	2	–
Paid to the King for the sheriff's aid for the year	–	17	–
Paid to the King's bailiff of the hundred for remission of suit to the hundred	–	1	–
Paid to the same King for "deseynsilver", for the year	–	6	–
Paid to the lord Pikot for remission of suit to the court for the year	–	2	–
Rent defaults for the holdings of John Holewell, John Wilgod, Thomas Neweman, John Smyth and Walter Aleyn, because they remained in the lord's hand this year, for "wodesilver" for the Christmas term, for each holding 2d	–	–	10
Rent defaults for the holdings of John Hened, Richard Hened, John Wilgod junior, Thomas Hened, and John Bonde, because they were at rent, for each holding 2d	–	–	10
Money allowance for rent reduction of John Wemme, whose rent used to be 13s 4d per year and is now only 8s	–	5	4
Money allowance for rent reduction of Alexander Jekes, for a place called le Mulneplace, which used to be rented at 7s per year and is now leased to the same Alexander for 5s, as appears above in the rents	–	2	–
Money allowance for rent reduction for a cottage lately Baldewynes, because leased to Robert Hened for 4d per year, as appears from the court roll and above in the rents	–	1	1
Money allowance for rent reduction of Nicholas Casse, because 8 acres of land remains in the lord's hand and therefore lies empty	–	4	–
Money allowance for rent reduction of John Wilgod, for one acre of land which he used to rent at 2s per year, because it is now leased to the same John for 16d per year, as appears above in the rents	–	–	8
Total	2	2	9

Upkeep of ploughs

	£	s	d
Iron and steel bought for 2 ploughs per year together with the smith's wages, and for iron and shoeing 4 cart horses and 4 affers on the forefeet	1	18	2
Shoeing 4 affers on the hindfeet, outside the smith's contract, and so much this year on account of much carting of malt to Luton	–	1	6

	£	s	d
Iron and steel bought for one new built plough for 3 seedtimes of the year for 24 weeks, together with the smith's wages	–	4	–
3 new ploughs bought	–	2	6
4 old ploughs re-boarded	–	1	4
4 hempen halters bought	–	–	4
1 wicker seed-basket bought	–	–	6
1 "Slyngge" for scaring crows	–	–	1
Total	2	8	5
Upkeep of carts			
1 pair of bare wheels bought	–	4	2
Fitting axles to 2 long carts for harvest, together with axles bought for same	–	–	8
10 clouts [metal plates] bought	–	2	1
Fitting axle to 1 dung cart, with axle bought for the same	–	–	4
4 clouts bought for the same	–	–	8
200 clout nails bought	–	–	8
Soap and grease bought for greasing carts	–	–	8
2 [horse] collars bought	–	2	–
1 pair of traces bought	–	–	8
1 new cart-ladder bought	–	–	6
2 leather halters bought for 2 cart horses	–	–	7
1 fork bought for lifting sheaves on to carts at harvest	–	–	3
1 new lynch pin bought	–	–	1
1 new dung cart bought	–	2	–
Whipcord bought	–	–	2
Total	–	15	6
Upkeep of buildings and mill			
One thatcher, hired at task work for 9 days, for thatching and repairing the mill house, the main building of the holding lately John Smyth's, and the main building and the bakehouse of the holding lately Walter Wildemore's, at 4d per head per day	–	3	–
The said thatcher, hired at task work for 19 days for thatching and ridging the malthouse, stable, goose-house, and henhouse, and for thatching faults in the barn, per head per day as above	–	6	4
The said thatcher, hired at taskwork for 4 days for thatching the bean stack, per head per day as above	–	1	4
One new axle bought for the mill wheel	–	8	4
Total	–	19	–

	£	s	d
Upkeep of folds			
4 gallons of tar, bought	–	2	8
Grease for the same, bought	–	–	8
20 wicker hurdles at 1¼d each	–	2	1
Total	–	5	5
Small necessaries			
Food and offerings for a bailiff and 8 manor servants at 2 main festivals, at 2d per head for each festival	–	3	–
3 quarters [lb] of wax bought for the manor servants for the day of the Purification of the B.V.M. [2 Feb]	–	–	6
3 lb of candles bought for turning malt by night in winter	–	–	6
2 sacks bought	–	2	6
1 bushel of salt for pottage for the manor servants	–	–	10
Parchment bought for the court roll and accounts	–	–	8
1 shovel with iron for the same, bought	–	–	5
1 bleached horse hide	–	–	9
1 new portable cask bought	–	–	9
1 dung fork bought, with iron for the same	–	–	4
Paid for title of a fifteenth and half of a fifteenth granted to the king this year	1	10	–
2 new fans bought	–	3	–
Total	2	3	3
Purchase of corn			
4 bu 3 pk of ground corn bought for making up the allowance for the manor servants, at 4½d per bushel	–	1	9¼
2 qr 5½ bu of corn bought for horse fodder, at 2s 8d per quarter	–	7	2
Total	–	8	11¼
Purchase of livestock			
2 carthorses bought at 23s per head	2	6	–
1 affer bought	1	–	–
Another affer bought		15	–
2 oxen bought at 17s 6d a head	1	15	–
2 other oxen bought at 16s a head	1	12	–
24 chickens bought for making into capons, at 1½d a head	–	3	–
Total	7	11	–

	£	s	d
Threshing and winnowing			
48 qr 2 bu 1 pk wheat, 22 qr 2 pk beans and peas, threshed by taskwork at 3d per quarter	–	17	6¾
158 qr 1½ bu dredge corn threshed by taskwork at 2½d per quarter	1	12	11
Nothing for winnowing because [done] by the dairyman and the manor servants	–	–	–
Total	2	10	5¾
Hoeing and mowing			
For hoeing corn, nothing here because [done] by customary services as appears outside	–	–	–
Usual gift to customary tenants for spreading hay in Fanmede	–	–	3
Defaults of 10 holdings now in the lord's hand and at rent this year, for gift to customary tenants in Fanmede, 2d for each holding	–	1	8
Given to the customary tenants for the said ten holdings now in the lord's hand and at rent, because they have to make and gather hay in the lord's meadow, 2d for each holding	–	1	8
Half an acre of meadow in the holding once John Wilgod senior's, mown by taskwork	–	–	2
Total	–	3	9
Cash payment for tithes of underwood sold			
Paid to the Prioress of Markyate for tithes of underwood sold in Strattlewode this year	–	4	–
Paid to the same Prioress of Markyate for tithes of bushes sold in Berdescoumbe	–	–	8
Paid to the rector of Hegham church for tithes of underwood sold in Pullokeshullewode	–	3	–
Paid to the same for tithes of underwood sold in Oxefolde	–	–	9
Total	–	8	5
Outside expenses			
Carting 43 quarters of malt to Luton to be sold	–	1	9½
Paid to customary tenants for carrying service as their "lodepannes"	–	–	8
Paid to a "rakyer"[1] in London	–	–	2

[1] raker = one who sweeps up straw in streets.

	£	s	d
Paid to customary tenants for 'panagesilver', viz for carting 15 quarters of wheat to London this year to be sold, with their carrying service, at ¼d for 5 bushels	—	—	5
Paid to the same customary tenants for the same, viz for carting 29 quarters of malt to London, with their carrying service, at ¼d per quarter	—	—	7¼
Expenses of the bailiff going to London 3 times to sell wheat and malt there, going and returning	—	4	—
Given as "remeneration" to manor servants	—	1	6
Total	—	9	1¾

Steward's fees and expenses

	£	s	d
Fees of the steward for the year	2	—	—
Expenses of the same steward for holding 3 courts	—	5	—
Total	2	5	—

Harvest expenses

	£	s	d
Ale, meat, herring fish, candles, cheese and other victuals bought for 6 boonworks, to each boonwork 42 men, viz: some customary tenants came with one man and others came with 2 men	2	2	6
9 pairs of gloves bought for a bailiff and 8 manor servants	—	1	6
One cow hired for the whole harvest as "sonylsilver" for the manor servants	—	1	—
One bushel of salt bought for the harvest	—	1	—
12 dishes bought for the harvest	—	—	4
One man hired at the lord's board from Lammas day [1 Aug] to Michaelmas for lifting sheaves to the carts and for stacking the lord's corn and other necessary work	—	8	—
One groom hired for the whole harvest for looking after the lord's oxen	—	2	—
96 reapers hired at the lord's board, separately as if for one day, for 8 holdings remaining in the lord's hand and at rent, which have to provide for each day's boonwork, 12 men for 6 day's boonwork at 2d per head	—	16	—
96 reapers hired at the lord's board separately as if for one day for the aforesaid 8 holdings remaining in the lord's hand and at rent which have to reap 96 harvest works, at 2d a head	—	16	—
Total	4	8	4

	£	s	d
Manor servants' wages			
(Wages of one bailiff for the year	2	–	–[c])
Wages of one carter for the year	–	13	4
Wages of four plough servants for the year, 10s a head	2	–	–
Wages of one shepherd for the year	–	10	–
Wages of one dairyman making malt and pottage for the manor servants, for 36 weeks	–	8	6
Wages of one warrener for the year	–	10	–
Wages of 2 plough servants, going with a new-built plough, for 24 weeks by turns in the year, 3s per head	–	6	–
(Wages of one clerk writing accounts	–	6	8[c])
Total	4	7	10

	£	s	d
Money payments			
Paid to Thomas Rolf, skinner of London for rent for St. Andrews term, by order of Nicholas Blus' as appears from a tally against the same	8	–	–
Paid to the lord's chest, from rent and from various manor proceeds, by the hand of Nicholas Blus' as appears from a tally	20	–	–
Paid to the lord's chest by the hand of the said Nicholas Blus' on 2 occasions without a tally	13	–	–
Paid to Thomas Rolf, skinner, of London without a tally, by order of the said Nicholas, on 2 occasions	14	–	–
Paid to John Cook for his annual fee, allowed to him by the lord	2	–	–
Total	57	–	–

	£	s	d
Sum Total of all expenses and allowances	88	7	2¾
Thus, by calculation, owing to the lord	2	1	2½
From which is allowed to the same [the bailiff] for his work, by the lord's favour this year	2	–	–
Thus so far owing to the lord	–	1	2¾

[1d]

HEGHAM

Proceeds of the grange there in the time of John Hened, bailiff, serving in the third year of the reign of Richard the second after the conquest [1379-1380]

Wheat	qr	bu	pk
Wheat from the whole proceeds of the grange, by level measure, besides 35 qr by heaped measure for sale, threshed by task work and by customary services without tally, of which by task work 48 qr 2 bu 1 pk	76	6	1
From heaped measure of the same	1	—	3
From the usual 21 customary tenants for their "bensed" for the Michaelmas term	1	2	2
Total	79	1	2
of which:—			
For seed on 87½ acres of land at seedtime for wheat this year, at 2 bushels per acre, and so much for seed for wheat this year because the holdings of John Holewell, John Wilgod, Thomas Neweman, John Smyth and Walter Aleyn remained in the lord's hand this year	21	7	—
For defaults from the holdings of John Holewell, John Wilgod, Thomas Neweman, John Smyth and Walter Aleyn, for their "benesed" because they remained in the lord's hand this year, for each holding ½ bushel	—	2	2
For defaults from the holdings of John Hened, Richard Hened, John Wilgod junior, Thomas Hened, and Robert Bonde for their "benesed", because they were at rent, for each holding ½ bushel	—	2	2
For bread baked for harvest expenses, viz. for customary boonworks	2	—	—
For allowances for manor servants below	18	4	3
Sold as below in London,	15	—	—
with heaped measure	—	3	3
Sold as below	20	—	—
with heaped measure	—	5	—
Total as above and it balances	[79	1	2]

Beans and peas	qr	bu	pk
Beans and peas from the whole proceeds of the grange, by level measure, besides 22 qr heaped measure for sale, threshed by task work and by customary services without tally, of which by task work 22 qr ½ bu	33	2	2

	qr	bu	pk
Heaped measure for the same	–	5	2
Total	34	–	–
of which:–			
For seed on 40 acres of land, at 2 bushels 1 peck per acre	11	2	–
Sold as below	22	–	2
with heaped measure	–	5	2
Total as above and it balances	[34	–	–]

Dredge Corn

	qr	bu	pk
Dredge corn from the whole proceeds of the grange, by level measure, threshed by task work and by customary services without tally, of which by task work 158 qr 1½ bu	194	1	2
From the same proceeds, in 350 sheaves of corn for ox fodder, of which 10 sheaves made one bushel	4	3	–
Total	198	4	2
of which:–			
For seed on 108 acres, at 3 bu ½ pk per acre, and so much in dredge corn seed this year because the holdings of John Holewell, John Wilgod, Thomas Newman, John Smyth and Walter Aleyn remained in the lord's hand this year	42	1	2
Set aside as oats below for ox fodder	4	3	–
For malting as below	152	–	–
Total as above and it balances	[198	4	2]

Oats

	qr	bu	pk
Oats from the usual 21 customary tenants at Christmas	5	2	–
In sheaves, per above estimate, for ox fodder	4	3	–
Bought as fodder for cart horses	2	5	2
Heaped measure for the same	–	–	2
Total	12	3	–
of which:–			
In default from the holdings of John Holewell, John Wilgod, Thomas Neweman, John Smyth and Walter Aleyn, because they remained in the lord's land this year, for each holding 2 bu	1	2	–

	qr	bu	pk
In default from the holdings of John Hened, Richard Hened, John Wilgod junior, Thomas Hened, and Robert Bonde, because they were at rent, for each holding 2 bu	1	2	–
For making flour for the manor servants' pottage for the year, and for harvest expenses	1	4	–
Fodder for 4 cart horses for the period of the account	4	–	–
For ox fodder as appears in the debit above	4	3	–
Total as above and it balances	[12	3	–]

Multure of the mill

	qr	bu	pk
Multure from rent of the lord's mill for the year, by level measure	18	–	–
Multure bought for the manor servants	–	4	3
Total	18	4	3

The whole amount was used for the allowance of mixed meal for the manor servants below

Dredge malt

	qr	bu	pk
Dredge malt for malting as above	152	–	–
Growth in making	19	–	–
Total	171	–	–

of which:

	qr	bu	pk
Sold as below in London	29	–	–
growth of the same, 1 quarter for 9 bushels	3	5	–
Sold as below	123	–	–
growth of the same, 1 quarter for 9 bushels	15	3	–
Total as above and it balances	[171	–	–]

Manor servants' allowances

	qr	bu	pk
Wheat	18	4	3
Multure for mixed meal for the manor servants as below	18	4	3
Total	37	1	2

of which:–

	qr	bu	pk
Allowances for one carter, 4 plough servants, one warrener and one shepherd, for the whole year, at 1 quarter of medium corn per head per 12 weeks	30	1	2

	qr	bu	pk
Allowances for one dairyman making malt and pottage for the manor servants from Michaelmas to 7 June, that is, for 36 weeks, per head as above	3	–	–
Allowances for 2 plough servants, going with a new-built plough for 24 weeks at 3 seedtimes in the year, per head as above	4	–	–
Total as above and it balances	[37	1	2]

ACCOUNT OF LIVESTOCK

Cart horses remaining 2, bought 2, total 4; and there remain	4 cart horses
Affers remaining 4, bought 2, total 6; of which there died of a murrain (as testified in the court roll) 1, sold 1 as below, total 2; and there remain	4 affers
Oxen remaining 12, bought 4, total 16; of which died of a murrain (as testified in the court roll) 2, sold 2 as below, total 4; and there remain	12 oxen
Ganders remaining 2, total 2; of which sold 1 as below, total 1; and there remains	1 gander
Young geese remaining 3, and no proceeds from these here because they were rented to the dairyman for money as appears below, total 3; and there remain	3 young geese
Cocks remaining 1, total 1; and there remains	1 cock
Hens remaining 12, and no proceeds from these here because they were rented to the dairyman for money, as appears below, & from 21 customary tenants as rent for the Christmas term 84, total 96; of which in default from the holdings of John Holewell, John Wilgod, Thomas Neweman, John Smyth and Walter Aleyn, because they were in the lord's hand this year 20, and in default from the holdings of John Hened, Richard Hened, John Wilgod junior, Thomas Hened and Robert Bonde, because they were at rent, 20, & sold as below, 44, total 84; and there remain	12 hens
Capons remaining 24, made from chickens as below, 24, total 48; of which sold as below, 24; and there remain	24 capons
Chickens bought for making into capons, 24, total 24, and used to make capons as above, and it balances.	
Eggs from 21 customary tenants, at 10 from each, of which in default from the holdings of John Holewell, John Wilgod, Thomas Neweman, John Smyth and Walter Aleyn, because they were in the lord's hand this year, 50 eggs, and in default from	210 eggs

the holdings of John Hened, Richard Hened, John Wilgod junior, Thomas Hened, and Robert Bonde, because they were at rent, 50 eggs; and sold as below 110 eggs, total as above, and it balances.	
Loaves from 21 customary tenants aforesaid at the Christmas term, from each tenant one loaf besides one bushel of wheat, total	21 loaves
of which in default from the holdings of John Holewell, John Wilgod, Thomas Neweman, John Smyth and Walter Aleyn, because they were in the lord's hand this year, 5 loaves; and in default from the holdings of John Hened, Richard Hened, John Wilgod junior, Thomas Hened and Robert Bonde, because they were at rent 5 loaves; and sold as below 11 loaves; total as above and it balances.	
Raw hides from an affer dead of a murrain as above, 1 hide; from oxen dead of a murrain as above, 2 hides, total	3 hides
of which sold as below, 2 ox hides, and kept for bleaching, 1 horse hide, total as above, and it balances.	
Bleached hides remaining 1 horse hide, kept as above 1 hide, total	2 hides
of which used for repairing harness this year, 1 hide, total 1 hide; and there remains	1 bleached horse hide

ACCOUNT OF SERVICES

Small services and ¾ services	Services
From the aforesaid 21 customary tenants, from each tenant 95 services. Total as it appears	1995
of which:–	
In default from the holdings of John Holewell, John Wilgod, Thomas Neweman, John Smyth and Walter Aleyn, because they were in the lord's hand this year, for each tenant 95 services	475
In default from the holdings of John Hened, Richard Hened, John Wilgod junior, Thomas Hened, and Robert Bonde, because they were at rent, for each tenant 95 services	475
For 3 assistants helping one thatcher, thatching the mill house and the main building of John Smyth's holding, remaining in the lord's hand, and the main building and bakehouse of the holding lately Walter Wildemor's, for 9 days for each day 3 services	27

	Services
For 3 assistants helping one thatcher thatching and ridging the malt house, stable, goose house and hen house, and repairing defects in the dredge corn barn, for 19 days, for each day 3 services	57
For 3 assistants helping one thatcher thatching the bean stack for 4 days, for each day 3 services	12
Allowed to the said customary tenants working with the lord at "bensed", for each tenant half a service	5½
Allowed to the said customary tenants for "malterth", for each tenant one service	11
For bundling straw this year, for each tenant 3 services	33
For spreading manure for the lord this year, for each tenant 2 services	22
Sold viz. to 11 customary tenants because they took demesne land, lying in various cultivated areas, at a price of ¾d per service, viz. for each tenant 20 services	220
Sold viz. to the said 11 tenants for harvest services for the aforesaid reason, viz. for each tenant 3 services	33
Allowed to the said customary tenants which is usually conceded to them for carrying services by ancient law, viz. for each tenant 12 services	132
For bringing the bean stack to the grange for threshing, for each tenant 2 services	22
For threshing 28 quarters 3 bushels of wheat by customary services, at 3 services per quarter	85½
For threshing 11 quarters 2 bushels of bean and peas by customary services, at 3 services per quarter	33½
For threshing 36 quarters of dredge corn by customary services, at 5 services per 2 quarters	90
For hoeing the lord's corn this year, for each tenant 7 services	77
For mowing the lord's meadow at Fanmede, making and gathering [hay], for each tenant 2 services	22
For mowing the lord's meadow at Southpond	9
For making and gathering hay in the said meadow for each tenant one service	11
For reaping, binding, and stooking, 16 acres of wheat, at 2 services per acre	32
For reaping, binding, and stooking 17 acres of beans and peas, at 4 services per acre	68
For reaping, binding, and stooking 15 acres 3 roods of dredge corn, at 2 services per acre	31½
Sold above the account	11
Total as above and it balances	[1995]

Ploughing services	Services ac	rd
The proceeds of the said 21 customary tenants ploughing for the lord, viz. 140 acres 3 roods of land at 3 seedtimes of the year, from each tenant 6 acres 3 roods per year		
Total as it appears	140	3
of which:–		
In default from the holdings of John Holewell, John Wilgod, Thomas Neweman, John Smyth and Walter Aleyn, because they were in the lord's hand this year, for each tenant 6 acres 3 roods	33	3
In default from the holdings of John Hened, Richard Hened, John Wilgod junior, Thomas Hened and Robert Bonde, because they were at rent, for each tenant 6 acres 3 roods	33	3
For ploughing the lord's land at 3 seedtimes of the year	73	1
Total as above and it balances	[140	3]

Carrying services	Services
Proceeds of the said 21 customary tenants, from each tenant 12 carrying services	252
of which:–	
In default from the holdings of John Holewell, John Wilgod, Thomas Neweman, John Smyth and Walter Aleyn, because they were in the lord's hand this year, for each tenant 12 carrying services	60
In default from the holdings of John Hened, Richard Hened, John Wilgod junior, Thomas Hened, and Robert Bonde, because they were at rent, for each tenant 12 carrying services	60
For carting 15 quarters of wheat to London for sale, 2 services per quarter	30
For carting 29 quarters of malt to London for sale, 2 services per quarter	58
Sold to the aforesaid 11 tenants, for the reason above, viz to each tenant 4 services price 6d per service	44
Total as above and it balances	[252]

Proceeds of the dove house

Proceeds of the dove house this year — 160 young pigeons

of which given in tithes 16, sold as below 144, and it balances.

Services

Rabbit warren

Proceeds of the warren, nothing this year because the lord granted the profits from it to Ralph FitzRichard	Total nil		

[2r]

HEGHAM

Account of John Hened, bailiff there, of all his receipts, expenditure, and allowances, made there from the day after Michaelmas in the fourth year of the reign of Richard the second after the conquest, up to the day after the same festival in the fifth year of the same king, that is for one whole year [1380-1381]

	£	s	d
Arrears			
Arrears from the last account, of the preceding year		1	2¾
Total		1	2¾

	£	s	d
Fixed rents			
Hegham cum Faldho, for St. Andrew's term [30 Nov]	1	6	1½
Strattele cum Scharpenho, for the same term	2	5	5
Hegham for Christmas term [25 Dec]	—	—	1½
A certain rent called "wodesilver", for the same term	—	3	4
Strattele for the same term	—	—	1½
Hegham for Lady Day term [25 Mar]	1	6	3
Strattele for the same term	2	7	10½
Hegham for Midsummer term [24 Jun]	1	6	1½
Strattele for the same term	2	5	5
Hegham for Michaelmas term [29 Sep]	2	7	3½
A certain rent called "langavel", coming from the customary tenants, for the same term	—	6	3
Strattele for the same term	2	7	10½
Concerning 4s from Walter Aleyn, for 1 ac 1 rd of land, nothing here because it was leased to Robert Hened at rent, as appears in the titles of rented land below and in the court roll, because of the incapacity of the said Walter	—	—	—
From Henry Longe for one croft of land called Horoldescroft, leased to him at rent for the year	—	4	—
From Simon Neweman for 3 sellions of land leased to him at rent for the year	—	2	—
From Richard Aleyn for 3 acres of land leased to him at rent in Southfeld and Oxefoldefeld for the year	—	7	—
Total	16	15	2½

	£	s	d
From John atte Brooke for one croft of land and 1 ac 3 rd of land, once held by John Aleyn, and which John Holewell held, thus leased to him this year	–	4	–
From John Yonge for the house of the said holding, thus leased to him at rent this year	–	2	–
Concerning the rest of the land of the said holding, nothing received here because it was taken for the lord's cultivation	–	–	–
From Robert Helder, for a house with a croft of land once held by Smyth, thus leased to him this year and no more received here in money because the rest of the land of the said holding was taken for the lord's cultivation	–	8	–
Concerning 8s from William atte Ston for a house with a croft of land and 1 acre of land, once held by John Wilgod, nothing this year because it remained in the lord's hand and therefore was taken for the lord's cultivation this year	–	–	–
From John Potton for herbage in the garden of the said house sold to him this year		1	4
Concerning 8s from Walter Aleyn for 3 acres of land lately leased to him at rent, nothing here because it was leased to Robert Hened, as in the court roll, because of the incapacity of the said Walter, as appears below	–	–	–
From Thomas Totegos for a cottage, once Cripses, leased to him at rent for a term of 40 years, this year being the 9th	–	2	–
Concerning 3s from Walter Aleyn for one acre of land lately leased to him on Wouwefurlong, nothing here because it was leased to Robert Hened, as in the court roll, as appears below, because of the incapacity of the said Walter	–	–	–
From Robert Hened, for 5 ac 1 rd of land, which Walter Aleyn lately held, thus leased to him at rent by the year, as in the court roll	–	5	–
From William Aleyn for a croft and 3 roods of land, once held by Thomas Neweman, thus leased for rent	–	6	8
From Israel Spynner, for the house and garden of the said holding, thus leased this year	–	2	–
Concerning the rest of the land of the said holding, nothing received here because it was taken for the lord's cultivation	–	–	–
From 16 customary tenants for 80 acres of demesne land leased to them at rent at the lord's will for 12d per acre, and no more because 20 acres of demesne land, which John Holewell, Thomas Neweman,			

	£	s	d
John Smyth and Walter Aleyn held, remained in the lord's hand this year and therefore was taken for the lord's cultivation	4	–	–
From John Priour for one rood of demesne land leased to him at rent at Littlewell this year	–	–	6
From Richard Aleyn for a holding once John Hened's, leased to him at rent	1	8	4
From Henry Longe, for a holding once Richard Hened's, leased to him at rent	1	8	4
From Thomas Hened, for a holding once John Hened's, leased to him at rent	1	8	4
Concerning 28s 4d from Geoffrey Whether, for a holding once Walter Aleyn's, nothing this year because the said holding remained in the lord's hand	–	–	–
From William Elis, for a holding once Robert Bonde's, leased to him at rent this year	1	8	4
From John Wilgod, for a holding once John Wilgod junior's, leased to him at rent	1	8	4
From Alexander Jekes, for a cottage with 1½ acres of land called le Mulnehous, thus leased to him at rent	–	5	–
From John Thurland, for a cottage which Walter Wildemore once held, thus leased to him at rent this year	–	3	–
For a house with a small croft of land once Walter Aleyn's, which Geoffrey Whether held, being in the lord's hand this year and thus leased at rent	–	2	–
Concerning the rest of the land of the said holding, nothing received here because it was taken for the lord's cultivation	–	–	–
Total	13	3	2

Strattele rents

	£	s	d
From various tenants in Strattele, for rent of the lord's meadows and land at Strattele and no more this year because the herbage of one meadow called Fannemede was granted to Ralph FitzRichard this year by the lord	6	17	10
Total	6	17	10

Perquisites of court

	£	s	d
For perquisites of 2 courts this year	–	15	8
Total	–	15	8

	£	s	d
Sale of underwood and old buildings			
For 4 acres of underwood sold in Strattelewode this year	2	—	—
For 3 roods of underwood sold in Oxefolde this year	—	7	6
For 2 acres of underwood sold in Pullokeshullewode this year	1	—	—
From Richard Southende for a part of a hedge sold to him in Oxefolde	—	2	—
From William Aleyn for an old barn sold to him, on the holding formerly Walter Aleyn's	—	10	—
Total	3	19	6

	£	s	d
Sale of pasture and herbage			
Concerning 2s for pasture sold at Eyebrok, nothing this year because it lay fallow	—	—	—
For pasture sold at Madefurlong this year	—	—	6
For pasture sold at Hulheg this year	—	—	8
For pasture sold at Estheg this year	—	—	6
For pasture sold at Hammenhaneden this year	—	—	6
For pasture round the garden ditch, nothing this year because the fence was newly cut down	—	—	—
For pasture sold at le Flete this year	—	4	—
Concerning 8d for half an acre of meadow sold at Colverhousmede, nothing here because it was leased to the lord's customary tenants, as appears below	—	—	—
Concerning 12d for pasture sold at Littleholm, nothing this year because it was depastured with sheep which stayed in the lord's fold	—	—	—
Concerning 13s 4d for herbage sold in le Newemede, nothing here because it was leased to the said customary tenants at rent, as appears below	—	—	—
For herbage sold in Wrastmede this year	1	—	—
Concerning 12d for pasture sold at Hexstounbroke, nothing here because it was leased to the lord's customary tenants at rent as appears below	—	—	—
Concerning pasture sold at Longelonde, nothing here for the aforesaid reason	—	—	—
Concerning 6d for pasture sold at Mersfurlong, nothing here because the headland was ploughed there this year	—	—	—
For pasture sold at Colverhousponde this year	—	1	8
For grazing animals going in the meadow called Estmede and Newemede and in half an acre of meadow at Colverhousmed for which the lord's customary tenants usually pay a rent of 26s 8d and no more this year because it was depastured by sheep which stayed in the lord's fold this year	—	15	—

	£	s	d
From Robert Hened, for a cottage lately Baldewynes, leased to him this year, for which the usual rent is 14d	—	—	4
Total	2	3	2

Proceeds of the manor

	£	s	d
Concerning 8d for mustard seed, nothing this year because none was grown	—	—	—
Concerning 12d for garden fruit, nothing this year because there were no apples	—	—	—
From nettles and herbage sold in the lord's garden this year	—	1	—
From the hire of 3 geese for the year at 12d a head	—	3	—
From the hire of 12 hens for the year at 12d [?6d] a head	—	6	—
From 24 capons sold at 4d a head	—	8	—
From 44 hens coming as rent, sold at a price of 2½d a head	—	9	2
From 110 eggs coming as rent, sold	—	—	5½
From 154 young pigeons sold at ½d a head	—	6	5
From one ox hide sold	—	1	2
From straw "stramen" sold this year	—	7	—
Total	2	2	2½

Sale of corn and malt

	£	s	d
From 7 qr of wheat sold in London at 8s per qr	2	16	—
From 26 qr of wheat sold in London at 7s 8d per qr	9	19	4
From 32 qr of beans and peas sold at 3s 4d per qr	5	6	8
From 80 qr of malt sold at 5s per qr	20	—	—
From 11 qr of malt sold in London at 5s 2d per qr	2	16	10
From 34 qr of malt sold at 4s 6d per qr	7	13	—
Total	48	11	10

Sale of livestock

	£	s	d
From one worn-out affer sold		2	8
Total		2	8

Sale of services	£	s	d
From 11 loaves coming from the proceeds of 11 customary tenants, sold at 8d per loaf	—	7	4
From 220 small services sold to 11 customary tenants at ¾d per service	—	13	9

	£	s	d
From 33 harvest services sold to the said 11 tenants, viz 3 services per tenant at 3d per service	–	8	3
From 44 carrying services sold to the said 11 tenants, viz 4 services per tenant at 6d per service	1	2	–
From 11 customary tenants for 2 days boonwork at harvest, sold to them, viz each of them comes each day for the said boonwork with 2 men	–	11	–
Total	3	2	4
Above the account			
From various items mentioned on the dorse and sold above the account[1]	1	6	9
Total	1	6	9
Sum total of receipts with arrears	99	1	6¾

1 This item probably includes the price of 2 affers mentioned under the account of livestock as 'sold above the account'.

EXPENSES

Rents paid with various allowances for holdings in the lord's hand or at rent

	£	s	d
Rent paid to the manor of Wraste, for the year	–	2	–
Paid to the King for sheriff's aid for the year	–	17	–
Paid to the same King for "deseynsilver" for the year	–	6	–
Paid to the King's bailiff for the remission of suit to the hundred, for the year	–	1	–
Paid to the lord Pikot for a fine for remission of suit to the court, for the year	–	2	–
Rent defaults for the holdings of John Holewell, John Wilgod, Thomas Neweman, John Smyth and Walter Aleyn, because they remained in the lord's hand this year, for "wodesilver" for the Christmas term, for each holding 2d	–	–	10
Rent defaults for the holdings of John Hened, Richard Hened, John Wilgod junior, Thomas Hened, and Robert Bonde, because they were at rent, for each holding 2d	–	–	10
Money allowance for rent reduction of John Wemme, whose rent used to be 13s 4d per year, because this year the rent was only 8s	–	5	4
Money allowance for rent reduction of Alexander Jekes, for a place called Mulnehous, which used to be rented at 7s per year, because it is now leased to him through the steward for 5s, as appears in the rents	–	2	–

	£	s	d
Money allowance for rent reduction for a cottage, lately Baldewynes, for the year, because it is now leased to Robert Hened at 4d per year, as appears from the court roll and in the rents above	–	–	10
Money allowance for rent reduction of Nicholas Casse, for 8 acres of land which he used to hold, because it remained in the lord's hand and lay empty	–	3	–
Money allowance for rent reduction of John Wilgod, for one acre of land which he used to rent at 2s per year, because it is now leased to him, as in the court roll and as appears above in the rents, for 20d per year	–	–	8
Rent default of Robert Hened, for 1½ acres of land which he held, because it remained in the lord's hand this year	–	4	–
Money allowance for rent reduction of John Wemme for a garden and le Launde at Strattle, formerly leased to him at 21s per year, and this year rented for only 14s 8d, as debited above in Strattle rents	–	6	4
Total	2	11	10

Upkeep of ploughs

	£	s	d
Iron and steel bought for 3 ploughs per year, together with the smith's wages, and for iron and shoeing 4 carthorses and 2 affers on the forefeet	2	13	2
Shoeing 2 affers on the hindfeet, outside the smith's contract	–	–	9
3 new ploughs newly bought	–	2	6
4 old ploughs re-boarded	–	1	4
Total	2	17	9

Upkeep of carts

	£	s	d
1 pair of bare wheels bought	–	4	2
Fitting axles to 2 long carts for harvest, together with axles bought for the same	–	–	8
8 clouts bought for the same	–	1	8
Fitting axle to 1 dung cart, with 1 axle bought for the same	–	–	4
6 clouts bought for the same	–	1	–
200 clout nails bought	–	–	8
Grease bought for greasing carts	–	–	6
1 pair of body traces bought	–	–	10
Another pair of traces bought	–	–	7
Whipcord bought	–	–	2

	£	s	d
1 leather halter bought	–	–	5
1 double hemp cord bought	–	1	2
Fitting hoops to 1 pair of wheels	–	–	3
Total	–	12	5
Upkeep of buildings and mill			
One thatcher, hired at taskwork for 20 days, thatching and ridging the barn, and thatching the dove house, at 4d per day	–	6	8
The said thatcher, hired at taskwork for 3 days, thatching the hall, price per day as above	–	1	–
One carpenter, hired at taskwork for 1 day on repairing the granary	–	–	4
One man hired at taskwork for 2 days for fitting new joists on the kiln at 4d per day	–	–	8
Two men hired at taskwork for 1 day on making a large hurdle, from the lord's wicker, for the kiln, at 3d per head per day	–	–	6
One carpenter hired at taskwork, wholesale, for mending and repairing faults in the building on the holding lately Richard Aleyn's	–	3	4
Total		12	6
Upkeep of folds			
4 gallons of tar, bought at 8d per gallon		2	8
Grease for the same, bought			10
40 wicker hurdles bought for the fold at 1¼d each		4	2
Total		7	8
Small necessaries			
Food and offerings for a bailiff and 9 manor servants at 2 main festivals, at 2d per head for each festival	–	3	4
1 lb of wax bought for the manor servants for the day of the Purification of the B.V.M. [2 Feb]	–	–	6
3 lb of candles bought for turning malt by night in winter	–	–	6
3 new sacks bought	–	3	6
1 bushel of salt for pottage for the manor servants	–	–	9
Parchment bought for the court roll and accounts	–	–	4
2 shovels with 2 irons for the same, bought	–	–	10
1 dung fork of iron bought for spreading the lord's manure	–	–	8
26 yds of "pann silic" [?sieve cloth] bought at 7½d per yard	–	16	3
Total	1	6	8

	£	s	d
Purchase of corn			
4 bushels of ground corn bought for making up the allowance for the manor servants, at 5d per bushel	–	1	8
4 qr 6 bu of corn bought for fodder for the lord's horses and for fodder for the carthorses, at 3s per quarter	–	14	3
Total		15	11
Purchase of livestock			
One affer bought	–	12	–
4 oxen bought at 14s a head	2	16	–
Total	3	8	–
Threshing and winnowing			
45 qr 4 bu 2 pk of wheat, 25 qr 2 bu of beans and peas, threshed by taskwork at 3d per quarter	(–	17	8¼[c])
(deduction for heaped measure	–	17	– [i])
125 qr 1 bu 3 pk dredge corn, threshed by taskwork at 2½d per quarter	(1	6	½[c])
(deduction for heaped measure	1	5	2½[i])
Nothing for winnowing because done by the manor servants	–	–	–
Total	2	2	2½
Hoeing and mowing			
For hoeing corn, nothing here because done by customary services as appears outside	–	–	–
Gift to customary tenants for spreading hay in Fanmede	–	–	2
Defaults of 10 holdings being in the lord's hand and at rent this year, for a gift to the customary tenants in Fanmede, 2d for each holding	–	1	8
Given to the said 10 customary tenants, being in the lord's hand and at rent, because they have to make and gather hay in the lord's meadow, 2d for each holding	–	1	8
Half an acre of meadow, in the holding once John Wilgod senior's, mown by taskwork	–	–	2
Total	–	3	8
Cash payments for tithes			
Cash paid for tithes of underwood sold above, nothing here in money, because delivered as underwood	–	–	–
Total		nil	

	£	s	d
Outside expenses			
Paid to customary tenants for carrying services as their "lodepanes"	—	—	8
Paid to a "rakier" in London	—	—	2
Paid to customary tenants for "panagesilver", viz for carting 33 quarters of wheat to London this year, with their carrying service, for sale, at ¼d for 5 bushels	—	1	1
Paid to the said customary tenants for the same, viz for carting 11 quarters of malt to London this year, with their carrying services, for selling, at ¼d per quarter	—	—	2¾
Expenses of the bailiff going to London 5 times to sell wheat and malt there, and for money paid there on the lord's authority	—	5	—
(Given to the manor servants as "remeneration"	—	2	— [c])
(For wages of one groom of the lord staying at Hegham 5½ days to take care of the lord's horse there, 2d per day	—	—	11 [c])
(For John Hospelord, the lord's servant, staying there for 10 days to take care of the lord's horse, at 1½d per day		1	3 [c])
One gallon and one pint of wine bought for the expenses of the lord staying at the house of Ralph FitzRichard on Whitsunday	—	1	2
Shoeing the lord's horse at the same time	—	—	4½
Paid for 2 discharges on the lord's behalf for John Carbonel and John Elisdon	—	—	4
(13s 2¼ [m])			
Total		8	3½[c])
	—	9	¼[i])

	£	s	d
Steward's fees and expenses			
Fees of the steward for the year	2	—	—
Expenses of the same steward coming there for holding 2 courts there	—	3	4
Total	2	3	4

	£	s	d
Harvest expenses			
Ale, meat, herring fish, candles, cheese, and other victuals bought for 6 boonworks, for each boonwork 42 men, viz: some customary tenants came with one man and others came with 2 men	2	2	6
10 pairs of gloves bought for a bailiff and 9 manor servants	—	1	8

	£	s	d
One cow hired for the whole harvest for "sonilsilver" for the manor servants	–	1	–
One bushel of salt bought for the harvest	–	–	10
One [?] ladle and eleven dishes bought for the harvest	–	–	5
One groom hired for the whole harvest for looking after the lord's oxen	–	2	–
One man hired at the lord's board for 4 weeks in harvest for stacking the lord's corn and also for lifting sheaves to the carts	–	6	–
96 reapers hired at the lord's board, separately as if for one day, for 8 holdings remaining in the lord's hand and at rent, which have to provide for each day's boonwork, 12 men for 6 days' boonwork, 2d per head per day	–	16	–
96 reapers hired at the lord's board separately as if for one day for the aforesaid 8 holdings remaining in the lord's hand and at rent, which have to reap 96 harvest services, 2d per head per day	–	16	–
Total	4	6	5

Manor servants' wages

	£	s	d
(Pay of one bailiff for the year according to agreement at 14d per head per week	3	–	8 [c])
Wages of one carter for the year	–	13	4
Wages of 5 plough servants for the year, at 10s per head	2	10	–
Wages of one shepherd for the year	–	10	–
Wages of one dairyman for 30 weeks	–	7	6
Wages of one warrener for the year	–	10	–
(Wages of one clerk writing account	–	6	8 [c])
Total	4	10	10

Money payments

	£	s	d
Paid to the lord's chest by the hand of Thomas Holewelle, from rents for St. Andrew's term, as appears from a tally	7	3	9
Paid to the lord's chest by the hand of the said Thomas before the feast of the Purification of the B.V.M., as appears from a tally	5	–	–
Paid to John Carbonel, through the lord's letter and seal, and as appears from a receipt from the said John on behalf of the lord	20	–	–
Paid to John Elisdone by order of the lord, and as appears from a receipt from the said John on behalf of the lord	20	–	–

	£	s	d
Paid to the lord on 2 occasions, as appears from a tally against the same	6	—	—
Paid to Richard Carlton for his fee, being in arrears, as appears from a sealed bill of John atte Hay	1	—	—
Paid to John Cook for his annual fee, allowed to him by the lord	2	—	—
Paid to John, bailiff of Hattele, for harvest expenses, without a tally	3	—	—
Total	64	3	9
Total of all expenses and allowances	90	11	11¾
Thus, by calculation, owing to the lord	8	9	7¼[1]

1 The actual difference is £8 9s 7d.

[2d]

HEGHAM

Proceeds of the grange there in the time of John Hened, bailiff there, serving in the fourth year of the reign of Richard the second after the conquest [1380-1381]

Wheat	qr	bu	pk
Wheat from the whole proceeds of the grange by level measure, threshed by taskwork and by customary services without tally, of which by taskwork 45 qr 3 bu 2 pk, besides 33 qr heaped measure for sale in London	73	4	2
From heaped measure for the same	1	—	1
From the usual 21 customary tenants for their "benesed" for the Michaelmas term	1	2	2
Total	75	7	1

of which:—

	qr	bu	pk
For seed on 83 acres of land at seedtime for wheat this year, at 2 bushels per acre, and so much for seed for wheat this year because the holdings of John Holewell, John Wilgod, Thomas Neweman, John Smyth and Walter Aleyn remained in the lord's hand this year	20	6	—
For defaults from the holdings of John Holewell, John Wilgod, Thomas Neweman, John Smyth and Walter Aleyn, because they remained in the lord's hand this year, for their "benesed", for each holding ½ bushel		2	2

	qr	bu	pk
For defaults in the holdings of John Hened, Richard Hened, John Wilgod junior, Thomas Hened and Robert Bonde, for their "benesed" because they were at rent, for each holding ½ bushel	–	2	2
For bread baked for harvest expenses, viz for customary boonworks	2	–	–
For mixed meal allowance for manor servants below	18	4	–
For sale in London as below	33	–	–
with heaped measure	1	–	1
Total as above and it balances	[75	7	1]

Beans and peas

	qr	bu	pk
Beans and peas from the whole proceeds of the grange, by level measure, threshed by taskwork and by customary services without tally, of which by taskwork 25 qr 2 bu besides 32 qr heaped for sale	43	2	–
Heaped measure for the same	1	–	–
Total	44	2	–

of which:–

	qr	bu	pk
For seed on 40 acres of land, at 2 bushels 1 peck per acre	11	2	–
Sold as below	32	–	–
with heaped measure	1	–	–
Total as above and it balances	[44	2	–]

Dredge corn

	qr	bu	pk
Dredge corn from the whole proceeds of the grange, by level measure, threshed by taskwork and by customary services without tally, of which by taskwork 125 qr 1 bu 3 pk besides 125 qr heaped measure for malting	165	1	3
Heaped measure	3	7	1
From the same proceeds, in 350 sheaves of corn for ox fodder, of which 10 sheaves make one bushel	4	3	–
Total	173	4	–

of which:–

	qr	bu	pk
For seed on 103 acres of land, at 3 bu ½ pk per acre, reduced in total by (½ pk[c]) 3½ pk and so much in dredge corn seed this year because the holdings of John Holewell, John Wilgod, Thomas Neweman, John Smyth and Walter Aleyn remained in the lord's hand this year	40	1	(3 [c])

	qr	bu	pk
Set aside as oats below for ox fodder	4	3	–
For malting as below	125	–	–
With heaped measure	3	7	1
(Sold above the account	–	–	3 [i])
Total as above and it balances	[173	4	–]

Oats

	qr	bu	pk
Oats from the usual 21 customary tenants at Christmas	5	2	–
In sheaves, per above estimate, for ox fodder	4	3	–
Bought as fodder for cart horses	4	6	–
Heaped measure for the same	–	1	–
Total	14	4	–

of which:–

	qr	bu	pk
In default from the holdings of John Holewell, John Wilgod, Thomas Neweman, John Smyth, and Walter Aleyn, because they remained in the lord's hand this year, for each holding 2 bu	1	2	–
In default from the holdings of John Hened, Richard Hened, John Wilgod junior, Thomas Hened, and Robert Bonde, because they were at rent, for each holding 2 bu	1	2	–
For making flour for the manor servants' pottage, and for harvest expenses	1	4	–
(Fodder for 5 horses of the lord, staying at Hegham 5½ days, and one other horse of the lord, staying there for 10 days	2	1	– [c])
(Because without warrant [i])			
Fodder for 4 cart horses for the period of the account	4	–	–
For ox fodder as appears in the above debit	4	3	–
Sold above the account	2	1	–
Total as above and it balances	[14	4	–]

Multure of the mill

	qr	bu	pk
Multure from rent of the lord's watermill for the year, by level measure	18	–	–
Bought for making up the manor servants' allowance	–	4	–
Total	18	4	–

The whole amount was used for the allowance of mixed meal for the manor servants below

	qr	bu	pk
Dredge malt	qr	bu	pk
Dredge malt for malting as above	125	–	–
Growth in making, for each quarter 1 bushel	15	5	–
Total	140	5	–
of which:–			
Sold as below in London	11	–	–
growth of the same, 1 quarter for 9 bushels	1	3	–
Sold as below	114	–	–
growth of the same, 1 quarter for 9 bushels	14	2	–
Total as above and it balances	[140	5	–]

	qr	bu	pk
Manor servants' allowances			
Wheat	18	4	–
Multure for mixed meal for the manor servants below	18	4	–
Total	37	–	–
of which:–			
Allowances for one carter, 5 plough servants, one warrener and one shepherd, for the whole year, 1 quarter of medium wheat per head per 12 weeks	34	4	–
Allowance for one dairyman making malt and pottage for the manor servants below from Michaelmas to 26 April, that is for 30 weeks, per head as above	2	4	–
Total as above and it balances	[37	–	–]

ACCOUNT OF LIVESTOCK

Cart horses remaining 4; total 4; and there remain	4 cart horses
Affers remaining 4, bought 1, total 5; of which – – – and sold as below, because worn out 1, sold above the account 2, total 3; and there remain	2 affers
Oxen remaining 12, bought 4, total 16; of which died of a murrain (as testified in the court roll) 1, total 1; and there remain	15 oxen
Ganders remaining 1, total 1; and there remains	1 gander
Young geese remaining 3, and no proceeds from these here because they were rented to the dairyman for money as appears below, total 3; and there remain	3 young geese
Cocks remaining 1, total 1; and there remains	1 cock

Hens remaining 12, and no proceeds from these here because they were rented to the dairyman for money as appears below, and from 21 customary tenants as rent for the Christmas term, 84, total 96; of which in default from the holdings of John Holewell, John Wilgod, Thomas Neweman, John Smyth and Walter Aleyn, because they remained in the lord's hand this year, 20; and in default from the holdings of John Hened, Richard Hened, John Wilgod junior, Thomas Hened, and Robert Bonde, because they were at rent, 20, and sold as below 44, total 84 and there remain — 12 hens

Capons remaining 24, made from chickens as below, 24, total 48; of which sold as below, 24; and there remain — 24 capons

Chickens bought for making into capons, 24 chickens, total 24, and used to make capons as above, and it balances

Eggs from 21 customary tenants, 10 from each — 210 eggs
of which in default from the holdings of John Holewell, John Wilgod, Thomas Neweman, John Smyth and Walter Aleyn, because they were in the lord's hand this year, 50 eggs, and in default from the holdings of John Hened, Richard Hened, John Wilgod junior, Thomas Hened and Robert Bonde, because they were at rent, 50 eggs, and sold as below 110 eggs, total as above, and it balances

Loaves from 21 customary tenants at the Christmas term, from each tenant 1 loaf besides 1 bushel of wheat, total — 21 loaves
of which in default from the holdings of John Holewell, John Wilgod, Thomas Neweman, John Smyth and Walter Aleyn, because they were in the lord's hand this year, 5 loaves; and in default from the holdings of John Hened, Richard Hened, John Wilgod junior, Thomas Hened and Robert Bonde, because they were at rent, 5 loaves; and sold as below 11 loaves, total as above, and it balances

Raw hides from an ox dead of a murrain as above, 1 hide, total 1 hide, and sold as below

Bleached hides remaining 1 bleached horse hide, total 1, which was used for repairing harness, leaving none

ACCOUNT OF SERVICES

Small services and $\frac{3}{4}$ services — Services

From the aforesaid 21 customary tenants, from each tenant 95 services. Total as it appears — 1995

of which:–

	Services
In default from the holdings of John Holewell, John Wilgod, Thomas Neweman, John Smyth and Walter Aleyn, because they were in the lord's hand this year, for each tenant 95 services	475
In default from the holdings of John Hened, Richard Hened, John Wilgod junior, Thomas Hened and Robert Bonde, because they were at rent, for each tenant 95 services	475
For 3 assistants helping one thatcher thatching the corn barn and ridging and thatching the dove house for 20 days, for each day 3 services	60
For 3 assistants helping one thatcher thatching the hall for 3 days, for each day 3 services	9
Allowed to the said customary tenants working with the lord at "bensed", for each tenant half a service	5½
Allowed to the said customary tenants for "malterth", for each tenant one service	11
Allowed to the same for "wodesilver" as usual, for each tenant one service	11
For bundling straw, for each tenant 2 services	22
For spreading manure this year, for each tenant 2 services	22
Sold viz. to 11 customary tenants because they took demesne land lying in various cultivated areas at rent, price per service ¾d for each tenant 20 services	220
Sold viz. to the aforesaid 11 tenants for harvest services for the aforesaid reason, viz for each tenant 3 services	33
Allowed to the aforesaid tenants services which are usually conceded to them for carrying services by ancient law, viz. for each tenant 12 services	132
For bringing the bean stack to the grange for threshing, for each tenant 2 services	22
For threshing 28 quarters of wheat by customary services, 3 services per quarter	84
For threshing 18 quarters of beans and peas by customary services, 3 services per quarter	54
For threshing 40 quarters of dredge corn by customary services, 5 services per 2 quarters	100
For hoeing the lord's corn this year, for each tenant 7 services	77
For mowing the lord's meadow at Fanmede, and making and gathering [hay], for each tenant 2 services	22
For mowing the lord's meadow at Southponde	9
For making and gathering hay in the said meadow, for each tenant one service	11

	Services
For reaping, binding and stooking 17 acres of wheat, 2 services per acre	34
For reaping, binding and stooking 16 acres of beans and peas, 4 services per acre	64
For reaping, binding and stooking 21 acres 1 rood of dredge corn, 2 services per acre	42½
Total as above and it balances	[1995]

Ploughing services	ac	rd
The proceeds of the aforesaid 21 customary tenants ploughing for the lord, viz. 140 acres 3 roods of land at 3 seed times of the year, from each tenant 6 acres 3 roods per year		
Total as it appears	140	3
of which:–		
In default from the holdings of John Holewell, John Wilgod, Thomas Neweman, John Smyth and Walter Aleyn, because they were in the lord's hand this year, for each tenant 6 acres 3 roods	33	3
In default from the holdings of John Hened, Richard Hened, John Wilgod junior, Thomas Hened and Robert Bonde, because they were at rent, for each tenant 6 acres 3 roods	33	3
For ploughing the lord's land at 3 seed times of the year	73	1
Total as above and it balances	[140	3]

Carrying services	Services
Proceeds of the said 21 customary tenants, from each tenant 12 carrying services. Total as it appears	252
of which:–	
In default from the holdings of John Holewell, John Wilgod, Thomas Neweman, John Smyth and Walter Aleyn, because they were in the lord's hand this year, for each tenant 12 carrying services	60
In default from the holdings of John Hened, Richard Hened, John Wilgod junior, Thomas Hened and Robert Bonde, because they were at rent, for each tenant 12 carrying services	60
Sold viz. to the 11 tenants aforesaid for the reason above, viz. to each tenant 4 services price 6d per service	44

	Services
For carting 33 quarters of wheat to London for sale, 2 services per quarter	66
For carting 11 quarters of malt to London for sale, 2 services per quarter	22
Total as above and it balances	[252]

Proceeds of the dove house

Proceeds of the dove house this year and no more here because of more expenses in the outgoings of the lord and others through the sheriff, but from the rest of the accounts of small items	171 young pigeons
Total	171
of which:–	
Given in tithes	17
Sold as below	154 young pigeons
Total as above and it balances	[171]

Rabbit warren

Proceeds of the warren, nothing this year because the lord granted the profits from it to Ralph FitzRichard this year	
Total	Nil

[3r]

HEGHAM

Account of John Hened, bailiff there, of all his receipts, expenditure and allowances, made there from the day after Michaelmas in the fifth year of the reign of Richard the second after the conquest, up to the day after the same festival in the sixth year of the same king, that is for one whole year [1381-1382]

	£	s	d
Arrears			
Arrears from the last account, of the preceding year	8	9	7¼
Total	8	9	7¼
Fixed rents			
Hegham cum Faldho, for St. Andrews term [30 Nov]	1	6	1½
Strattele cum Scharpenho, for the same term	2	5	5

	£	s	d
Hegham, for Christmas term [25 Dec]	—	—	1½
A certain rent called "wodesilver", for the same term	—	3	4
Strattele, for the same term	—	—	1½
Hegham, for Lady day term [25 Mar]	1	6	3
Strattele, for the same term	2	7	10½
Hegham, for Midsummer term [24 Jun]	1	6	1½
Strattele, for the same term	2	5	5
Hegham, for Michaelmas term [29 Sep]	2	7	3½
A certain rent "langavel", coming from the customary tenants, for the same term	—	6	3
Strattele, for the same term	2	7	10½
Concerning 4s from Walter Aleyn for 1 ac 1 rd of land per year, nothing here because it was leased to Robert Hened at rent, as appears in the titles of rented land below, in the court roll, because of the incapacity of the said Walter	—	—	—
From Henry Longe for a croft of land called Horoldescroft, leased to him at rent for the year	—	4	—
From Simon Neweman, for 3 sellions of land leased to him at rent for the year	—	2	—
From Richard Aleyn, for 3 acres of land leased to him at rent in Southfeld and Oxefoldefelde for the year	—	7	—
Total	68	15	2½

Hegham rents

	£	s	d
From Nicholas Carlton, for a house with one croft of land and for 1 ac 3 rd of land of the holding once held by John Aleyn and which John Holewell once held, thus leased to him this year	—	8	—
Concerning the rest of the said land, nothing here in money, because it was taken for the lord's cultivation			
From Robert Helder, for a house with a croft of land of the holding once John Smyth's thus leased to him this year	—	8	—
and no more here in money because the rest of the said land was taken for the lord's cultivation			
From Nicholas Crane, for a house and a croft of land, and for one acre of land of the holding once held by John Wilgod senior, thus leased to him at rent this year	—	8	—
and no more here in money because the rest of the said land was taken for the lord's cultivation			
Concerning 8s from Walter Aleyn for 3 ac of land lately leased to him at rent, nothing here because it was leased to Robert Hened as in the court roll, by reason of the incapacity of the said Walter, as appears below	—	—	—

	£	s	d
From Thomas Totegos, for a cottage once Cripses, thus leased to him for a term of 40 years, this year being the 10th	–	2	–
Concerning 3s from Walter Aleyn for one acre of land lately leased to him on Wouwefurlong, nothing here because it was leased to Robert Hened as in the court roll as appears below, by reason of the incapacity of the said Walter	–	–	–
From Robert Hened for 5 ac 1 rd of land which Walter Aleyn once held, thus leased to him at rent for the year as appears in the court roll	–	5	–
From William Aleyn, for a croft and 3 roods of land held by Thomas Neweman, thus leased to him at rent for the year	–	6	8
From Israel Spynner, for the house and garden of the said holding, thus leased to him this year	–	2	–
Concerning the rest of the land of the said holding, nothing here because it was taken for the lord's cultivation			
From 16 customary tenants for 80 acres of demesne land leased to them at rent at the lord's will at 12d per acre and no more because 20 acres of demesne land, which John Holewell, Thomas Neweman, John Smyth and Walter Aleyn formerly held, remained in the lord's hand and therefore was taken for the lord's cultivation	4	–	–
From John Priour, for 1 rood of demesne land leased to him at Littlewell this year	–	–	6
From Richard Aleyn for a holding once John Hened's, thus leased to him this year and no more because the lord allowed him 6s 8d this year from the usual rent per year for this holding	1	1	8
From the same Richard by the hand of the bailiff for the said allowance of 6s 8d	–	3	4
From Henry Longe, for a holding once Richard Hened's, thus leased to him at rent for the year	1	8	4
From the same Henry for 2 acres of land allowed to him this year in correction of his rent	–	6	8
Concerning 28s 4d from Geoffrey Whether, for a holding once Walter Aleyn's, nothing this year because it remained in the lord's hand	–	–	–
From Hugh Clerke, for a house with 2 acres of land of the said holding thus leased to him this year	–	9	–
and no more here because the rest of the land of the said holding was taken for the lord's cultivation	–	–	–
From Thomas Hened, for a holding once John Hened's, thus leased to him at rent for the year	1	8	4

	£	s	d
Concerning 28s 4d from William Elis, for a holding once Robert Bonde's, nothing from this because it remained in the lord's hand and therefore was taken for the lord's cultivation this year	–	–	–
From John Priour, for having accommodation to store his corn in the barn of the said holding	–	1	–
From John Wilgod, for a holding once John Wilgod senior's, thus leased to him at rent for the year	1	8	4
From Alexander Jekes, for a cottage with one and a half acres of land, called "le Mulnehouse" thus leased to him at rent	–	5	–
From John Yonge for a cottage, which Walter Wildemor once held, thus leased to him at rent this year	–	3	–
From John Priour, for a cottage with an adjoining croft of land, lately Ann Bonde's thus leased to him at rent this year	–	4	–
From Thomas Totegos, for 4½ roods of land lying at Little Innyngg, thus leased to him at rent for the year	–	1	–
From John Potton, for three half-acres of demesne land leased to him with a cottage formerly John Mulward's, for the term of his life	–	1	–
From John Priour for 3 ac 3 rd of land in various holdings, being in the lord's hand and leased to him for one crop	–	3	4
From Geoffrey Whether, for one rood of land lying under his croft, thus leased to him at rent for the year	–	–	4
Total	13	4	6
Strattele rents			
From various holdings in Strattele, for rent of the lord's meadows and land at Strattele for the year, and no more this year because one meadow called Fannemede, which was usually rented at 10s per year, was mown for the lord's livestock this year	6	17	10
Total	6	17	10
Perquisites of court			
From perquisites of court for the year	2	8	7
Total	2	8	7
Sale of underwood			
From William Mile for 9 ac 1 rd of underwood sold to him wholesale in Pullokeshullewode through the lord's warrant	11	–	–

	£	s	d
From John Adam for 9 ac 1 rd of underwood sold to him wholesale in Strattlewode through the lord's warrant	11	–	–
From Philip Totegos for a piece of hedge sold to him at Oxefold	–	1	6
From Richard Coke for a piece of hedge sold to him in the same place	–	–	6
From John Cooke and Richard Coke for a piece of hedge sold to him in the same place	–	1	10
For half an acre of underwood sold in Oxefold	–	5	–
For bushes sold in the lord's garden which spoilt the pasture of the said garden	–	4	–
From William Carlton for a branch of a tree sold to him in Oxefold	–	1	–
From Nicholas Carlton for a branch of a tree sold to him in the same place	–	1	–
From John Pope for a piece of hedge sold round the lord's close	–	1	4
Total	22	16	2

Sale of pasture and herbage

	£	s	d
For pasture sold at Eyebrook this year	–	2	–
Concerning 6d for pasture sold at Madefurlong, nothing this year because it lay fallow	–	–	–
For pasture sold at Hulheg this year	–	–	8
Concerning 6d for pasture sold at Estheg, nothing because it became woodland	–	–	–
Concerning 6d for pasture sold at Hammenheneden, nothing this year because it lay fallow	–	–	–
Concerning 6d for pasture sold round the garden ditch, nothing this year because it lay fallow	–	–	–
Concerning 4s for pasture sold at le Flete, nothing this year because it lay fallow	–	–	–
Concerning 8d for half an acre of meadow sold at Colverhousmed, nothing here because it was leased with other meadows to customary tenants of the lord, as appears below	–	–	–
For pasture sold at Littleholm this year	–	–	8
Concerning 13s 4d for herbage sold in le Newemed, nothing this year because it was leased to customary tenants of the lord at rent, as appears below	–	–	–
For herbage sold in Wrastmede this year	1	–	–
Concerning 12d for pasture sold at Hexstounbrok, nothing here because it was leased to customary tenants of the lord at rent as appears below	–	–	–
Concerning pasture sold at Longelond, nothing here for the reason aforesaid	–	–	–

	£	s	d
Concerning 6d for pasture sold at Mershfurlong, nothing here because the headland there was ploughed	—	—	—
For pasture sold at Colverhouspond this year	—	1	8
From William Mulward for herbage sold to him in le Newemed this year	—	13	4
For pasture sold in le Estmede this year and no more because the rest of the pasture was depastured with the lord's oxen and sheep	—	5	—
Concerning pasture sold in Colverhousmed, nothing this year in money because it was depastured by the lord's sheep	—	—	—
From Robert Hened for a cottage once Baldewynes leased to him this year, which is usually rented at 14d per year	—	—	4
For pasture sold in Fanmed and Shortmed	—	2	6
Total	2	6	2

Proceeds of the manor

	£	s	d
Concerning 8d for mustard seed, nothing this year because none was grown	—	—	—
Concerning 12d for garden fruit, nothing this year because there was no fruit	—	—	—
From nettles and herbage sold in the lord's garden this year	—	1	—
From the hire of 3 geese for the year at 12d a head	—	3	—
From the hire of 12 hens for the year at 6d a head	—	6	—
From 12 capons sold at 4d a head	—	4	—
From 40 hens coming as rent from customary tenants, sold at 2½d a head	—	8	4
From 100 eggs coming as rent from customary tenants, sold	—	—	5
From 132 young pigeons sold at ½d a head	—	5	6
From straw "stramen" sold	—	3	4
From straw "stipula" sold	—	5	—
Total	1	16	7

Sale of corn and malt

	£	s	d
From 24 qr of wheat sold in London at 6s 8d a quarter	8	—	—
From 5 qr of wheat sold in the same place at 6s a quarter	1	10	—
From 21 qr of beans and peas sold at 3s 4d a quarter	3	10	—
From 20 qr of dredge corn sold at 3s 6d a quarter	3	10	—
From 11 qr of malt sold in London at 5s 2d a quarter	2	16	10

	£	s	d
From 85 qr of dredge malt sold at 4s 6d a quarter	19	2	6
Total	38	9	4
Sale of livestock			
From one aged ox sold	–	6	8
Total	–	6	8
Sale of services			
From 10 loaves coming from the proceeds of 10 customary tenants, sold at 7d per loaf	–	5	10
From 200 small services sold to the said 10 customary tenants at ¾d per service	–	12	6
From 30 harvest services sold to the said 10 tenants, viz. 3 services to each tenant at 3d per service	–	7	6
From 40 carrying services sold to the said 10 tenants, viz 4 services to each tenant at 6d per service	1	–	–
From 10 customary tenants for 2 days boonwork at harvest, sold to them, viz each of them comes each day for the aforesaid boonwork with 2 men	–	10	–
Total	2	15	10
Above the account			
From various items put on the dorse and sold above the account	–	2	4½
Total	–	2	4½
Sum total of receipts with arrears	116	4	10¼

EXPENSES

Rents paid, with various allowances for holdings in the lord's hand or at rent

	£	s	d
Rent paid to the manor of Wraste, for the year	–	2	–
Paid to the King for sheriff's aid for the year	–	17	–
Paid to the King for "deseynsilver", for the year	–	6	–
Paid to the King's bailiff for remission of suit to the hundred, for the year	–	1	–
Paid to the lord Pikot for remission of suit to the court, for the year	–	2	–
Rent defaults for the holdings of John Holewell, John Wilgod, Thomas Neweman, John Smyth, Walter Aleyn, and Robert Bonde, because they remained in the lord's hand this year, for "wodesilver" for the Christmas term, for each holding 2d	–	1	–

	£	s	d
Rent defaults for the holdings of John Hened, Richard Hened, John Wilgod junior, Thomas Hened, and John Southend, because they were at rent, for each holding 2d	–	–	10
Money allowance for rent reduction of John Wemme, whose rent used to be 13s 4d per year, because it is now only 8s	–	5	4
Money allowance for rent reduction of Alexander Jekes for a place called le Mulnehous, which used to be rented at 7s per year, and is now leased to him at 5s, as appears above in the rents	–	2	–
Money allowance for rent reduction for a cottage lately Baldewynes, because it is leased to Robert Hened at 4d per year, as appears from the court roll and above in the rents	–	1	1
Money allowance for rent reduction of Nicholas Casse, for 8 acres of land which he used to hold because it remains in the lord's hand and now lies empty, taken in default	–	4	–
Money allowance for rent reduction of John Wilgod, for one acre of land, which he used to rent at 2s per year, because it is now leased to the same John at 16d as appears above in the rents	–	–	8
Rent default of Robert Hened for 1½ acres of land, because it remained in the lord's hand and was therefore taken for the lord's cultivation	–	4	–
Money allowance for rent reduction of John Wenne, for a garden in Strattle, and for le Launde, which he used to rent at 21s per year and this year he rents at only 17s, as debited above in the rents of Strattle	–	4	–
Total	2	10	11

Upkeep of ploughs

	£	s	d
Iron and steel bought for 3 ploughs per year, together with the smith's wages, and for iron and shoeing 4 cart horses and 2 affers on the forefeet	2	13	3
Shoeing 2 affers on the hindfeet, outside the smith's contract	–	–	9
3 new ploughs bought	–	2	6
4 old ploughs re-boarded	–	1	4
Total	2	17	10

Upkeep of carts

	£	s	d
2 pairs of bare wheels bought for carts	–	8	6
Fitting 2 long carts with axles for harvest, and axles bought for the same	–	–	8

	£	s	d
16 clouts bought for the same	–	2	8
Fitting axle to one dung cart, with axle bought for the same	–	–	4
200 clout nails bought	–	–	8
Grease for greasing carts	–	–	6
A pair of body traces bought	–	–	10
Another pair of traces bought	–	–	6
4 hempen halters bought	–	–	4
2 short hemp ropes bought, for binding carts	–	1	–
Fitting hoops to one pair of wheels	–	–	2
Whipcord bought	–	–	2
Mending a long cart body and a cart ladder	–	–	4
4 new leather [horse] collars bought	–	2	4
1 bleached horsehide bought for mending harness	–	1	6
Total	1	0	6

Upkeep of buildings and mill

	£	s	d
One thatcher hired at taskwork for 12 days for thatching and repairing the dredge corn grange, defects in the hall, and the dove house at 4d per head per day	–	4	–
For assistants, nothing here, because through customary services, as appears on dorse	–	–	–
The said thatcher hired at taskwork for 5 days, for thatching and repairing defects in the buildings on the holdings of Walter Aleyn, and John Aleyn, per head as above	–	1	8
For assistants, nothing here because through customary services, as appears outside	–	–	–
The said thatcher, hired at taskwork for 3 days for thatching the bean stack, per head as above	–	1	–
For assistants, nothing here for the reason as above	–	–	–
One carpenter, hired at taskwork for one day for mending the great gate	–	–	4
The said carpenter, hired at taskwork, wholesale, for making a new bridge called Eyebrugge from the lord's timber	–	1	–
Paid for 2 new bars, made from the lord's iron, for the great gate of the manor, new hung and repaired	–	–	2
One new long ladder bought	–	1	–
400 spikenails bought for fixing boards to the wheel of the watermill, and for mending the waterwork	–	2	–
One carpenter hired at taskwork, wholesale, for mending a barn on the holding of John Aleyn, now in the lord's hand	–	2	–

	£	s	d
The said carpenter, hired at taskwork, wholesale, for repairing the main building on the holding of John Wilgod, senior, now in the lord's hand	–	1	2
Total	–	14	4

Upkeep of folds	£	s	d
32 wicker hurdles, bought for the fold at 1¼d each	–	3	4
4 gallons of tar, bought	–	2	8
Grease for the same, bought	–	–	10
Total	–	6	10

Small necessaries			
Food and offerings for a bailiff and 9 manor servants at 2 main festivals at 2d per head for each festival	–	3	4
1 lb of wax bought for the manor servants for the day of the Purification of the B.V.M. [2 Feb]	–	–	8
3 lb of candles bought for turning malt by night in winter	–	–	6
3 new sacks bought	–	3	6
1 bushel of salt bought for pottage for the manor servants	–	–	9
Parchment bought for the court roll and accounts	–	–	6
2 shovels with 2 irons for the same, bought	–	1	–
1 sling bought for scaring crows	–	–	1
1 cooper hired at taskwork for mending 2 large casks and another wooden bowl, at 4d per head per day	–	–	8
4 hoops bought for mending 2 large casks	–	–	4
5 hoops for mending a portable cask	–	–	2½
1 wicker seedbasket bought	–	–	6
2 fans bought	–	3	–
2 "skoteles" bought	–	–	7
2 pairs of fetters with 2 locks and keys for horses, bought	–	2	4
1 quarter 3 bushels of corn, defective and made into flour	–	–	6
Total	–	18	5½

Purchase of corn			
2 qr 2½ bu of "tollcorn" bought for making up the allowance for the manor servants, at 3s 4d per quarter	–	7	8½
3 qr 7 bu 1 pk corn bought for fodder for horses at 2s per quarter	–	7	9¾
Total	–	15	6¼

	£	s	d
Purchase of livestock			
24 chickens bought for making into capons, at 1d a head	–	2	–
Total	–	2	–
Threshing and winnowing			
50 qr 2 bu of wheat, 27 qr 5 bu of beans and peas, threshed by task work at 3d per quarter		(16	11¼[c])
(deduction for heaped measure	–	16	5¼[i])
97 qr 7 bu 3 pk of dredge corn, threshed by task work at 2½d per quarter	(1	–	7 [c])
(deduction for heaped measure		19	8½[i])
Nothing for winnowing because done by the manor servants	–	–	–
Total	1	16	1¾
Hoeing and mowing			
For hoeing the lord's corn, nothing this year because done by customary works, as appears outside	–	–	–
Gift to customary tenants for spreading hay in Fanmede	–	–	2
Defaults of 11 holdings being in the lord's hand and at rent this year, 2d per holding	–	1	10
Given to the said 11 customary tenants, being in the lord's hand and at rent, because they have to mow, make, and gather hay in the lord's meadow, 2d per holding	–	1	10
Half an acre of meadow in the holding once John Wilgod senior's, mown by task work	–	–	2
Total	–	4	–
Cash payments for tithes of underwood sold			
Cash paid for tithes of underwood sold above, nothing here because delivered in underwood	–	–	–
Total		nil	
Outside expenses			
Paid to customary tenants for carrying services as their "lodepanes"	–	–	8
Paid to a rakyer in London	–	–	2
Paid to customary tenants for "panagesilver", viz. for carting 29 quarters of wheat to London this year, with their carrying service, for sale, at ¼d for 5 bushels	–	–	11½

	£	s	d
Paid to the said customary tenants, viz. for carting 11 quarters of malt to London this year, with their carrying service, at ¼d per quarter	—	—	2¾
Expenses of the bailiff going to London 6 times to sell wheat and malt there, and for money paid there on the lord's authority	—	6	—
6 geese bought and sent to Dunstable for the lord's expenses staying there for the assizes at Michaelmas with Hugh Spenser, knight, at 4d a head	—	2	—
(Given to the manor servants for "remeneration"	—	2	— [c])
Total	—	10	¼

Steward's fees and expenses	£	s	d
Fees of the steward for the year	2	—	—
Expenses of the same for holding 5 courts and no more because 2 courts were at the house of Ralph FitzRichard with the lord		3	4
Total	2	3	4

Harvest expenses	£	s	d
Ale, meat, herring fish, candles and other victuals bought for 6 boonworks, for each boonwork 42 men, viz. some customary tenants came with one man and others came with 2 men	2	2	6
9 pairs of gloves bought for a bailiff and 8 manor servants	—	1	6
One cow hired for the whole harvest as "sonilsilver" for the manor servants	—	1	—
One bushel of salt bought for harvest expenses	—	—	10
26 dishes and plates bought for harvest	—	—	8
One groom hired for the whole harvest for looking after the lord's oxen	—	2	—
96 reapers hired at the lord's board, separately as if for 1 day, for 8 holdings remaining in the lord's hand and at rent, which have to provide for each day's boonwork, 12 men for 6 days' boonwork, 2d per head	—	16	—
96 reapers hired at the lord's board, separately as if for 1 day, for the aforesaid 8 holdings remaining in the lord's hand and at rent, because they have to reap 96 harvest services, 2d per head	—	16	—
Total	4	—	6

	£	s	d
Manor servants' wages			
(Pay of one bailiff for the year at 14d per head per week	3	–	8 c)
Wages of one carter for the year	–	13	4
Wages of 5 plough servants for the year, at 10s per head	2	10	–
Wages of one shepherd for the year	–	10	–
Wages of one dairyman for 27 weeks	–	7	–
Wages of one warrener for the year	–	10	–
(Wages of one clerk writing the account	–	6	8 c)
Total	4	10	4

	£	s	d
Money payments			
Paid to the lord's chest by the hand of John Helesden, as appears from a sealed tally	60	–	–
and also including £20 paid to the same John last year			
Paid to Thomas Rolf, skinner, London by order of the lord and by the lord's letter	13	15	4½
Paid to John Cook for his annual fee, allowed to him by the lord	2	–	–
(Paid on one occasion without tally to Sir Ralph FitzRichard, on the word of John Cook	2	–	– c)
Paid to Joanna, wife of John Drone, by order of John atte Hay	1	–	–
Total	76	15	4½

	£	s	d
Total of all expenses and allowances	99	6	1¼
Thus, by calculation, owing to the lord of which,	16	18	9
allowed to the same bailiff for his pay for that year and the previous year viz. 14d per week	6	1	4
(Allowed to the same, what was paid for the lord without tally to Sir Ralph FitzRichard, because witnessed	2	–	– c)
Allowed to the same for fodder for the lord's horse and wages of the lord's groom	–	10	6½
Thus so far owing to the lord	10	6	10½
Allowed to the same, what was paid for the lord without tally to Sir Ralph FitzRichard, because witnessed	2	–	–
Thus so far owing to the lord	8	6	10½

[3d]

HEGHAM

Proceeds of the grange there in the time of John Hened, bailiff there, serving in the fifth year of the reign of Richard the second after the conquest [1381-1382]

	qr	bu	pk
Wheat			
From the whole proceeds of the grange, by level measure, threshed by taskwork and by customary services, without tally, of which by taskwork 50 qr 2 bu 1 pk, besides 29 qr heaped measure for sale in London	70	2	—
From heaped measure of the same	—	7	1
From the usual 21 customary tenants for their "benesed" for the Michaelmas term	1	2	2
From "cornbote" for transgressions made in the lord's corn, as appears in the court roll	—	2	—
Total	72	5	3

of which:—

	qr	bu	pk
For seed on 87 acres of land, at seedtime for wheat this year, at 2 bushels per acre and so much seed wheat this year because the holdings of John Holewell, John Wilgod, Thomas Neweman, John Smyth, Walter Aleyn and Robert Bonde remained in the lord's hand this year	21	6	—
For defaults from the holdings of John Holewell, John Wilgod, Thomas Neweman, John Smyth, Walter Aleyn, and Robert Bonde, for their "benesed", because they remained in the lord's hand this year, for each holding ½ bushel	—	3	—
For defaults from the holdings of John Hened, Richard Hened, John Wilgod junior, Thomas Hened, and John Southende, for their "benesed", because they were at rent this year, for each holding ½ bushel	—	2	2
For bread baked for harvest expenses, viz. for customary boonworks	2	—	—
For mixed meal allowance for manor servants below	18	3	—
Sold in London as below	29	—	—
with heaped measure	—	7	1
Total as above and it balances	[72	5	3]

	qr	bu	pk
Beans and peas			
Beans and peas from the whole proceeds of the grange, by level measure, threshed by taskwork and by customary services without tally, of which by task-work 17 qr 5 bu besides 21 qr heaped measure for sale	31	5	–
Heaped measure for the same	–	5	1
From "cornbote", for transgressions made in the lord's beans, as appears in the court roll	–	5	–
Total	32	7	1
of which:–			
For seed on 40 acres of land, at 2 bu 1 pk per acre	11	2	–
Sold as below	21	–	–
with heaped measure	–	5	1
Total as above and it balances	[32	7	1]
Dredge corn			
Dredge corn from the whole proceeds of the grange by level measure, threshed by taskwork and by customary services without tally, of which by task-work 97 qr 7 bu 3 pk besides 20 qr heaped measure for sale	155	7	3
Heaped measure for the same and besides 96 qr heaped measure for making into malt	–	5	–
Heaped measure for the same [96 qr]	3	–	–
From the same proceeds, in 350 sheaves for ox fodder, of which 10 sheaves make one bushel	4	3	–
From "cornbote", for transgressions made in the lord's corn, as appears in the court roll	–	2	–
Total	164	1	3
of which:–			
For seed on 103 acres of land, at 3 bu ½ pk per acre (reduced in total by ½ pk [c])	40	1	(3 [c])
and so much in dredge corn seed this year because the holdings of John Holewell, John Wilgod, Thomas Neweman, John Smyth, Walter Aleyn, and Robert Bonde remained in the lord's hand this year			
Set aside as oats below for ox fodder	4	3	–
For malting as below	96	–	–
with heaped measure	3	–	–
Sold as below	20	–	–
with heaped measure	–	5	–

	qr	bu	pk
Sold above the account	—	—	3
Total as above and it balances	[164	1	3]
Oats			
Oats from the usual 21 customary tenants at Christmas	5	2	—
In sheaves, per above estimate, for ox fodder	4	3	—
Bought as fodder for horses	3	7	1
Heaped measure for above	—	—	3
Total	13	5	—
of which:—			
In default from the holdings of John Holewell, John Wilgod, Thomas Neweman, John Smyth, Walter Aleyn, and Robert Bonde, because they were in the lord's hand this year, for each holding 2 bu	1	4	—
In default of the holdings of John Hened, Richard Hened, John Wilgod junior, Thomas Hened, and John Southend, because they were at rent, for each holding 2 bu	1	2	—
For making flour for the manor servants' pottage, and for harvest expenses, for the year	1	4	—
Fodder for cart horses for the period of the account	4	—	—
Fodder for the lord's horse coming to Hegham 3 times this year	1	—	— [c])
(because without warrant [i])			
Fodder for oxen as appears in debit above	4	3	—
(Sold above the account	1	—	— [i])
Total as above and it agrees	[13	5	—]
Tolcorn			
Tolcorn from rent of the lord's watermill for the year, by level measure, as leased at rent	16	—	—
Tolcorn bought to make up the allowance for the manor servants	2	2	2
Heaped measure for the same	—	—	2
Total	18	3	—
the whole amount used for the allowance of mixed corn for the manor servants below			
Dredge malt			
Dredge malt for malting as above	96	—	—
Growth in making, for each quarter one bushel	12	—	—
Total	108	—	—

	qr	bu	pk
of which:–			
Sold as below in London	11	–	–
growth of the same, 1 quarter for 9 bushels	1	3	–
Sold as below	85	–	–
growth of the same, 1 quarter for 9 bushels	10	5	–
Total as above and it balances	[108	–	–]
Manor servants' allowances			
Wheat	18	3	–
Tolcorn for mixed meal for the manor servants below	18	3	–
Total	36	6	–
of which:–			
Allowances for one carter, 5 plough servants, one warrener, and one shepherd for the whole year, at 1 quarter of medium wheat per head per 12 weeks	34	4	–
Allowance for one dairyman making malt and pottage for the manor servants from Michaelmas to 5 April, that is for 27 weeks, per head as above	2	2	–
Total as above and it balances	[36	6	–]

ACCOUNT OF LIVESTOCK

Cart horses remaining 4, total 4; and there remain	4 cart horses
Affers remaining 2, total 2; and there remain	2 affers
Oxen remaining 15, total 15; of which sold as below because worn out, 1, total 1; and there remain	14 oxen
Ganders remaining 1, total 1; and there remains	1 gander
Young geese remaining 3, and no proceeds from these here because they were rented for money as appears below, total 3; and there remain	3 young geese
Cocks remaining 1, total 1; and there remains	1 cock
Hens remaining 12, and no proceeds from these because they were rented to the dairyman for money, as appears below, and from 21 customary tenants as rent for the Christmas term, 84, total 96; of which in default from the holdings of John Holewell, John Wilgod, Thomas Neweman, John Smyth, Walter Aleyn and Robert Bonde because they were in the lord's hand this year, 4 for each holding, 24; and in default from the holdings of John Hened, Richard Hened, John Wilgod junior, Thomas Hened, and John Southend because they were at rent, 20; and sold as below, 40, total 84; and there remain	12 hens

Capons remaining 24 capons, made from the chickens as below, total 24; of which sent to Dunstable, for the lord staying there at the Assizes at Michaelmas with Hugh Spenser, knight, 12, and sold as below, 12, total 24; and there remain — 24 capons

Chickens bought for making into capons, 24, total 24; and used for capons made above.

Eggs from 21 customary tenants, 10 eggs from each, total — 210 eggs

of which in default from the holdings of John Holewell, John Wilgod, Thomas Neweman, John Smyth, Walter Aleyn and Robert Bonde because they were in the lord's hand this year, 60 eggs, and in default from the holdings of John Hened, Richard Hened, John Wilgod junior, Thomas Hened and John Southend, because they were at rent, 50 eggs, and sold as below, 100 eggs; total as above, and it balances.

Loaves from 21 customary tenants at the Christmas term, from each tenant 1 loaf besides 1 bushel of wheat, total — 21 loaves

of which in default from the holdings of John Holewell, John Wilgod, Thomas Neweman, John Smyth, Walter Aleyn and Robert Bonde because they were in the lord's hand this year, one loaf for each tenant, 6, and in default from the holdings of John Hened, Richard Hened, Wilgod junior, Thomas Hened, and John Southend, because they were at rent, 5 loaves, and sold as below, 10 loaves; total 21 as above, and it balances.

Hides Bought for repairing harness, 1 bleached hide, and used for repairing harness, leaving none.

ACCOUNT OF SERVICES

Small services and ¾d services	Services
From the aforesaid 21 customary tenants, from each tenant 95 services, Total as it appears	1995
of which:–	
In default from the holdings of John Holewell, John Wilgod, Thomas Neweman, John Smyth, Walter Aleyn, and Robert Bonde, because they were in the lord's hand this year, for each tenant 95 services	570
In default from the holdings of John Hened, Richard Hened, John Wilgod junior, Thomas Hened, and John Southend, because they were at rent, for each tenant 95 services	475

	Services
For 3 assistants helping one thatcher thatching the dredge corn barn, the dove house and the hall, for 12 days, for each day 3 services	36
For 3 assistants helping one thatcher thatching the holding lately Walter Aleyn's for 3 days, for each day 3 services	9
For 3 assistants helping one thatcher thatching the holding lately John Aleyn's for 2 days, for each day 3 services	6
For 3 assistants helping one thatcher thatching the bean stack for 3 days, for each day 3 services	9
Allowed to the said tenants for "malterth", for each tenant one service	10
Allowed to the said tenants helping the lord at "bensed", for each tenant half a service	5
Allowed to the same for "wodesilver" as usual, for each tenants one service	10
For bundling straw, for each tenant 2 services	20
For spreading manure for the lord this year, for each tenant 2 services	20
Sold viz. to 10 tenants because they took demesne land lying in various cultivated areas at rent, price per service ¾d, viz for each tenant 20 services	200
Sold viz. to 10 tenants aforesaid for harvest services for the aforesaid reason, viz for each tenant 3 services	30
Allowed to the aforesaid 10 tenants services which are usually conceded to them for carrying services by ancient law, viz for each tenant 12 services	120
For bringing the bean stack into the grange for threshing, for each tenant one service	10
For threshing 20 quarters of wheat by customary services, 3 services per quarter	60
For threshing 16 quarters of beans and peas by customary services, 3 services per quarter	48
For threshing 58 quarters of dredge corn by customary services, 5 services per 2 quarters	145
For hoeing the lord's corn this year, for each tenant 7 services	70
For mowing the lord's meadow at Fanmede and making and gathering hay, for each tenant 2 services	20
For reaping, binding and stooking 11 acres of wheat, 2 services per acre	22
For reaping, binding and stooking 10 acres of beans and peas, 4 services per acre	40

	Services	
For reaping, binding and stooking 30 acres of dredge corn, 2 services per acre	60	
Total as above and it balances	[1995]	

Ploughing services	ac	rd
The proceeds of the aforesaid 21 customary tenants ploughing for the lord, viz. 140 acres 3 roods of land at 3 seedtimes of the year, from each tenant 6 ac 3 rd. Total as it appears	140	3
of which:–		
In default from the holdings of John Holewell, John Wilgod, Thomas Neweman, John Smyth, Walter Aleyn and Robert Bonde, because they were in the lord's hand this year, for each tenant 6 acres 3 roods	40	2
In default from the holdings of John Hened, Richard Hened, John Wilgod junior, Thomas Hened, and John Southend, because they were at rent, for each tenant 6 acres 3 roods	33	3
For ploughing the lord's land at 3 seedtimes of the year	66	2
Total as above and it balances	[140	3]

Carrying services	Services
Proceeds of the said 21 customary tenants, from each tenant 12 carrying services Total as it appears	252
of which:–	
In default from the holding of John Holewell, John Wilgod, Thomas Neweman, John Smyth, Walter Aleyn and Robert Bonde, because they were in the lord's hand this year, for each tenant 12 carrying services	72
In default from the holdings of John Hened, Richard Hened, John Wilgod junior, Thomas Hened and John Southende, because they were at rent, for each tenant 12 carrying services	60
Sold to 10 tenants for the reason above, viz to each tenant 4 services price 6d per service as appears below	40
For carting 29 quarters of wheat to London for sale, 2 services per quarter	58
For carting 11 quarters of malt to London for sale, 2 services per quarter	22
Total as above and it balances	[252]

Proceeds of the dove house

Proceeds of the dove house this year	186 young pigeons
Total as it appears	
of which:–	
Given in tithes	18
Sent to Dunstable for the expenses of the lord staying there at the Michaelmas assizes with Hugh Spenser, knight, with the capons above	36
Sold as below	132
Total as above and it balances	[186]

Rabbit warren

Profits of the warren, nothing this year because the lord granted the profits of it to Ralph FitzRichard.	
Total	Nil

BLUNHAM RECTORY ACCOUNTS

The study of the economic position of the beneficed clergy in the early sixteenth century is hindered by the scarcity of surviving accounts. Assessments for taxation, such as the *Valor Ecclesiasticus* of 1535, can tell us a great deal about the comparative values of benefices but they provide little detail about the sources of revenue, the means by which that revenue was collected, or the various items of expenditure which had to be met out of the incumbent's income. In his survey of medieval clerical accounts, Mr Heath described six documents, ranging in date from 1414 to 1520.[1] The three Blunham accounts printed here, dated 1520, 1534 and 1538-9, bear many similarities to those discussed by Mr Heath and they provide valuable evidence for a study of the finances of a comparatively wealthy benefice during the Reformation period.

They were among the archives of the Grey family of Wrest Park deposited at the Bedfordshire County Record Office by the Rt Hon the Lady Lucas, and have the catalogue numbers L 26/232, L 254 and L 26/1407.

The rectory of Blunham was one of the wealthiest livings in Bedfordshire. At the time of the Taxation of Pope Nicholas IV of 1291, it was one of the ten most valuable benefices in the archdeaconry of Bedford; its assessment of £20 annual value was exceeded only by the rectories of Felmersham and Shillington. The *Valor Ecclesiasticus* of 1535 assessed Blunham at £46 13s 4d, a valuation exceeded in Bedfordshire only by the rectory of Shillington.[2]

The rector of Blunham during the period covered by these three accounts was Master William Wittur. An Oxford graduate, he had by 1514 attained the degree of Doctor of Canon Law. He was instituted to the rectory of Blunham in March 1514, on the presentation of Henry Grey esquire, and held the living until his death in 1542.[3] It would seem unlikely, however, that Wittur was responsible for the compilation of these three accounts. The 1520 document records the receipt of tithes and offerings by John Cawt, the parochial chaplain or, as he described himself, 'gubernator animarum'. The account for 1534 was clearly drawn up by the bailiff of Sir Henry Grey of Wrest, the patron of the living, and the same would appear to be true of the 1538-9 account. The 1534 accounts contain numerous references to the conveyance of produce from the rectory to the Grey household at Wrest. These references suggest that Wittur had, like many clergy of the period who held valuable livings, farmed (or leased) the benefice, receiving a fixed annual sum from the lessee (Sir Henry Grey) who was then entitled to receive all the income from glebe, tithes and offerings. This suggestion is confirmed by a note in the diocesan visitation book for 1543. After recording that the rector Master Roger Tong (Wittur's successor) was non-resident, being absent at Cambridge, the register added that Sir Henry Grey was the farmer of the benefice.[4]

Dr Wittur's reason for farming the rectory was almost certainly his non-residence. At the bishop's visitation in 1540, he was described as being in Lancashire, and it would seem likely that he was absent during the earlier years of his incumbency as well.[5] He evidently visited Blunham from time to time, and there are occasional references to him in the accounts. In 1534, a pig and eight pigeons were consumed 'when Master Thomas was at Blounham with Maister Doctor'; the 1538-9 accounts record that four pigs, four dozen pigeons and two bushels of pease were delivered to Dr Wittur. It is possible that the lease of the rectory may have included a clause reserving to the rector the use of certain rooms and stabling at the parsonage whenever he should visit Blunham, as was done in a lease of the prebend of Leighton Buzzard in 1535.[6]

The evidence of the accounts, therefore, suggests that Dr Wittur had farmed the rectory to Sir Henry Grey of Wrest. This arrangement made economic sense for both parties. Wittur was able to receive a regular income from his benefice without the burden (for a non-resident incumbent) of overseeing the farming of the glebe or the collection of the tithes and oblations. Grey, on the other hand, had his bailiff and other servants conveniently placed to farm the glebe and collect the tithes; the produce no doubt played an important part in the provisioning of the household at Wrest, the surplus being sold for cash.

The Grey family acquired the manor and advowson of Blunham in 1389 when Reynold de Grey inherited, through his mother, many of the estates of John de Hastings, last earl of Pembroke.[7] On the death of George Grey, second earl of Kent, in 1503, the Blunham property went to Henry, the eldest son of his second wife. The bulk of the earl's estates were inherited by the only son of his first marriage, Richard, about whom his father expressed the fear that 'he will not thrive but will be a waster'. Richard, who became third earl of Kent, died without heirs in 1523, by which time he had confirmed his father's fears by losing much of the inherited property. He was succeeded by his half-brother Henry who declined to use the title earl of Kent, 'by reason of his slender estate'. It is clear, however, that by careful management he was able to recover some of the lost estates, and to acquire others. The farming of Blunham rectory, and the care with which these accounts were kept, can therefore be seen as part of the efforts of Sir Henry Grey to restore the prosperity of his family.[8]

In common with most rectories, Blunham's income came from three sources: glebe, tithes and offerings. Its status as one of the richest livings in the county was due in part to the size of its glebe. Apart from a note of glebe rents in the 1534 document, these accounts make little mention of the income produced by the lands belonging to the benefice. Fortunately, however, a glebe terrier of 1607 survives to give an indication of the extent of these lands. The terrier lists the parsonage house 'of tenn bayes buylt of tymber and covered with tyle, seven of them beinge chambred over and boarded, contrived into twoo storyes and disposed into xxij roomes (that is to saie) the hall twoo parlors eighteene other chambers and roomes, withe the kitchin one brewehowse and one backhowse'. Around the parsonage there were barns, a malthouse, dovecote, stable and other outbuildings. Two cottages in the village belonged to the rectory. The glebe land consisted of 3 acres of pasture, 4½ acres of meadow and 71 acres 3 roods of arable.[9]

Tithes, defined as the tenth part of the annual produce of each parishioner, or of the profit from his labours, were a potentially fruitful source of income for the incumbent but were also particularly liable to produce disputes and lawsuits. The all-embracing nature of the demand for tithes is well illustrated by the Blunham accounts. Arable crops (wheat, rye, pease, hay), wood, all manner of livestock (cows, calves, pigs, lambs, geese), eggs (collected on Good Friday) were all liable. The 1520 account suggests that tithes of livestock were frequently paid in money rather than in kind (2d for a cow, ½d for a lamb); it is probable that these payments represent cases where the parishioner had fewer than ten animals. This account also indicates that most parishioners paid personal tithes in respect of their labour; even the poorest widow paid 1d, while other parishioners paid as much as 8d. Craftsmen paid 4d, and the miller 10s 8d. Payment was also due from each garden (1d), and from each hive of bees in respect of wax (½d).

The third source of income for the rector came from the offerings made in the church. These included the oblations collected at the major festivals, traditionally Christmas, Easter, Whitsun, and the dedication of the church. The 1520 account records the sums offered at 'Sir Thomas masse' on Maundy Thursday, to the cross on Good Friday, and at the masses on Easter Day. The offerings on the day of the church's dedication in 1534, and at Christmas 1538, amounted to 4s 4d on each occasion. In addition to these seasonal payments, fees were received all through the year for weddings, churchings and funerals. Offerings at weddings varied from 2d (Thomas Dawes, 1538-9) to 11d (William Passlew's wife, 1534); the fee for the churching of women was usually 1d or 2d, while at a burial the priest received sums ranging from 1d (Robert Ossburne's child) to 18d (William Passlew), the amount no doubt reflecting the wealth and status of the deceased. There were two other sources of income arising from the deaths of parishioners: the mortuary (often the second-best beast or gown left by the deceased), and the sums left for the celebration of masses on the anniversary of the death. In 1538-9 a payment of 3s 4d was made by Margery Hyllys for a mortuary (presumably that of Richard Hyllys whose burial is recorded in the same account); during the course of the same year, sums were received at the anniversaries of Sir Edmund Lucy knight (8d), Thomas Pecke (1d), Tumlyn Smythe (1d), John Peke (1d), T Farthyng (1d), Simon Beynet (1½d), William Fyschar (1½d) and Thomas Yerrell (2d). The most regular of the oblations received was the weekly sum of 2d for the 'Holy Loaf', the bread blessed during the mass and shared out after the service.

From the sum of these receipts, there were certain outgoings to be met. The parsonage and glebe needed to be kept in good repair. It was no doubt in the parsonage that one Wypperley was paid 6d in 1539, for work in the kitchen: laying a sill, and making a 'dog-piece' in the entry (perhaps to keep the dogs out). Later in the same year, Thomas Wakefield was paid 3s 4d for making 46 bays (possibly of fencing) about the parsonage. The chancel had to be repaired when necessary, and the stipend of the parochial chaplain had to be paid. The 1534 account records two quarterly payments of 33s 4d to 'Sir Edward', who can be identified as Edward Steroppe, still chaplain at the time of the bishop's visitation in 1540.

The accounts include many items of expenditure for the services of the church. Wine for the communion was regularly purchased: a pint of 'mawesse', or malmsey, bought at Potton or St Neots, usually lasted a fortnight, but for Easter 1539 four gallons were needed, at a cost of 3s 4d. The communion wafers, variously described as 'syngyng brede' or 'howsyllyng brede', were also bought, 200 for Christmas and 300 for Easter. Other necessities included incense, lamp oil and the Paschal candle, and in 1539 the sum of 8d was spent 'for bred and drynke when we waschyd the auterys'. The expenses involved in attending the periodic diocesan visitations were also recorded. The sum of 7s in respect of Peter's Pence was handed over at the bishop of Lincoln's visitation at Northill in April 1534; in October of that year, the archbishop of Canterbury held a metropolitical visitation at Shefford, when 10s 6d was paid 'for seneg and proxys' (?procurations and synodals) and the sum of 5s was contributed to the cost of the visitation dinner.

The form of the three accounts varies. The 1520 document records the tithe receipts from 136 men and 48 women, together with a levy of 1d for each hearthstone; this is followed by an account of receipts from offerings over the Easter period. The account for 1534 is divided into sections for offerings, rents from glebe, receipts of produce from tithes (and presumably glebe), and for the payment of expenses. The 1538-9 account consists of sections for the quarterly receipts (beginning at Christmas, Lady Day and Midsummer) from offerings and miscellaneous sales of tithe produce, with separate sections for receipts from pigeons, straw, hay, pease, barley and malt. These are followed by quarterly accounts of payments made, beginning at Michaelmas, Christmas, Lady Day and Midsummer.

The 1534 account in particular provides much information about the provisioning of the Grey household. From the tithe eggs collected on Good Friday, nine score were sent to Wrest; these were followed by 5 capons on Tuesday in Easter week, by another capon on Low Sunday and, during the following week, ten green geese, six more capons and another 400 eggs. The subsequent months saw a steady procession of carts and livestock along the roads between Blunham and Wrest, carrying wheat, rye, malt, hay, pease, fresh fish in Whitsun week, calves, pigs, poultry and pigeons (including, on 31 July, five live pigeons for the hawks at Wrest).

Nicholas H. Bennett

1 P. Heath, *Medieval Clerical Accounts* (St Anthony's Hall Publications No 26, 1964), pp 3-6.
2 *Taxatio ecclesiastica Angliae et Walliae auctoritate P. Nicholai IV, circa A.D.1291*, ed T. Astle, S. Ayscough and J. Caley (London, 1802); *Valor Ecclesiasticus*, ed J. Caley and S. Hunter (London 1810-34), vol iv, pp 187-214. Appropriated rectories have been excluded.
3 LAO, Reg 25 fo 4; Reg 27 fo 270; A. B. Emden, *Biographical Register of the University of Oxford, A.D.1500 to 1540* (Oxford, 1974), p 633.
4 LAO, Vj 11 fo 38.
5 LAO, Vj 12 fo 32.
6 *Lincoln Diocese Documents, 1450-1544*, ed A. Clark (Early English Text Society No 149, 1914), p 186.
7 *Calendar of Inquisitions Post Mortem*, vol xvi, p 344.
8 G. E. Cockayne, *Complete Peerage* (revised edition, 12 vols, London, 1910-59), vol vii, pp 166-70.
9 BCRO ABE 1 (Blunham).

Tithe Account 1520

This document, L 26/232, is a booklet of 6 folded sheets, the pages found separated and much in need of repair. It has been transcribed but not translated. Nearly all entries are abbreviated, and so unless there is other evidence, it is sometimes difficult to decide if an entry is in the singular or plural, in which case the abbreviation is not extended. The heading, translated, reads: "These are the offerings and ancient emoluments with all other Easter tithes belonging to the parish church of Blunham which I sir John Cawt governor of the souls, have received in the year of our Lord 1520." Pages 1r and 1v are blank.

pro:		for:	
	agnis		lambs
	aratro		a plough
	arte		his craft
	aucis		geese
	anserulis		goslings
	cera		wax
	colombis		pigeons
	decimis oblitis		tithes forgotten
	decimis secretis		hidden tithes
	lana		wool
	oblacionibus		offerings
	orto		an orchard
	ovibus		sheep
	personalibus		personal (tithes)
	petra		the hearthstone
	porcellis (porc')		piglets
	vacca, vaccis		a cow, or cows
	vacca sterili, vaccis sterilibus		a store beast or store beasts
	vellere, velleribus		a fleece or fleeces
	vendito, venditis		sold
	vitulo, vitulis (vit')		a calf or calves

[L 26/232]

[2r] Haec sunt oblaciones nec antiqua emolumenta cum cunctis aliis decimis pascalibus ecclesie parochiali de Blonam pertinentibus quas ego dominus John Cawt animarum predic' gubernator recepivi viz anno Domini M^{mo} ccccc^{mo} xx^{mo}.

In primis

Johannes Biton	pro arte	iiij^{d}		
	pro vacca	ij^{d}		
	pro petra	j^{d}		
	pro orto	j^{d}		
	pro cera		ob	viij^{d} ob
Johannes Grimsdiche	pro personalibus	iiij^{d}		
	pro vacca	ij^{d}		
	pro vacca sterili	j^{d}		
	pro vitulo		ob	
	pro petra	j^{d}		
	pro orto	j^{d}		
	pro cera		ob	x^{d}
Johannes Brinley	pro personalibus			iij^{d}
Johannes Kokes	pro personalibus	iiij^{d}		
	pro petra	j^{d}		
	pro orto	j^{d}		
	pro cera		ob	vj^{d} ob

Johannes Yey	pro orto	j^{d}		
	pro petra	j^{d}		
	pro cera		ob	ij^{d} ob
Johannes Lavander	pro personalibus			ij^{d}
Johannes Chessam	pro duabus vaccis	iiij^{d}		
	pro duobus vitulis	iiij^{d}	ob	
	pro personalibus	ij^{d}		
	pro sex agnis	iij^{d}		
	pro porcellis	ij^{d}	ob	
	pro aucis	ij^{d}		
	pro petra	j^{d}		
	pro orto	j^{d}		
	pro cera		ob	xx^{d} ob
Johannes Baker	pro aratro	j^{d}		
	pro duabus vaccis	iiij^{d}		
	pro duobus vitulis	j^{d}		
	pro petra	j^{d}		
	pro orto	j^{d}		
	pro cera		ob	viij^{d} ob
Johannes Benet	pro vacca	ij^{d}		
	pro vit'	ij^{d}	ob	
	pro petra	j^{d}		
	pro orto	j^{d}		
	pro cera		ob	vij^{d}
	(Item: the same Benyt for tyth wod rec' a j^{d} [c])			
		Summa		vj^{s} j^{d}

[2v]

Johannes Peke	pro aratro	j^{d}		
	pro duabus vaccis	iiij^{d}		
	pro vacca sterili	j^{d}		
	pro duobus vitulis	iiij^{d}		
	pro petra	j^{d}		
	pro orto	j^{d}		
	pro cera		ob	jxj^{d} ob [sic]
	(rebat' ij^{d} for pygges and woole [i])			
Johannes Okley	pro personalibus			ij^{d}
Johannes Raulyn	pro duabus vaccis	iiij^{d}		
	pro vitulo vendito	j^{d}	ob	
	pro vitulo alio		ob	
	pro agno		ob	
	pro petra	j^{d}		
	pro cera		ob	viij^{d} (jx^{d} [i])
Johannes Warner	pro personalibus			ij^{d}
Johannes Hyllard	pro personalibus	j^{d}		

Johannes Benet	pro aratro	j^{d}		
	pro tribus vaccis	vj^{d}		
	pro tribus vitulis	j^{d}	ob	
	pro duobus agnis	j^{d}		
	pro petra	j^{d}		
	pro cera		ob	xj^{d}
			(rec' xiij$^{d\ i}$)	
Johannes Scherpe	pro personalibus	ij^{d}		
	pro petra	j^{d}		
	pro orto	j^{d}		
	pro cera		ob	iiij^{d} ob
Johannes Newcun	pro vacca	ij^{d}		
	pro vit'	ij^{d}		
	pro tribus velleribus	j^{d}	ob	
	pro agno		ob	vj^{d}
Johannes Sclad	for Barford vater	xvj^{d}		
	for the clos	ij^{s}		
	for Oxholm	j^{d}	ob	
	pro duabus vaccis sterilibus	ij^{d}		
	pro petra	j^{d}		
	pro orto	j^{d}		
	pro cera		ob	
	pro personalibus	vj^{d}		iiij^{s} iiij^{d}
Johannes Osburn	pro aratro	j^{d}		
	pro tribus vaccis	vj^{d}		
	pro vit'	ij^{d}		
	pro petra	j^{d}		
	pro orto	j^{d}		
	pro cera		ob	xj^{d} ob [?]
Johannes Fels	pro vacca	ij^{d}		
	pro vit'	ij^{d}		
	pro porcellis	j^{d}		
	pro duabus vaccis sterilibus	ij^{d}		
	pro petra	j^{d}		
	pro cera		ob	viij^{d} ob
				(rec' xij$^{d\ i}$)
(Johannes Lavender	pro personalibus	iij$^{d\ c}$)(nichull ^{i})		
Johannes Lavander	pro personalibus	ij^{d}		
				[summa] x^{s} iiij^{d} ob

[3r]

Johannes Verdew	pro personalibus	iiij^{d}		
	pro duabus vaccis	iiij^{d}		
	pro vit'		ob	
	pro petra	j^{d}		
	pro cera		ob	x^{d}

Johannes (Bat^{c}) Batell	pro iiij^{or} vaccis	viij^{d}		
	pro porcellis	iij^{d}	ob	
	pro aratro	j^{d}		
	pro petra	j^{d}		
	pro orto	j^{d}		
	pro cera		ob	xv^{d}
(Nota: vij shep ^{m})				
Johannes Towrs	pro personalibus			iiij^{d}
Johannes Warde	pro personalibus			iiij^{d}
Johannes Fyn	pro duabus vaccis	iiij^{d}		
	pro vit'		ob	
	pro porc'		ob	
	pro ancerulis		ob	
	pro vit'	ij^{d}		
	pro petra	j^{d}		
	pro aratro		ob	
	pro cera		ob	(xvij^{d} ob ^{c})
				(ix^{d} ob ^{i})
Johannes Thomas	pro vacca	ij^{d}		
	pro vit'	ij^{d}		
	pro personalibus	ij^{d}		
	pro petra	j^{d}		
	pro cera		ob	vij^{d} ob
Johannes Vekery	pro vij vaccis	xiiij^{d}		
	pro tribus vaccis sterilibus	iij^{d}		
	pro duobus vitulis venditis	iij^{d}		
	pro duodecim porcellis	vj^{d}		
	pro agnis	j^{d}	ob	
	pro aratro	j^{d}		
	pro petra	j^{d}		
	pro cera		ob	ij^{s} vj^{d}
(nota: a tyth calf ^{m})				
Johannes Turner	pro personalibus	ij^{d}		
	pro - - [? petra]	j^{d}		
	pro cera		ob	iij^{d} ob
Johannes Northe	petra	j^{d}		
	pro cera		ob	
	pro arte	ij^{d}	ob	summa iiij^{d}
Johannes Underwood	petra	j^{d}		
	pro cera		ob	
	pro arte	iiij^{d}		
	quinque oves	ij^{d}	ob	summa viij^{d}
				summa vij^{s} xj^{d}

[3v]

Willelmus Fyscher	pro vacca	ij^{d}		
	pro vacca sterili	j^{d}		
	pro vit'	ij^{d}	ob	

	pro petra	j^{d}		
	pro cera		ob	vij^{d}
				(rec' jx^{d} [i])
Willelmus Hyllys	pro aratro	j^{d}		
	pro vacca	ij^{d}		
	pro vit'		ob	
	pro petra	j^{d}		
	pro orto	j^{d}		
	pro cera		ob	
	pro decimis oblitis	iiij^{d}		x^{d}
(nota: a tyth calf [m])				
Willelmus Bradfeld	pro personalibus	iiij^{d}		
	pro vacca	ij^{d}		
	pro vit'	ij^{d}		
	pro vit' [sic]			
	pro petra	j^{d}		
	pro orto	j^{d}		
	pro cera		ob	xjx^{d} ob [sic]
Willelmus Wahyon [?]	pro aratro	j^{d}		
	pro iiij^{or} vaccis	viij^{d}		
	pro vacca sterili	j^{d}		
	pro iiij^{or} vitulis	xj^{d}		
	pro petra	j^{d}		
	(pro orto	j^{d} [c])		
	pro cera		ob	(xxiij^{d} ob [c])
				(xxij^{d} ob [i])
Willelmus Witter	pro personalibus			iiij^{d}
Willelmus Smalwode	pro aratro	j^{d}		
	pro duabus vaccis	iiij^{d}		
	pro duobus vitulis	j^{d}		
	pro petra	j^{d}		
	pro cera		ob	vij^{d} ob
Willelmus Yardley	pro aratro	j^{d}		
	pro tribus vaccis	vj^{d}		
	pro personalibus	iiij^{d}		
	pro petra	j^{d}		
	pro cera		ob	xij^{d} ob
Willelmus Topschall	pro vacca	ij^{d}		
	pro vit'	ij^{d}		
	pro petra	j^{d}		
	pro orto	j^{d}		
	pro cera		ob	(vj^{d} ob [c])
				(vij^{d} ob [i])
(nota: for shep [m])				

Willelmus Eyr	pro aratro	j^{d}		
	pro tribus vaccis	vj^{d}		
	pro vit'		ob	
	pro petra	j^{d}		
	pro cera		ob	ix^{d}
Willelmus Gybson	pro personalibus			iiij^{d}
				Summa viij^{s} ix^{d} ob

[4r]

Willelmus Warde	pro duabus vaccis	iij^{d}		
	pro vit'	iij^{d}		
	pro petra	j^{d}		
	pro cera		ob	viij^{d} ob
Willelmus Thomas	pro duabus vaccis	iiij^{d}		
	pro duobus vitulis	iiij^{d}		
	pro vacca sterili	j^{d}		
	pro petra	j^{d}		
	orto	j^{d}		
	pro cera		ob	xj^{d} ob
Willelmus Weyte	pro personalibus			vj^{d}
Willelmus Peke	pro aratro	j^{d}		
	pro iiij^{or} vaccis	viij^{d}		
	pro iiij^{or} vitulis	ij^{d}		
	pro petra	j^{d}		
	pro cera		ob	xij^{d} ob
Willelmus Parslewe	pro aratro	j^{d}		
	pro iiij^{or} vaccis	viij^{d}		
	pro tribus vitulis	vj^{d}		
	propter sexdecem oves venditis	viij^{d}		
	pro petra	j^{d}		
	pro cera		ob	ij^{s} ob
Willelmus Hanskom	pro personalibus	iij^{s}		
	pro vacca	ij^{d}		
	pro vit'		ob	
	pro petra	j^{d}		
	pro cera		ob	iij^{s} iiij^{d}
Willelmus Sandon	pro vacca sterili	j^{d}		
	pro vit'		ob	
	pro petra	j^{d}		
	pro cera		ob	iij^{d}
Willelmus Luffe	pro aratro	j^{d}		
	pro duabus vaccis	iiij^{d}		
	pro vit'		ob	
	pro petra	j^{d}		
	pro cera		ob	vij^{d}

Willelmus Holms	pro vacca una	ij^{d}		
	pro duabus vaccis sterilibus	ij^{d}		
	pro vit’	ij^{d}		
	pro petra	j^{d}		
	pro orto	j^{d}		
	pro cera		ob	
	pro personalibus	ij^{d}		rec’ x^{d} ob
	[original total deleted and illegible]			(summa x^{s} iij^{d} ob [i])

[4v]

Willelmus Ward	pro vacca sterili	j^{d}		
	pro arte	ij^{d}		
	pro orto	j^{d}		
	pro petra	j^{d}		
	pro cera		ob	v^{d} ob
Willelmus Crows	pro arte			iiij^{d}
Willelmus Parslewe	pro personalibus			iiij^{d}
Willelmus Cowper	pro duabus vaccis	iiij^{d}		
	pro vit’	ij^{d}		
	pro vit’		ob	
	pro aratro	j		
	pro petra	j^{d}		
	orto	j^{d}		
	pro cera		ob	x^{d}
Willelmus Jhons	pro arte	ij^{d}		
	pro iiij^{or} vaccis	viij^{d}		
	pro vit’		ob	
	pro aratro	j^{d}		
	pro petra	j^{d}		
	pro cera		ob	xiij^{d}
Willelmus More	pro personalibus	j^{d}		
	petra	j^{d}		
	pro cera		ob	ij^{d} ob
Willelmus Joons	pro columbis	viij^{d}		
	pro orto	iiij^{d}		
	pro petra	j^{d}		
	pro cera		ob	xiij^{d} ob
Willelmus Benet	pro v vaccis	x^{d}		
	pro vit’	ij^{d}		
	pro duobus vitulis	j^{d}		
	pro aratro	j^{d}		
	pro petra	j^{d}		
	pro cera		ob	xv^{d} ob
Willelmus Yerell	pro personalibus			iiij^{d}
Willelmus Vycary	pro personalibus			iiij^{d}

Willelmus Smythe	pro vacca	ij^{d}		
	pro duobus vitulis	j^{d}		
	pro petra	j^{d}		
	pro orto	j^{d}		
	pro cera		ob	v^{d} ob
(Item: rec' of Thomas	Drynge j^{d} ^{i})			
				Summa vj^{s} ix^{d} ob

[5r]

Thomas Ward	pro aratro	j^{d}		
	pro vacca una	ij^{d}		
	pro vit' vend'	iij^{d}		
	pro tribus vaccis sterilibus	iij^{d}		
	pro porc'	ij^{d}	ob	
	pro personalibus	iiij^{d}		
	pro petra	j^{d}		
	orto	j^{d}		
	cera		ob	xviij^{d}
Thomas Uriell	pro aratro	j^{d}		
	pro vacca	ij^{d}		
	pro vit'		ob	
	pro petra	j^{d}		
	pro orto	j^{d}		
	pro cera		ob	vj^{d}
Thomas Pulter	pro personalibus	viij^{d}		
	pro vacca	ij^{d}		
	pro duobus vitulis	j^{d}		
	pro petra	j^{d}		
	pro cera		ob	xij^{d}(ob^{c})
Thomas Malley	pro personalibus	ij^{d}		
	petra	j^{d}		
	orto	j^{d}		
	pro cera		ob	iiij^{d} ob
Thomas Towrs	pro personalibus			iiij^{d}
Thomas Everat	pro vacca	ij^{d}		
	pro vacca sterili	j^{d}		
	pro duobus vitulis venditis	v^{d}		
	pro petra	j^{d}		
	pro aratro	(ob^{c}) j^{d}		
	pro orto	j^{d}		
	pro cera		ob	xj^{d} ob
Thomas Austyn	pro personalibus			ij^{d}
Thomas Fermary	pro vacca	ij^{d}		
	pro duabus vaccis sterilibus	ij^{d}		
	pro vit'	ij^{d}		
	pro petra	j^{d}		
	pro aratro	j^{d}		
	pro orto	j^{d}		
	pro cera		ob	ix^{d} ob

Thomas Ade	pro personalibus	iiij^{d}	
	pro agnis	iij^{d}	
	pro lana	ij^{d}	viij^{d}
			[illegible deletions]
Thomas Est	pro petra	j^{d}	
	pro cera	ob	j^{d} ob
Thomas Wake	pro orto	j^{d}	
	petra	j^{d}	
	pro cera	ob	ij^{d} ob
Thomas Cros	for the mylne	x^{s} viij^{d}	
	pro petra	j^{d}	
	pro orto	j^{d}	
	pro cera	ob	x^{s} x^{d} ob
		summa xvij^{s} vj^{d}	

[5v]

Thomas Luffyn	pro petra	j^{d}	
	pro cera	ob	j^{d} ob
Thomas Coliar	pro duabus vaccis	iiij^{d}	
	pro vit'	ij^{d}	
	pro petra	j^{d}	
	pro orto	j^{d}	
	pro cera	ob	viij^{d} ob
Thomas Uriell	pro aratro	j^{d}	
	pro duabus vaccis	iiij^{d}	
	pro duobus vitulis	iij^{d}	
	pro petra	j^{d}	
	orto	j^{d}	
	pro cera	ob	x^{d} ob
Thomas Roger	pro aratro	j^{d}	
	pro iiij^{or} vaccis	viij^{d}	
	pro tribus vitulis	vj^{d} ob	
	pro porc'	ij^{d}	
	pro petra	j^{d}	
	pro orto	j^{d}	
	pro cera	ob	xx^{d}
			(rec' xxij^{d} [i])
Thomas Farthyng	pro aratro	j^{d}	
	pro tribus vaccis	vj^{d}	
	pro duobus vitulis	iiij^{d}	
	pro porcis	iij^{d} ob	
	pro decimis secretis	v^{s}	
	pro petra	j^{d}	
	pro orto	j^{d}	
	pro cera	ob	vj^{s} v^{d}
Thomas Baumford	pro personalibus		ij^{d}

Thomas Pek	pro aratro	j^{d}		
	pro vij vaccis	xiiij^{d}		
	pro tribus vitulis	vj^{d}		
	pro tribus vitulis	j^{d}	ob [sic]	
	pro porc’	iij^{d}		
	pro petra	j^{d}		
	pro orto	j^{d}		
	pro cera		ob	ij^{s} iiij^{d}
(nota [m])	(Item: the mnst’ rec’ a tyth calf [i])			
Thomas Blyth	pro aratro	j^{d}		
	pro x vaccis	xx^{d}		
	pro duobus vitulis	iiij^{d}		
	(pro vacca sterili	j^{d} [c])		
	pro petra	j^{d}		
	pro orto	j^{d}		
	pro cera		ob	ij^{s} iij^{d} ob
(nota [m])	(Item: a tyth calf [i])			
Thomas Grey	pro aratro	j^{d}		
	pro quinque vaccis	x^{d}		
	pro duobus vitulis	iij^{d}	ob	
	petra	j^{d}		
	orto	j^{d}		
	cera		ob	xvij^{d} ob
				[illegible deletion]
		summa xvj^{s} ij^{d}	ob	

[6r]

Thomas Hall	pro aratro	j^{d}		
	pro iiij^{or} vaccis	viij^{d}		
	pro vit’	ij^{d}		
	pro duobus vitulis	j^{d}		
	pro personalibus	iiij^{d}		
	pro petra	j^{d}		
	pro orto	j^{d}		
	pro cera		ob	xviij^{d} ob
Thomas Bur	pro aratro	j^{d}		
	pro iiij^{or} vaccis	viij^{d}		
	pro petra	j^{d}		
	pro cera		ob	x^{d} ob
Thomas Carpenter	pro petra	j^{d}		
	pro orto	j^{d}		
	pro cera		ob	ij^{d} ob
Thomas Mathew	pro personalibus			ij^{d}
Thomas Cley	pro aratro		ob	
	pro duabus vaccis	iiij^{d}		
	pro duobus vitulis	iiij^{d}		
	pro petra	j^{d}		
	pro arte	xij^{d}		

	pro cera	ob	xxij^{d} (rec' xx^{s} ^{i})
Thomas Jent	pro vacca	ij^{d}	
	pro vit'	ij^{d} ob	
	pro agno	ob	
	pro petra	j^{d}	
	pro cera	ob	
	porc'	j^{d}	
	pro orto	j^{d}	
	pro decimis secretis	xij^{d}	xx^{d} ob
(Item: of John Inggyll	[or Juggyll] pro decimis	iiij^{d} ^{i})	
			summa vj^{s} x^{d}

[6v]

Richardus Swynstow	pro petra	j^{d}	
	pro cera	ob	
	pro orto	j^{d}	
	pro vacca una	ij^{d}	
	pro quinque vaccis sterilibus	v^{d}	
	pro vit' vend'	iij^{d}	
	pro decimis secretis	iiij^{s}	v^{s} ob
	(pro iiij porcellis	ij^{d} ^{i})	
Ricardus Hyllys	pro personalibus	ij^{d}	
	pro vacca (sterilis)	(ij^{d} ^{c}) j^{d}	
	pro vit'	ob	
	pro petra	j^{d}	
	pro cera	ob	(vj^{d} ^{c}) v^{d}
Richardus Gostweke	pro personalibus	ij^{d}	
	petra	j^{d}	
	orto	j^{d}	
	cera	ob	iiij^{d} ob
Ricardus Coliar	pro personalibus	viij^{d}	
	pro vacca	ij^{d}	
	vit'	ij^{d}	
	pro duobus agnis	j^{d}	
	petra	j^{d}	
	orto	j^{d}	
	pro cera	ob	xvj^{d} ob
Ricardus Wryght	pro vacca	ij^{d}	
	pro vit'	ob	
	pro aratro	j^{d}	
	pro petra	j^{d}	
	pro orto	j^{d}	
	pro cera	ob	vj^{d}
Ricardus Tyler	pro personalibus	(viij^{d} ^{c}) iiij^{d}	

Ricardus Emerson	pro tribus agnis	j^{d} ob	
	pro aucis	ij^{d}	
	pro petra	j^{d}	
	pro orto	j^{d}	
	pro cera	ob	vj^{d}
			(rec' v^{d} ^{i})
	(debt' a goose of last yere ^{i})		
Ricardus Warde	pro aratro	j^{d}	
	pro iiij^{or} vaccis	viij^{d}	
	pro vacca sterili	j^{d}	
	pro duobus vitulis	iiij^{d} ob	
	pro tribus velleribus	j^{d} ob	
	pro petra	j^{d}	
	pro orto	j^{d}	
	pro duobus agnis	j^{d}	
	pro cera	ob	xix^{d} ob
Ricardus Mereweder	pro duabus vaccis	iiij^{d}	
	(pro duobus vitulis	iiij^{d} ob ^{c})	
	pro aratro	j^{d}	
	petra	j^{d}	
	pro cera	ob	vj^{d} ob
Ricardus Uriell	pro vacc'	ij^{d}	
	pro vit'	ob	
	pro petra	j^{d}	
	pro orto	j^{d}	
	pro cera	ob	v^{d}
		(summa xj^{s} xj^{d} ob ^{c})	
		(summa xij^{s} j^{d} ob ^{i})	

[7r]

Ricardus Samwell	pro aratro	j^{d}	
	pro vacca sterili	j^{d}	
	pro vit'	ij^{d}	
	pro petra	j^{d}	
	pro orto	j^{d}	
	cera	ob	vj^{d} ob
Ricardus Hesylden	pro petra	j^{d}	
	pro orto	j^{d}	
	pro cera	ob	ij^{d} ob
Ricardus Sutton	pro petra	j^{d}	
	pro orto	j^{d}	
	pro cera	ob	ij^{d} ob
Ricardus Angell	pro aratro	j^{d}	
	pro tribus vaccis	vj^{d}	
	pro vacca sterili	j^{d}	
	pro tribus vitulis	j^{d} ob	
	pro orto	(ob^{c}) j^{d}	
	pro petra	j^{d}	
	pro cera	ob	xij^{d}
			(rec' xiij$^{d i}$)

Ricardus Odam	pro petra	j^{d}	
	orto	j^{d}	
	pro cera	ob	ij^{d} ob
Ricardus Barn'	pro arte	iiij^{d}	
	pro petra	j^{d}	
	cera	ob	v^{d} ob
Ricardus Wymynton	pro oblacionibus	ij^{d}	
[7v]			
Robertus Leceter	pro personalibus		iiij^{d}
Robertus Thomas	pro vacca	ij^{d}	
	pro aratro	j^{d}	
	pro petra	j^{d}	
	pro cera	ob	iiij^{d} ob
Robertus Thorpe	for the mylne	x^{s} viij^{d}	
	pro vacca	ij^{d}	
	pro vit'	ob	
	pro orto	j^{d}	
	pro petra	j^{d}	
	pro cera	ob	xj^{s} j^{d}
Robertus Person	pro duabus vaccis	iiij^{d}	
	pro vit'	j^{d} ob	
	pro petra	j^{d}	
	pro cera	ob	viij^{d}
Robertus Samwell	pro aratro	j^{d}	
	pro duabus vaccis	iiij^{d}	
	pro vit'	j^{d} ob	
	pro petra	j^{d}	
	pro orto	j^{d}	
	pro cera	ob	ix^{d}
Robertus Spenser	pro aratro	j^{d}	
	pro viij vaccis	xvj^{d}	
	pro columbis	iiij^{d}	
	pro petra	j^{d}	
	pro orto	j^{d}	
	cera	ob	xxiij^{d} ob
Robertus Fyscher	pro aratro	j^{d}	
	pro duabus vaccis	iiij^{d}	
	pro porc'	ij^{d}	
	pro petra	j^{d}	
	pro cera	ob	ix^{d} ob
Robertus Dode	pro personalibus	ij^{d}	
	petra	j^{d}	
	orto	j^{d}	
	cera	ob	iiij^{d} ob
Robertus Mortimyr	pro petra	j^{d}	
	orto	j^{d}	
	cera	ob	ij^{d} ob

Robertus Spell	pro personalibus	iiij^d		
	pro petra	j^d		
	pro cera		ob	v^d ob
Robertus More	pro duabus vaccis	iiij^d		
	pro duobus vitulis	v^d	ob	
	petra	j^d		
	pro cera		ob	xj^d
			(rec' xij^d [i])	
				Summa xvij^s xj^d
[8r]	Divers names			
Radulphus Williams	pro personalibus	ij^d		
	pro petra	j^d		
	pro orto	j^d		
	pro cera		ob	iiij^d ob
Laurentius Brown	pro personalibus	ij^d		
	pro vacca	ij^d		
	pro petra	j^d		
	orto	j^d		
	pro cera		ob	vj^d ob
Clemens' Kyng	pro personalibus	vj^d		
	petro	j^d		
	pro cera		ob	vij^d ob
Walterus Parslewe	pro aratro	j^d		
	pro vacca	ij^d		
	pro vit'	ij^d		
	pro vacca sterili	j^d		
	petra	j^d		
	pro orto	j^d		
	pro cera		ob	viij^d ob
Walterus Awstyn	pro vacc'	ij^d		
	pro personalibus	iiij^d		
	pro petra	j^d		
	orto	j^d		
	pro cera		ob	viij^d ob
Simon Benet	pro duabus vaccis	iiij^d		
	pro vit'	ij^d		
	pro vit'		ob	
	pro cera		ob	vij^d
				(rec' xiiij^d [c])
Simon Benet junior	pro tribus vaccis	vj^d		
	pro vacc'	j^d		
	pro j vellere		ob	
	pro porc'	iij^d		
	pro duobus vitulis	j^d		
	pro aratro	j^d		
	petra	j^d		
	cera		ob	xiiij^d

Edwardus Bown	pro arte	iiij^{d}		
	petra	j^{d}		
	cera		ob	v^{d} ob
Gylbertus Fyscher	pro personalibus			ij^{d}
Jacobus Baker	pro personalibus			ij^{d}
Jacobus Cam	pro vacca	ij^{d}		
	pro vit'	ij^{d}	ob	
	pro petra	j^{d}		
	pro orto	j^{d}		
	pro cera		ob	vij^{d}
	Summa vj^{s} ij^{d}			

[8v]

Walterus Butler	pro aratro	j^{d}		
	pro duabus vaccis	iiij^{d}		
	pro vacca sterili	j^{d}		
	pro duobus vitulis	iiij^{d}		
	pro vit'		ob	
	petra	j^{d}		
	pro orto	j^{d}		
	cera		ob	xiij^{d}
Galfridus Osburn'	pro aratro	j^{d}		
	pro vacca sterili	j^{d}		
	pro vit'		ob	
	pro petra	j^{d}		
	pro cera		ob	iiij^{d}
Walterus Scharpe	pro personalibus			ij^{d}
Henricus Kotyn'	pro personalibus			j^{d}
Gy' Strong	pro petra	j^{d}		
	pro cera		ob	j^{d} ob
Stephanus Byrd'	personalibus	iiij^{d}		
	pro petra	j^{d}		
	cera		ob	v^{d} ob
Henricus Towrs	pro petra	j^{d}		
	pro cera		ob	j^{d} ob
Henricus Cole	pro personalibus			iiij^{d}
	Summa ij^{s} viij^{d} ob			

[9r]

Elezabetha Wotton	pro petra	j^{d}		
	pro cera		ob	j^{d} ob
Agnes Butler	pro aratro	j^{d}		
	pro tribus vaccis	vj^{d}		
	pro duobus vitulis	j^{d}		
	pro porc'	ij^{d}		
	pro petra	j^{d}		
	pro orto	j^{d}		
	pro cera		ob	xij^{d} ob

Issabella Ryche	petra	j^{d}	
	pro cera	ob	j^{d} ob
Emma Malyns	pro personalibus	xij^{d}	
	pro vit'	ob	
	petra	j^{d}	
	orto	j^{d}	
	pro cera	ob	xv^{d}
Agnes Ecope	pro personalibus	ij^{d}	
	petra	j^{d}	
	pro cera	ob	iij^{d} ob
Elinora Reyncok	pro personalibus		ij^{d}
Agnes Hall	pro personalibus	ij^{d}	
	pro orto	j^{d}	
(Mergeria Fyscher	pro orto	j^{d} ^{c})	
Dionisius [sic]	orto	j^{d}	
Raulynson	petra	j^{d}	
	cera	ob	ij^{d} ob
Alicia Cley	pro personalibus	vj^{d}	
	orto	j^{d}	
	porc'	ob	vij^{d} ob
Agnes Tibe	pro vacca	ij^{d}	
	pro vit'	ob	
	porc'	ij^{d}	$iiij^{d}$ ob
(Item: the same Agnes for fleces and lames		v^{d} ^{i})	
Agnes Hanskom	pro personalibus		ij^{d}
Cristina Uriell			j^{d}
Elizabetha Benet	pro orto	j^{d}	
	pro ancerulis	ob	j^{d} ob
(Felys Thomas	pro orto ^{c}) (in a noder place ^{i})		j^{d}
Johanna Towrs	pro orto		j^{d}

[9v]

Agnes Carpenter	pro orto		j^{d}
Issabella Luffe	pro orto		j^{d}
Elizabetha Forthe	propter sex oves venditas		iij^{d} (rec' $iiij^{d}$ ^{i})
Elizabetha Brown	pro orto		j^{d}
Agnes Tyler	pro personalibus		ij^{d}
Emma Fox	pro personalibus		ij^{d}
(Mergar' Wylliams	pro orto	j^{d} ^{c})	
Mergeria Bur'	pro orto		j^{d}
Cristina Benet	pro orto		j^{d}
(Elizabetha Jons	orto	j^{d} ^{c})	
Johanna Pulter	pro vacca sterili	j^{d}	
	pro aucis	j^{d}	ij^{d}

Johanna Sandon	pro orto	j^{d}	
	pro aucis	j^{d} ob	ij^{d} ob
(Alicia Batyll	orto	j^{d} [c])	
Mergeria Parsleue	pro personalibus		$iiij^{d}$
Johanna Underwood'			j^{d}
Johanna Peke			j^{d}
Elizabetha Chessam			j^{d}
Isabella Eyr			j^{d}
(Isabella[c]) Elizabetha Holms			j^{d}

[10r]

(Johanna Awstyn		j^{d} [c])	
Mergeria Hylles	pro orto et personalibus		iij^{d}
Matilda Yerell			j^{d}
Agnes Ward	pro orto et aucis		ij^{d}
Alicia Rawlyn	pro vacca sterili	j^{d}	
	pro orto	j^{d}	
	petra	j^{d}	
	pro cera	ob	iij^{d} ob
Cristina Yerell'	pro aucis	ij^{d}	
	orto	j^{d}	iij^{d}
(Agnes Tyler	pro personalibus	ij^{d} [c])	
Alicia Mereweder			j^{d}
Johanna Awngell			j^{d}
Johanna Benet			j^{d}
Ame Ward	pro aucis		j^{d}
Agnes Vykery			j^{d}
Agnes Andrewe			j^{d}

(summa [illegible] [c])

Summa iij^{s} x^{d}

Summa vij^{li} . . . [illegible deletions and corrections]
(vj^{li} $xiij^{s}$ ij^{d} ob [i])

[10v]

Item on Mawndy Thorsday offered at Sir Thomas masse	v^{d}ob
Item offeryd to the crosse on Gud Fryday	x^{d}
Item payd to th' sommter that broght owyll and creme	$iiij^{d}$
Item on (Ester evyn [i]) offerd at howslyng	ij^{s} j^{d}
Item th' offryng at fryst masse on Ester day and seconnd	vj^{s} ob
Item payd to the clerkes	iij^{d}

(Summa $xiiij^{s}$ v^{d} [i])

Item delivered of th'Eyster book to Agnes Gyry	vij^{li} $viij^{s}$ ij^{d} ob
Item to the sayd Agnes for tythe egges delivered	xij^{s} $viij^{d}$

debethe vj^{s} iij^{d} ob

Rectory Account 1534
These accounts are in a booklet of 6 folded sheets, catalogue no. L 254. The accounts seem to be for over half a year from April to October 1534, for the dates of the payments for the holyloaf agree with the dates of Sundays in that year. However, strictly speaking, the 4 April 26 Henry VIII was in the year 1535.

[L 254]
[1] The boke off offerynges and other profettes comyng off the parsonage off Blonnham begone apone (Lady day ^{c}) the iiij^{ty} [?4] day of Aprill in the xxvj yere off the rene off Kyng Harry the eightt. [1534/5]

Item resaved the viij day off Aprill at the bureyng off John Brownell' chyld iij^{d}
Item rec' the xij day off Aprill for the holyloyff ij^{d}
Item rec' the sayd day at the bureyng off Bays iij^{d} ob
Item rec' the xix day off Aprill for the holyloyff ij^{d}
Item rec' for the holyloyff the xxvj day off Aprill ij^{d}
Item rec' at the purificacion off Paternoster wyff a crisum ij^{d}
Item rec' the iij day off Maij for the holyloyff ij^{d}
Item rec' the vij day off Maij at the buryall off Mother Bennet v^{d}
Item rec' the x day off Maij for the holyloyff ij^{d}
Item rec' the sayd day at anniversarij off (byyo^{c}) Wyll' Bays ij^{d}
Item rec' the xiiij day off Maij at the purificacion off Wardew wyff and off Hawkyynges wyff ij crysumys v^{d}
(delivered jd^{m}) Item rec' the (xviij^{c}) xvij day of Maij for the holyloyff ij^{d}
Item rec' the xviij day off Maij at the purificacion off John Angell wyff a crisum ij^{d}
Item rec' off a strange woman that dyd ly in at Qweperlays at the purificacion off the sayd stranger a crisum and a j^{d}
Item rec' the layst day off Maij for the holyloyff ij^{d}
Item rec' the vij day off (Maij^{c}) (Julij^{ic}) for the holyloyff ij^{d}
Item rec' the xiiij day off (Jul^{c}) Junij for the holyloyff ij^{d}
Item rec' the xviij day off Junij at the buriall off Thomas Clarke iiij^{d} ob
Item rec' the xxj day of Junij for the holyloyff ij^{d}
Item rec' at the buriall off Wyllm' Passlow xviij^{d}
Item rec' the xxviij day off Junij for the holyloyff ij^{d}
Item rec' the sayd day at the purificacion off a pore woman off Mogeranger ij^{d}

Summa vs xd

[2]
Item rec' the v day of (Julij^{c}) Julij for the holyloyff ij^{d}
Item red' the xij day off Julij for the holyloyff ij^{d}
Item rec' the xix day off Julij for the holyloyff ij^{d}
Item rec' the sayd day at the purificacion off a powre woman a crysum with on j^{d}
Item resaved the xxiij day of Julij at the (mary^{c}) weddyng off Robert Cranke ij^{d}

Item re' the xxvj day off Julij for the holyloyff		ij^{d}
Item re' (off^{c}) for old Wyllm' Passlewys mortuarij	iij^{s}	iiij^{d}
Item re' the secund day off August for the holyloyff		ij^{d}
Item rec' the same day at the maryage off yone Wyllm' Passlew wyff		xj^{d}
Item rec' the iiij day off August at the buryeng off Robert Ossburne chyld		j^{d}
Item re' the ix day off August for the holyloyff		ij^{d}
(Ihn^{m}) [?] Item re' owyt off the boxe the sayd day		xij^{d}
Item re' the xxiij^{ty} day off August for the holyloyff		ij^{d}
Item re' at the buryeng of Jone Passlew chylld		j^{d}
Item re' the xxix day off August at the purificacion off Ryc' Taler wyff a crisum and		j^{d}
Item rec' the vj day off September for the holiloyff		ij^{d}
Item rec' the xiij day off September for the holyloyff		ij^{d}
Item rec' the xx day off September for the holyloff		ij^{d}
Item rec' the xxvij day off September for the holyloyff		ij^{d}
Item rec' at the purificacion off Wyllm' Butler wyff a crsum		j^{d} ob
Item rec' the iiij day off October for the holyloyff		ij^{d}
Item rec' the v day off October at the buriall off Wardew wyff mother		j^{d}
Item rec' the sayd day at the buriall off the hyrdman chyld off Mogeranger		j^{d} ob
Item rec' at the dedicacion day in offeryng	iij^{s}	iiij^{d}
Summa xj^{s} v^{d}		

[3]

Rec' for Michaellmes rent off the glebe lond for cottyges (long^{c}) belongyng to the parsonage		
Fyrst off Robert Bokkyngum for on part off lond and medew	ix^{s}	viij^{d}
Item rec' off Rychard Samwell for on part	ix^{s}	viij^{d}
Item rec' off Wyllm' Wotton on part	ix^{s}	viij^{d}
Items off old Mother Passlew for on partt	ix^{s}	viij^{d}
Item rec' off John Brownell for the howysse in the Northend	iij^{s}	iiij^{d}
Item rec' off John Bowygtton for the vicarege	iij^{s}	iiij^{d}
Item resaved for halyff a old hare [harrow?] sold to Yereld off the northe end price		xx^{d}
Memorandum that I have re' off Maister Spenser to pay warkemen in harvest tyme with iiij^{li}		
Summa vj^{li} vij^{s}		

[4]

Lambertes floke

Mother Homes, a lame
Water Butler, on lame
Jesera Ossburne, ij lames
Thomas Boston, iiij lames
Robert Wottun, ij lames
Thomas Powter, ij lames

Owell floke

Ryc' Odam, on lame
Ryc' Samwell, on lame
Ryc' Hylles on lame
(Thomas, on lame^{c})
Thomas Hull, on lame
John Stele, on lame
John Ossburne, iij lames

Mogeranger syde

Ryc' Pecke, on lame
Maister Batell, on lame
Mathew off Sowmylne, viij lames
Thomas Ward, iij lames
Thomas Grae, on lame
Old Samwell wyff, on
Thomas Blythe, ij lames
Thomas Pecke, ij lames
Robert Thomas, on lame for Gowser
Wyllm' Peck, on lame
Robert Thomas, on lame
Wyllm' Peck for Gowser, on lame
John Benett, ij lames
Maister Spenser, iiij lames
Robert Thorpe, on lame

Item, sold to the sayd Robertt iij lames that wer drevene to Bassmede owit off Blonham paryst before Ester — iij^{s} iiij^{d}
Tomas Peck for Gowser, on lame
John Angell, on lame
Thomas Grey the junior, on lame
Thomas Fecher, ij lames
Thomas Bure, on
Spenser off Gerforthe, on lame
Memorandum: that I have re' for od lames and od wolle all thenges deduckyd and pay to Henery Man — ij^{s} v^{d}

Summa v^{s} ix^{d}

[5]

Tethe wode sold

Item sold to Thomas Powter halyff a rowyd, price with the fellyng — iiij^{s}
Item sold to John Thomas and Thomas Wakefeld xvij polles price — iij^{s} iiij^{d}
Item sold to (old^{c}) old Passlew x polle price — xxij^{d}
Item sold to Torney off Mogeranger vij polle price — xiiij^{d}
Item sold to John Pette iiij polle price — ix^{d}
Item sold to the Brotherhede on lode price — x^{d}
Item fet in to the (parsel^{c}) parsonage yerd iij lodes to hege the pesse reke and to mende the heges withall

Tethe hay sold

Item sold to Maister Spenser Stekebeke and the Fene price — vij^{s}
Item sold to John Thomas the heddes price — viij^{d}
Item sold to Blythe hys pece price — xij^{d}
Item sold to John Gostweke the Kowemede price — ij^{s} iiij^{d}
Item sold to Hawkynges off Charyllton the mown kys howyd price — ij^{d}
Item sold to Wodam the che' mede price — ij^{s}
Item sold to John Syme Barcar mede price — ij^{s}
Item to Harry Ossburne Kow howme price — xij^{d}
Item sold to Queperlay the Ox howme — xij^{d}
Item Robert Bockyngham and Robert Samwell for on closse — ij^{s}
Item Thomas Powter for on closse — ij^{s}

Item Wyllm' Wottun for the parsons closse v^{s}
Item resaved for the Rychys off a man off Everton xx^{d}

Summa xxxix^{s} ix^{d}

[6]

Malt sent to Wrast

Item sent to Wrast the xvij day off Aprill by Wyllm' Thomas and John Peto xxj^{ty} buschelles off malt

(Item sent to^{c})

Item delivered to the cherchewordonys off Blounham ij busschell off maltt for ther Maij ale

Item delivered to the fremason that mayd my maisteres chapel' at Wrast by a redytokyn a quarter off malt

Item sold to John Bowyghton on buschell off malt price vj^{d}

Item deleveryd to the wyffys off Blounham for the prosescion weke (to^{c}) a bz malt

Item sent to Wrast the viij day off Maij by Wyllm' Thomas xviij buschelles malt

Item delivered to the cherchewardonys off Mogeranger syde ij buschelles malt to ther Maij

Item sent to Wrast the xj day off Maij by Wyllm' Thomas and John Petto vj quarterys malt

Item sent to Wrast the xxix off Maij by Wyllm' Thomas iiij quarteres of malt

Item sent to Wrast xviij day of Junij v quarteres and v bz off malt by Wyllm' Thomas and John Petto

Item sent to Wrast the xj day off Julij by Wyllm' Thomas xij buschelles malt

Item sent to Wrast the layst day off Julij v quarterys malt by John Naler and John Loyssyng

[illegible erasure of 1½ lines]

Item sold to Wakefeld on buschell price vj^{d}

Summa xij^{d}

[7]

Whett and rye sent to Wrast

Item sent to Wrast the xvij day off Aprill by Wyllm' Thomas and John Petto ij quarter off whett and v buschell off rye

Item sent to Wrast the v day off Maij by (Wll^{c}) Wyllm' Thomas and John Petto hallyff a quarter off whett

Item sent to Wrast the viij day off Maij by Wyllm' Thomas and John Petto ij quarterys off whett and ij quarterys off rye

Item sent to Wrast the xj day off Maij by Wyllm' Thomas and John Petto x buschelys whett and iij buscheles off talynges off the sayd whett

Item deleveryd to Wrast and the sayd day v buschelles rye

Item sent to Wrast the xxix day off Maij by Wyllm' Thomas xij bz off rye

Item sent to Wrast the secund day off Julij xiiij buschelles rye by Wyllm' Thomas

Item sent to Wrast the xj day off Julij ij quarterys off whett
Item sent the sayd day ij quarter rye by Wyllm' Thomas
Item sent to Wrast the xviij day off Julij by John Petto v bz off whett and halyff a quarter rye
Item sent to Wrast the last day off Julij halyff a quarter rye
Item sent to Wrast the xxiiij day off August v buschelles whett
Item sent the sayd day x buschelles rye by John Loyssyn
Item sent to Wrast the xj^{ty} day off September by John Naler ij bz off rye and ij and a halyff off whett

[8]

(Peson sold[c])

(Item sold to Thorogood servand ij buschell peson price	xij^{d} [c])
(Item sold to John Ossburne on buschell price	v^{d} [c])
(Item sold to Bloke off Hechyng halyff a buschell price	iij^{d} [c])
(Item sold to Wyllm' Ade a buschell	vj^{d} [c])

Tethe egges

Item resaved off Margett Powter for egges at Ester xiij^{s} iiij^{d}
Item resaved at the (crowyng[c]) crechyng off the crosse ix skore egges and sent thame to Wrast

Tethe gesse

Mother Hylles the wedew	ij	Rychard Ward	j
Wyllm' Mores wyff	j	Ares wyff	j
Mother Homes	j	Boge wyff	j
Wylkockys wyff	j	Mother Farmery	j
Coper wyff	j	Mother Passlew	j
Margett Powter	j	Chessam wyff	j
Bokyngham wyff	ij	Fynns wyff	j
Robert Samwell wyff	ij	Maisterys Spenser	j
Fecher wyff	j		

Summa xiij^{s} iiij^{d}

[9]

Tethe pyges sold

Item sold to Qwekys wyff on pege price	iij^{d}
Item sold to Thomas Blythe on pege price	iiij^{d}
Item sold to Annes Qweke on pege price	iij^{d}
Item sold to Water Butler hys tethe pege price	iiij^{d}
Item sold to Paternoster a tethe pege price	iiij^{d}
Item sold to sir Edward a pege price	iiij^{d}
Item delivered a pege to the bale and sir Edward when the dyd geder the tethe woll	
Item sold to Margery Hylles a tethe pyge price	iiij^{d}
Item spent on pyge when Maister Thomas was at Blounham with Maister Doctor	
(delivered[m]) Item sold on pyge to Thomas Bamforthe price	ij^{d}
Item sold on to Wakefeld price	j^{d} ob
Item sold to Margery Hylles on pyge price	iiij^{d}

Item sold to Yereld off Northe end on pyge price iij^{d}
Item send to Wrast the xiij day off September ij tethe pyges
Item sold to Thomas (Fy^{c}) Fecher a tethe peg price iij^{d}

Summa iij^{s} iii^{d} ob

[10]

Hencorne sold

Item sold to John Wardew on buschell price iiij^{d}
Item sold to Thomas Powter on buschell off hencorne price iiij^{d}
Item sold to John Wardew iij buschell price xij^{d}
Item (sod^{c}) sold to Robert Samwell halyff a quarter off hencorne price xiiij^{d}
Item sold to Margett (Pw^{c}) Powter on buschell of hencorne iij^{d} ob[1]
Item deleveryd to Wrast xxix day off Maij by Wylm' Thomas xiij^{te} bz off hencorne
Item sold to Rychard Hylles on bz off hencorne price iiij^{d}
Item sold to Thomas Powter on bz off hencorne price iiij^{d}
Item sold to Annenes Qweke a pecke off hencorne j^{d}
Item sold to Fesand wyff a pecke price j^{d}
Item sold to Ryc' Hylles and John Bowne the powter ij buschell of hencorne price vij^{d}
Item sold to Wakefeld on bz off malt price vj^{d}
Item sold to Meriweder wyff a peke off hencorne j^{d}
Item sold to Margett Powter a bz off hencorne price iiij^{d}
Item deleveryd to Wrast the xviij day off Julij by John Petto vj bz hencorne
Item sold to John Ossburne wyff halyff a bz price ij^{d}
Item sold to Scharpys wyff and Fesand wyff iij price iij^{d}
Item sent to Wrast Wrast [sic] the layst day off Julij halyff a quarter hencorne

Summa v^{s} x^{d} ob

[11]

Peson sold and sent to Wrast

Item deleveryd to Wyllm' Wytcherche for my Maisteres geldyng when (whe^{c}) he was at Blounham for on weke ij buschell and a halyff
Item delivered for the cart horsys the sayd weke when they fett hay at Blounham halyff a buschell
Item sent to Wrast the xxviij day off Aprill by Wyll' Thomas (half^{c}) halyff a quarter off peson
Item sent the sayd day to Wrast v buschell off hencorne
Item sold to John Ossburne on buschell price v^{d}
Item deleveryd to Wyllm' Thomas for the cartt horssys the iiij day off Maij a bz off peson
Item sold to Thomas Powter ij buschell peson price x^{d}
Item sold to Rychard Hylles on buschell price v^{d}
Item sold to John Ossburne iij buschell off peson the viij day off Maij xv^{d}

Item sent to Wrast the xj day off Maij by Wyllm' Thomas and John Petto halyff a quarter off (malt^{c}) peson and deleveryd to tham the sayd day for the cartt horsys halyff a bz peson

Item sold to Thomas Powter on bz off peson price v^{d}

Item sold to Robert Samwell on buschell off peson vj^{d}

Item sold to Wyllm' Ade on bz off peson vj^{d}

Item sold to the sayd Wyllm' a peke price j^{d} ob

Item sold to Thorogood servandes ij buschell off peson price xij^{d}

Item sold to John (Ossbr^{c}) Ossburne on bz price v^{d}

Item sold to Bloke off Hechyng halyff a bz price iij^{d}

Item sold to Wyllm' Ade a bz vj^{d}

Item delivered to Maister Doctor servand for hys horsys when he lay at (Blob^{c}) Blounham the xij day off Julij on bz off peson

Item delivered to John Naler whe he fett malt and other stoyff at Blounham for the cart horsys halyff a bz peson

Item sold to Ryc Hylles a bz off peson price vj^{d}

Item sold to the powter a buschell peson price vj^{d}

Item sold to Thomas Powter on buschell vj^{d}

Item sold to Master Colbeck halyff a buschell price iij^{d}

Summa viij^{s} iiij^{d} ob

[12]

Tethe cauves

Item rec' off Mathewe off Sowmyllne a tethe cauyff and sold to hymme for xxij^{d}

Item rec' off Maister Spenser a tethe cawyff and sen to Wrast by Thomas Wakefeld

(weder^{m}) Item re' for a weder skyne that dyyd off Harry Samwell v^{d}

Item sent to Wrast on Wytsoneven John Benett tethe cawyff by the boye Mat

(sent the mony to Wrast by Thomas Wakefeld^{m})

(Item sold Jesera Ossburne tethe cawyff the the [sic] taterys for price xxj^{dc})

Item sold Blythe tethe cawyff to Harry Samwell price xxij^{d}

Pydgons sold

Item rec' off Thomas Powter wyff for ij dosan pedgons x^{d}

Item sold to Eme Joyns vj pydgonys price ij^{d} ob

Item sold to Robert Wottun wyff iij pydgons j^{d}

Item delivered to olde Passlowe on dosan pydgonys for dressyng off a geldyng for the jandes

Item spent when master Thomas was at Blounham with Maister Doctor viij pydgonys

Item sent to Wrast the last day off Julij v qwke pydgons for the hawkys

Item sent to Wrast the secund day off August ij dosan pydgonys

Item sent to Wrast the xv day off August by Mat the boye iiij dosan pydgons

Item sent to Wrast the xxiiij day off August iij dosan pydgonys
Item sent to Wrast the xxx day off August ij dosan pedgons
Item sent to Wrast the vj day off September iij and a halyff off pydgons [sic]
Item sent to Wrast the xiij day off September iiij dosan pydgons
Item sent to Wrast the xx^{ty} day off September ij dosan and vj pydgons
Item sent to Wrast the xxvij off September ij dosan and iij pydgons
Item sent to Wrast the vj day off October by John Warner xviij pydgons
Item sold to Harry Samwell halyff a dosan pydgons ij^{d}
(Schepe^{m}) Memorandum: that I have sent to Wrast the secund day off Julij xl (vij^{l}) wedderys (and vij^{c})
Item sent the sayd day to Wrast by Wakefeld and Bowyghtton lx lames lackyng on lame

Summa v^{s} iiij^{d} ob

[13]

Ordynarij chargys and exspences (conse^{c}) concernyng the parsonage off Blounham

(Payd^{m}) Item payd for pyntt off mawesse fett at Norhyll the ix day off Aprill		j^{d} ob
Item paid at my lord off Lyncoln visitacion keppyt at Norhyll the xv day off Aprill for Peter pensse	vij^{s}	
Item paid to syr Edward for hys quarter wages off Sanc' Elyn even the thyrd day off May	xxxiij^{s}	iiij^{d}
Item paid for a pynt of mawesse fet at Sanc' Nedes by Harry Samwell		j^{d} ob
Item paid for a pynt of mawesse fet at Bedforthe on Wetson even		ij^{d}
Item paid for a pynt of mawesse for fett at Sanc' Nedes the iiij day off Junij by Harry Samwell		j^{d} ob
Item paid for a pynt of mauesse fet at Potton the xx day off Junij		j^{d} ob
Item paid for a pynt off mauesse that Sir Edward fett when I was fro home		j^{d} ob
Item paid for a pynt off mawesse the xj day off Julij fett at Pottun		j^{d} ob
Item paid for a pynt off red wyn fett at Scheforth the xxiiij^{ty} off Julij		j^{d}
Item paid for a pynt of mauesse fet at Potton the fryst day off August		j^{d} ob
Item paid to Sir Edward paryssh preyst for hys wages the iij day off August	xxxiij^{s}	iiij^{d}
Item paid for a pynt off mawesse fett at Potton the xv day off August		j^{d} ob
Item paid for a pottell off lampe ole fett att Bedforthe		iiij^{d}

Item paid for a pynt off mawesse fett at Potton the xxix day off August — j^{d} ob

Item paid for a pynt off mawese fet at Sanc' Nedes the xvij day off September — j^{d} ob

Item paid for a pynt off mawesse fett at Sanc' Nedes the fyrst day off October — j^{d} ob

Item paid at my lord off Canterbure visitacion for seneg and proxys the ix day off October — x^{s} vj^{d}

Item paid the sayd day at Scheforthe to the v marke for that denre — v^{s}

Summa iiij^{li} xj^{s} i^{d} ob

Item re' xj^{li} vij^{s}

Summa iiij^{li} x^{s} x^{d} ob

Rec' of Sor Rychard of Maister Doctors mony left for the barn — iij^{li} vj^{s} viij^{d}

thes som alowed to Sor Rechard

[p 14 is blank]

[15]

Item payd for Wyllm' Thomas and John Petto dener the xvij day off Aprill when tha fett malt and whett at Blounham the — iij^{d}

Item paid to Wakefeld for caryneng off gren gesse to Wrast — ij^{d}

Item paid for Wyllm' Thomas and John Peto soper when tha fett hay at Blounham — iij^{d} ob

Item paid for Mat the boye the sayd tyme when he lay seke ij day at Blounham for hys soper and other charges — iij^{d}

Item paid for Wyllm' Thomas and John Petto with othare men off Blounham that (fett^{c}) dyd cary hay to Wrast the xxij day off Aprill for thare drenkeng in the mornyng when they hade lode thare carttes — ix^{d}

Item paid for Wyllm' (for Wyllm^{c}) Whetcherche weke bord when he cyppytt my maisteres geldynges at Blounham — x^{d}

Item payd for John Warner when he fett the besse at Blounham — j^{d}

Item paid for Rychard the boye when he fett ij C egges for hys dener — j^{d}

Item paid for Wyllm' Thomas dener the xxviij day off Aprill when he fett hencorne and peson at Blownham — j^{d} ob

Item paid for ij pare schowne on pare off dobyll solyd for the coke and a pare for Rychard the boye, price off bothe pareys — xiij^{d}

Item paid for Wyllm' Thomas and John Petto and Matte soper and dener when the fett hay and schepe at Blounham the v day off Maij — viij^{d}

Item paid to Bowyghttun for ij maundes — vij^{d}

Item paid to hymme for mendyng off the bothoym off the clothe (baskytt^{c}) basskytt and makyng off a panyer lyed — iij^{d}

Item paid for a pare off fortrays and sent to Wrast by Wyllm' Thomas and John Peto the viij day of Maij — iiij^{d}

Item paid for Wyllm' Thomas and John Petto soper off Thoryssday at neghtt and for thare drenkyng on Friday in the mornyng the viij day off Maij — vj^{d}

Item paid for Wyllm' Thomas and John Petto the xj day off Maij for thare dener and the boye Rychardes dener when tha fett whett and rye — v^{d}

Item paid for thred to mend the tranell and for mendyng off the sayd trannell to Ranold boye off Sanday — vij^{d}

Summa vij^{s} iij^{d}

[16]

(paid[m]) Item payd to Wyllm' Ward for caryeng off ij lodys off wod frome the lady wod — viij^{d}

Item paid the Wakefeld for caryeng off a C and a halyff off egges to Wrast and vj grene gesse with a pecorell for hyss wages — ij^{d}

Item paid for iiij bownettes to the barber off Pottun — ij^{s}

Item paid to Thomas Wakefeld for goyng too tyme to Wrast — iiij^{d}

Item paid for ij denerys the Fryday before Wytsunday and the Tuyssday foloyng — ij^{d}

Item to Thomas Wakefeld for goyng to Wrast ij tymes with (vj[l]) grene gesse and ij C off egges with other stoyff — iiij^{d}

Item paid for fresche feche and sent to Wrast for Wytsonweke — vj^{d}

Item paid to Wardew off Blounham for iiij hary (tedderys[c]) ropys to tye horsys with in the felde at Wrast — xiiij^{d}

Item paid for peche and tare to marke the schepe at Blounham the fryst day off Junij — iij^{d}

Item paid to Thomas Bamforth for scheryng off xlviij^{ty} schepe — x^{d}

Item paid for bred and ale (for[c]) and for gederyng upe off losse woll and for wyndyng off the sayd wole — iij^{d}

Item paid to Thomas Wakefeld for kepyng off ij fat oxne frome Ester to Wytsonday — xij^{d}

Item paid for John Petto and Wyllm' delivered the xviij day off Junij when they fett malt at Blounham — iij^{d}

Item paid for Wyllm' Thomas delivered the ij day off Julij — ij^{d}

Item paid to Wakefeld and Bowghtton for dryveng off schepe to Wrast the secund day off Julij — iiij^{d}

Item payd to Roger Qweke the xj day off Julij for iij pare off schowne on pare for the cowke and ij pare for plowboyeys price — xviij^{d}

Item payd for Wyllm' Thomas dener and a servand off my Maister the sayd day when they fett whett and rye at Blownham — iij^{d}

Item paid for John Pette dener the xvij day off Julij when he fett whett and rye — j^{d}

Item paid to Thomas Wakefeld for caryeng off egges caponys and chekynges to Wrast iij tymes — vj^{d}

Item paid for John Naler John Boweyn dener the layst day off Julij ij^{d}

Summa x^{s} xj^{d}

[17]

(paid^{m}) Item paid to Thomas Wakefeld for caryeng off (p^{c}) ij dosan pydgons and C egges to Wrast the fryst day of August ij^{d}
Item payd to Wyllm' Wottun for careyng off iiij lodes off clay iiij^{d}
Item paid for Mattes dener the xv day off August when he fett gesse with other stowyff at Blounham j^{d}
Item paid to Thomas Wakefeld for caryeng feche to Wrast the sayd xv day for hys wages ij^{d}
Item paid for Lossyn my Maister servand soper bede and dener the xxiiij day off August when he fett whett and rye at Blounham ij^{d}
Item paid to Thomas Wakefeld for goyng ij tymes to Wrast with pydgons and chekynges iiij^{d}
(Item for payd for Naler^{c})
Item paid for John Naleres dener the xj day off September when he fett whett and rye at Blounham j^{d}
Item payd (Qweke^{i}) for a pare off schone for John Wattes and tham to Wrast by Thomas Wakefeld vj^{d}
Item paid for a pare off schowne for the cooke to (Roger^{i}) Qweke and sent to Wrast by Thomas Wakefeld viij^{d}
Item paid for ij pare off schowne to Qweke on pare for Matte and nother pare for the plowbowye the v day off October xij^{d}
Item paid for Mattes dener the say day j^{d}
Item paid for John Warneres dener vj day off October when he browyg' the fatt oxene to Blounham j^{d}
Item to Thomas Wakefeld for hegeyng off the swan pen and inlardgeyng off it iiij^{d}

Summa iiij^{s}

[18]

Hay tyme

Item paid to Harry Samwell for mowyng off ij closys, the pertre cloysse and the (grett^{i}) aylandes iiij^{s} ij^{d}
Item paid to Thomas Wakefeld and Thomas Bamforthe for makyng off xiij lodes off hay in the sayd closys ij^{s} viij^{d} ob
Item paid to Thomas Wakefeld and Thomas Bamforthe for makyng off xx^{ty} lodys off (th^{c}) tethe hay in the medys v^{s}
Item spent off the cartys that caryd hay to Wrast on Tuyssday the xxj day off Julij when they lodyd thare carttes and off the morowe at Scheforthe for viij carttes xj^{d}
Item on Thoryssday for v carttes over neghtt and in the mornyng at Scheforthe viij^{d}
Item paid to Thomas Yereld for caryeng off on lode iiij^{d}
Item paid to Thomas Pecke for careyng off ij lodys viij^{d}
Item paid to Robert Peck for a lode careyng iiij^{d}

Item paid to Angell for a lode careyng iiij^{d}
Item paid to Welwyn for caryeng off a lode iiij^{d}
Item paid to Thomas Wakeffeld and Thomas Bamforthe for makyng off xv lodys off tethe hay iij^{s} ix^{d}
Item paid to Thomas Powter for careng off xxiiij^{ty} lodys off tethe hay viij^{s}

Summa xxvij^{s} ij^{d} ob

[19]

Harvest

Item paid to Hodam for gederyng off tethe corne off Mogeranger syde vj^{s}
Item paid to Willm' (Wytt^{c}) Wotton for caryeng off the sayd syde xlvj^{s} viij^{d}
Item paid to Ryc' Boge for gederyng off Blounham part vj^{s}
Item paid to Thomas Powter for careyng off Blounham syde xxxviij^{s} iiij^{d}
Item paid to Thomas Wakefeld for kepyng off the mowys viij^{s}
Item paid to Thomas Bamforth for kepyng off the mowys viij^{s}
Item paid to John Bowgghtton for kepyng off the mowys viij^{s}
Item paid to Wakefeld wyff and to Bowgghtton wyff to helpe to trede the pesse reke iiij^{d}
Item paid to Claton the thacar for ij days thakyng off the pesse reke ix^{d}
Item paid to Wyllm' More for serveng off hym vj^{d}
Item paid to Wakefeld for hegeng off the sayd reke iiij^{d}
Item paid to Wakefeld yelmeyng off ij lodys off straw to thake the pesse reke with iiij^{d}
Item paid to Haukynges for ij lodes off straw to thake the sayd reke with xvj^{d}
Item payd to Wyllm' Wotton for caryeng off the sayd straw frome Charyllton to Blounham viij^{d}

Summa vj^{li} v^{s} iij^{d}
(Summa vj^{li} iv^{s} ix$^{d\ c}$)

[20]

Malt sold to Thorogud off Hechyn

Fryday — Item delivered to Thorogud servandes the xxix day off Maij viij quarterys malt

Saturday — Item delivered to Thorogood servandes the xxx day off Maij ix quarterys malt

Monday — Item delivered to Thorogood servandes Wyllm' Fage and Wyllm' Ade the fryst day off Junij delivered to tham ix quarterys off malt

Tuyssday — Item delivered to Wyllm' Fage and Wyllm' Ade with other ij lades servandes to the sayd Wyllm' Fage the xxiij^{ty} day of Junij viij quarterys malt

Fryday — Item delivered to Wyllm' Fage servand the xxvj day of Junij viij quarterys malt

Satturday Item delivered to Wyllm' Fage and hys servandes the xxvij day off Junij
viij quarterys malt

Tuyssday Item delivered to Wyllm' Ade the layst day off Junij
viij quarterys malt

Fryday Item delivered to Thorogudes servand and to felay that ys cawlyd Bloke off Hechyng the iij day off Julij
ix quarterys malt

Saturday Item delivered (off[c]) to Wyllm' Fage the iiij day off Julij
ix quarterys off malt

Item delivered the sayd day to Ryc' Bloke and Thorogudes servand
ix quarterys malt

Tuyssday Item delivered to Wyllm' Ade the vij day of Julij
viij quarteres malt

Fryday Item delivered to Wyllm' Fage and hys servand Wyllm' Ade the x day off Julij
viij quarterys malt

Munday Item delivered to Wyllm' Fage (the[c]) and Wyllm' Ade the xiij day off Julij
viij quarterys and a halyff of malt

Wedynyssday Item delivered to Wyllm' Fage servandes as [sic] Wyllm' Ade and other ij bowyeys the xv day off Julij
viij quarterys malt

Saturday Item delivered to Wyllm' Ade the xviij day off Julij
viij quarterys and a halyff a quarter off malt

[21]

Whett and rye thresschyd sens Ester

Items payd to Thomas Wakkfeld and John Ward for threschyng of v quarterys off Whett the layst day off Aprill and payd to tham for thare wages xx[d]

Item paid to Thomas Wakefeld for threscheyng off ij quarterys off rye the viij day off Maij and payd to hym for hys wages viij[d]

Item paid to Thomas Wakefeld for thresschyng off ij quarterys off rye the xxj day off Maij and payd to hym for hys wages viij[d]

Item re' off Thomas Wakefeld the xxvij off Junij iij quarterys off whett and a halyff quarter and payd for threschyng xvij[d] ob

Item re' off Thomas Wakefeld and off Ryc' Boge the iij day off Julij v quarterys (off[c]) and v bz off rye at thare dressyng and payd to tham for thare wages ij[s]

Newe rye threscheyd before Michaellmes thys yere

(Rye[m]) Item sent to Wrast the xix[ty] day off September (xix day off[c]) by Loyssyn my Mr' servand ix buschell off newe rye

Item payd to Wakefeld and John Bowygton for threschyng off newe rye and whett before Michaellmes ij days and a halyff xv[d]

Item sent to Wrast the vj day off October by Matt the (boye[c]) bowye ix buschelles off rye

Item to John Bronyng and Thomas Wakfeld for threschyng off x buschelles off rye viij^{d}

Item sent to Wrast off Sanc' Luce even x buschelles off rye by Matt the plow boye

Item paid for thressyng off the sayd rye to Wakefeld and John Ward vj^{d} ob

Summa viij^{s} xj^{d}

[22]

Powtry ware sent to Wrast

Item sent to Wrast the vij day off Aprill by Wakefeld v caponys

Item sent to Wrast the xiiij day off Aprill by Thomas Wakefeld x grene gesse and ij C egges and paid for the sayd x gesse to Samwell wyff off Sowmylle xx^{d}

Item sent to Wrast on Low Sonday by Matt the boye on (capon[c]) capon and on spent when my lady was at Blounham

(Item sent to Wrast by Thomas Wakefeld vj caponys[c])

Item sent to Wrast the xvij day off Aprill by Wyllm' Thomas and John Peto vj caponys and ij C egges and payd to Margett Powter for the egges xviij^{d}

Item (payd[c]) sent to Wrast the sayd day a dosan pydgonys and v oder

Item sent to Wrast (the[c]) on Sanc' Markes day by Rychard Gasqwyne the boye ij C egges and (ij tethe pyges[l]) payd for the sayd egges xviij^{d}

(London[m]) Item sent to London the frist day off May by Thomas Powter iiij caponys

Item sent the sayd day on C egges and payd for the sayd egges ix^{d}

(Item sent to Wrast Sanc' Marke day ij tethe pyges by Rychard the plow boye [c])

Item sent to Wrast the iiij day off Maij by Thomas Wakefeld ij C egges and paid to Margett Powter for the sayd egges xviij^{d}

Item sent the sayd day ij dosan pydgonys by the (sy[c]) sayd Thomas

Item sent to Wrast the xij day off Maij by Thomas Wakefeld (x[c]) vj grene gesse and paid for thaym to Margett Powter xij^{d}

Item sent the sayd day C and a halyff off egges and payd (for[c]) to the sayd Marg' Powter xiij^{d} ob

Item sent to Maister Harry and to the chyldyr on pecorell

Item sent to Maister Harry and to the chylder a chewen the xiiij off Maij

Item sent to Wrast the xxij day of Maij by Thomas Wakefeld ij C egges xviij^{d}

Item sent the say day iiij caponys and payd for the sayd caponys xvj^{d}

Item sent the sayd day xvj chekyns pay for the sayd chekyns xvj^{d}
Item sent the sayd day (a the[c]) a tethe pege wened and a pecorell
(Item sold to Qweky wyff on pyge price iij^{d} [c])
(Item sold to Thomas Blythe a tethe pege price iiij^{d} [c])
(Item sold to Annenes Qweke a tethe pyg price iiij^{d} [c])
(Item sold to Water Butler a tethe pege price iiij^{d} [c])

Summa xiij^{s} ij^{d} ob

[23]

(Item sold to Paternoster a tethe pyge off John Ossburnes price iiij^{d} [c])
(Item sold to sir Edward a tethe pege price iiij^{d} [c])
Item paid to Margett Powter for a C egges and sent to Wrast the v^{ty} day off Junij by Thomas Wake and paid for the sayd egges x^{d}
Item sent the sayd day to Wrast on capon
Item sent to Wrast the xviij day of Junij (by[i]) Wyllm' Tomas and John Petto on C egges and payd for tham to Margett Powter ix^{d}
Item sent to Wrast the xx day off Junij by Thomas Wakefeld vj gesse xij^{d}
Item sent the sayd day x chekynges price x^{d}
Item paid to Thomas Powter for xij caponetes the xxvij day off Junij ij^{s}
Item paid to Margett Powter for xiij chekynges and sent to Wrast the xxviij day off Junij by Thomas Wakefeld xiij^{d}
Item sent the sayd day ij tethe pygges and vj gesse
Item sent to Wrast the iij day off Julij by Thomas Wakefeld vj caponys
Item sent the sayd day to Wrast a C and a halyff off egges and payd for the sayd egges to Margett Powter xv^{d}
Item sent to Wrast the xvij day (off Wrast[c]) off Julij by Thomas Wakefeld a C egges price x^{d}
Item sent to Wrast the xix day off Julij by Thomas Wakefeld iij capons xv^{d}
Item sent the sayd day ij dosan chekyns and viij price ij^{s} viij^{d}
Item sent to Wrast the xxv day off Julij by Thomas Wakefeld iij capons, ij off the sayd iij war my ladys and on bowgght off Margery Hylles price v^{d}
Item sent the sayd day of C egges price x^{d}
Item sent the sayd day xij chekynges price xij^{d}
Item sent the sayd day vj gesse price xviij^{d}
Item sent to Wrast the laysst day off Julij a C egges by John Neler price x^{d}

Summa xvij^{s} j^{d}

[24]

Powtry ware bowgghtt remanyng unsent to Wrast

(Item paid to Samwell wyff for x gesse grene gesse xx^{d} [c])
Item paid to Margett Powter for x chekynys x^{d}

Item paid to Hyllys wyff the wedew for vij grene gesse		xiiij^{d}
Item payd to Rychard Hylles for iij caponys		xij^{d}
Item paid to Margett Powter for a C egges		ix^{d}
Item paid to Annes Scharp for vij chekyns		vij^{d}
Item paid to Margett (Powter^{i}) for ij caponys		viij^{d}
Item paid to the sayd Marget for iiij caponettes		xij^{d}
Item paid to Rychard Hylles for vj chekyng' abyll to carve		ix^{d}
Item paid to Rychard Hylles for iij chekyng' (alby^{c}) abyll to carve		iiij^{d} ob
Item paid to Thomas Powter for viij gesse and sent to Wrast the xv day off August	ij^{s}	iiij^{d}
Item paid to the sayd Thomas for vj chekynges and sent the sayd day		vj^{d}
((Pydgons^{m}) Item sent the sayd day by Matt the boye iiij dosan pydgons ^{c})		
Item sent the sayd day on C egges price		x^{d}
Item paid for viij chekyns to Thomas (Pecke^{i}) wyff and iiij caponys and sent to Wrast the sayd (day^{c}) xv day August price		xx^{d}
Item paid to Marget Powter the xviij day off August for iiij capons		xij^{d}
Item paid for iiij caponettes to Robert Thomas wyffe off Mogeranger the xxiiij day off August and sent to Wrast the sayd day		xiij^{d}
Item paid for xvj chekynges to Rychard Hylles the xxx day off August and sent to Wrast the sayd by Thomas Wakefeld		xviij^{d}
Item sent to Wrast the vj day off September iiij caponys by Thomas Wakefeld		
Item sent to Wrast the xx day off September on C egges and paid to John Ossburne for the sayd egges		x^{d}
Item paid to old Mother Passlew for ij kockerelles abyll to carve		iij^{d}
Item sent to Wrast the vj day off October by John Warner on C egges and pay for thame to John Ossburne		x^{d}

Summa xvij^{s} xj^{d} ob

(The summa off the ^{c}) paimentes (xvj^{li} ij^{s} xj^{d} ^{c})

Rectory Account 1538-9

This document, L 26/1407, is a booklet of 5 folded sheets. The receipts in the account run from Christmas 1538 to Michaelmas 1539: the payments from Michaelmas 1538 to Michaelmas 1539.

crysom = chrisom, a white cloth put on a new-born child.
d. = dimidium, a half.
hole loffe = bread blessed and distributed to the congregation after mass.
howsyllyng brede = the wafers used in the administration of the eucharist.
syngyng brede = see 'howsyllyng brede' above.
tramell = fishing net.

[L 26/1407]

[1]

The reyt' begynyng at Crystnmas

Imprimis the offeryng the same day	iiij^{s}	iiij^{d}
Item at the bereyng of Ryc' Hyllys the offeryng		vj^{d} ob
Item the fyrste Sunday for the holeloffe		ij^{d}
Item of the same man bequethyd to the hye autar		xij^{d}
Item the second Sunday for the holeloffe		ij^{d}
Item at the (yeretyde^{c}) (aneversary^{i}) of syr Edmunde Lucy knygth		viij^{d}
Item at the purificacion of the wyffe of Kyng		j^{d} ob
Item the iij Sunday for the holeloffe		ij^{d}
Item at the weydyng of Goldesmythe the offeryng		vj^{d}
Item a pygke of Fynne and solde to Th. Pulter the price		ij^{d} ob
Item the iiij Sunday for the holyloffe		ij^{d}
Item at the purificacion of the wyffe of (chr^{c}) Cleyton		j^{d}
Item the v Sunday for the holeloffe		ij^{d}
Item the vj Sunday for the holeloffe		ij^{d}
Item at weydyng of Thomas Dawys the offeryng		ij^{d}
Item at the aneversar' of Thomas Pecke		iij^{d} ob
Item the vij Sunday for the holeloffe		ij^{d}
Item recd. of Margere Hyllys for the mortuare	iij^{s}	iiij^{d}
	xij^{s}	v^{d}

[2]

Item the viij Sunday for the holeloffe		ij^{d}
Item of Margere Hyllys odde money for pygkes		j^{d} ob
Item at bereyng of a chylde of the myller		j^{d}
Item the ix Sunday for the holeloffe		ij^{d}
Item the x Sunday for the holeloffe		ij^{d}
Item at the yeretyde of Tumlyn Smyythe		j^{d}
Item at the aneversar' of Jhon' Peke		j^{d}
Item the xj Sunday for the holeloffe		ij^{d}
Item of Porter for offeryng		j^{d}
Item the xij Sunday for the holeloffe		ij^{d}
Item rec' for the tythe hempe	xiiij^{s}	
Item of Jhon' Osburne for growndhey		ij^{d}
Item for the lope of a tre yn the heylande		v^{d}

Item the xiij Sunday for the holeloffe		ij^{d}
	xvj^{s}	ob

[3]

The rec' begynnyng at Sente Mare day

Imprimis at the (yeret^{c}) aneversar' of T. Farthyng the offeryng		j^{d}
Item of the Kyrbe for a pygke		iiij^{d}
Item rec' oddemoney for pygkys		j^{d} ob
Item of Hanyscam' for a tythe pygke		v^{d}
Item owt of (of^{c}) the Estur boke	xx^{s}	
Item of Fynne for a tythe pygke		iiij^{d}
Item at the bereyng of T. Cleyton the offeryng		ij^{d}
Item at the purific' of the wyffe of Henr' Osburne a crisum		j^{d}
Item a the purific' of the wyffe of W. Porter		iij^{d}
Item at the bereyng of a chyld of Meyys the offeryng		iij^{d}
Item at the purific' of the wyffe of Kyrbe a crysum		j^{d}
Item rec' for the dunngke yn the duffehowse	ij^{s}	vj^{d}
Item for vij Sundayys for the holyloffe		ij^{d}
Item at the weydyng of the bayle the offeryng		vj^{d} ob
Item at the purific' of the wyffe of J. Angell a crysum		j^{d} ob
Item the viij Sunday for the holeloffe		ij^{d}
	xxv^{s}	vij^{d} ob

[4]

Item at the aneversar' of Symon Beynet the offeryng		j^{d} ob
Item at the yeretyte of Wyllm' Fyschar		j^{d} ob
Item the ix Sunday for the hole loffe		ij^{d}
Item of John Cowper for a tythe pygke		iij^{d}
Item a tythe calfe of the myller and sold to the same man		xviij^{d}
Item of Thomas Pulter for the tythe eygys	xiij^{s}	iiij^{d}
Items at weydyng of Ranold the offeryng		iiij^{d}
Item (for^{c}) the x Sunday for the hole loffe		ij^{d}
Item at the bereyng of wyffe of Thomas Bawmford		iij^{d} ob
Item at the weydyng J. Blythe the offerng		iiijd ob
Item the xj Sunday for the holeloffe		ij^{d}
Item rec' of W. Porter for viij poyle of tythe wode		xvj^{d}
Item for xx poyle of (th^{c}) tythe wode	iij^{s}	iiij^{d}
Item the xij Sunday for the holeloffe		ij^{d}
	xxj^{s}	viij^{d}

[5]

The rec' begynnyg' at Mydsomer

Imprimis the same day for the offeryng		xix^{d} ob
Item the fyrste Sunday for the holeloffe		ij^{d}
Item the secunde Sunday for holeloffe		ij^{d}
Item at the bereyng of Modyr Angelle the offeryng		vj^{d}
Item at the aneversar' of Thomas Yerrell the offeryng		ij^{d}
Item the iij Sunday for the holeloffe		ij^{d}
Item the iiij Sunday for the hole loffe		ij^{d}
Item the v Sunday for the holeloffe		ij^{d}

Item at the purific' of the wyffe of Garrett a crysum			ij^{d}
Item a pygke of Schomaker and solde to Quycke the price			iij^{d}
Item the vj Sunday for the holeloffe			ij^{d}
Item the vij Sunday for the holeloffe			ij^{d}
Item the viij Sunday for holeloffe			ij^{d}
Item a pygke of Fyschar and sold to the same man the price			iij^{d}
Item the ix Sunday for the holeloffe			ij^{d}
Item at the purific' of the wyffe of T. Samwell a crysum			j^{d}
		iiij^{s}	vj^{d} ob

[6]

Item the x Sunday for the holeloffe			ij^{d}
Item a the purific' of the wyffe of T. Bawmford a crysum			j^{d}
Item a pygke of Marger' Hyllys and sold the same woman			iij^{d} ob
Item the xj Sunday for the holeloffe			ij^{d}
Item the xij Sunday for the holeloffe			ij^{d}
Item the xiij Sunday for the holeloffe			ij^{d}
Item a pygke of Gefferey and sold to Annes Quycke			iij^{d}
Item the xiiij Sunday for the holeloffe			ij^{d}
Item rec' of Porter for the mortuar' of Hullys Hyllys		iij^{s}	iiij^{d}
Item rec' for the mortuare of Symon Beynet		iij^{s}	iiij^{d}
Item sold to Master Lucy xx pygkys the price		v^{s}	
Item delyveryd to Maystur Doctur iiij pygkes			
Item rec' for xij stone of woole iiij^{s} vj^{d} a stone the summe		lvj^{s}	iij^{d}
	iij^{li}	ix^{s}	iiij^{d} ob

[7]

The receytes for pygyns

Imprimis of Mayster Lucy for ij dosyn the price			x^{d}
Item of Annes Quycke for ij dosen			x^{d}
Item of Masteres Malyns a dosen the price			iiij^{d}
Item of Flynt wyfe a dosen the price			v^{d}
Item of Byrde a dosen the price			v^{d}
Item of Marget Pulter (a^{c}) ij dosen the price			x^{d}
Item of T. Pecke ij dosen the price			viij^{d}
Item of Master Lucy iij dose the price			xij^{d}
Item of Thomas Pulter ij dosen and d. price			xij^{d} ob
Item of Annes Quycke ij dosen the price			x^{d}
Item of Thomas Pulter ij dosen the price			ix^{d}
Item of Byrde for ij dosen			x^{d}
Item of Masteres Gostewycke for v dosen the price		ij^{s}	j^{d}
Item delyvered to Master Doctur iiij dosen			
Item (del^{c}) of Annes Quycke iij dosen the price			xij^{d}
Item of Masteres Gostewycke xviij dosen the price			vj^{d} vij^{s}
Item of Annes Quycke (price^{c}) a dosen the price			iiij^{d}
		xix^{s}	viij^{d} ob

[8]

The rec' for straw and chaffe

Imprimis for barle straw (and^{c}) rec' of J. Paternoster for d. a day			v^{d}
Item of W. Bocher for a day			x^{d}

Item of the myller for haffe a day	v^{d}
Item of H. Gullyn for halfe a day	v^{d}
Item of Bonde for halfe a day	v^{d}
Item of Byrde for halfe a day	v^{d}
Item of the pulter of Lundun for halfe a day	v^{d}
Item of R. Hyllys for for a day	x^{d}
Item of T. Sawer for a kenche of straw	iiij^{d}
Item of Peyte for halfe a day	v^{d}
Item of Cleyton for halfe a day	v^{d}
Item of the potter for a day	x^{d}
Item of Hasylden for a day	x^{d}
Item of W. Warde for d. a day	v^{d}
Item of H. Samwell for d. a day	v^{d}
Item of the schomaker for a day	x^{d}
Item of Master Lucy for d. a day	v^{d}
Item of Henr' Gullyn d. a day	v^{d}
Item of J. Ward for d. a day	v^{d}
Item of W. Cowper for a kenche of straw	ix^{d}
	x^{s} viij^{d}

[9]

Item of R. Hyllys for d. a day	v^{d}
Item of J. Ward for d. a day	v^{d}
Item of Byrd for d. a day	v^{d}
Item of Boge for for d. a day	v^{d}
Item of J. Morter for d. a day	v^{d}
Item of J. Warne for d. a day	vj^{d}
Item of Micaell Spenser for for d. a day	vj^{d}
Item of H. Osburne for d. a day	vj^{d}
Item for Master Lucy for d. a day	vj^{d}
Item of Masteres Malyns for d. a day	vj^{d}
Item of J. Warde for d. a day	vj^{d}
Item of Hasylden for d. a day	vj^{d}
Item of W. Warde for d. a day	vj^{d}
Item of W. Cowper for d. a day	vj^{d}
Item of Peyte for d. a day	vj^{d}
Item of W. Bocher for for d. a day	vj^{d}
Item of H. Gullyn for d. a day	vj^{d}
Item of R. Hyllys for d. a day	vj^{d}
Item of J. Potter for d. a day	vj^{d}
	ix^{s} j^{d}

[10]

Peyse straw

Imprimis of Henr' Samwell for a day	ix^{d}
Item of R. Smart for a parcell of straw	iiij^{d}
Item of Quick for d. a day	v^{d}
Item of Porter for a day	xij^{d}
Item of Paternoster for a day	xij^{d}
Item of R. Kox for d. a day	vj^{d}
Item of H. Gullyn for d. a day	vj^{d}

Item of Mergar' Hyllys for d. a day		vj[d]
Item of W. Bocher for d. a day		vj[d]
Item for Peyte for for d. a day		vj[d]
Item for J. Ward for d. a day		vj[d]
Item of Scheltun for d. a day		vj[d]
Item for the myler for d. a day		vj[d]
Item to Modyr Neyvell for a parcel of straw		ij[d]
Item of Maystur Lucy for the weyte peyse straw		ij[d]

For chaff

Imprimis of R (R[c]) Hyllys for x quarter		xviij[d]
Item of W. Cowper for chaffe		xvj[d]
Item of the myller for xv quarter	ij[s]	iiij[d]
Item of Schorte Pecke for chaffe		
Item of W. Cowper for x quarter		xviij[d]
Item of T. Pulter for chaffe	vj[s]	vj[d]
Item of the fuller for v quarter		viij[d]
Item of Flyt for chaffe	iij[s]	viij[d]
Item for the wenoyng peyse chaffe		xij[d]
	xxix[s]	viij[d] [sic]

[11]

The rec' for Meyde

Imprimis for the Swanpenclose	xvj[s]	
Item of Mastur Lucy for ij lowdys of hey in the Bereclose	v[s]	iiij[d]
Item of Henr' Gullyn for hey owt of the same close	iij[s]	iiij[d]
Item careyd whom a lowde owt of the same close		
Item of Mastur Lucy (of Mastur Lucy[c]) for the tythe of hys close	ij[s]	

The Weste Meyde

Imprimis of John Verdew for the tythe of ix acre	iij[s]	ij[d]
Item of J. Peyte for acre		viij[d]
Item Angnes Scharp for iij acre and a rode		xiij[d]
Item of Henr' Keytyns a acre and halfe		vj[d]
Item of Gefferey Osburne a acre and d.		vj[d]
Item of Bokyngam a acre and d.		vj[d]
Item of Ric' Samwell a acre and d.		vj[d]
Item of Watur' Boteler for a acre		iiij[d]
Item of Scheltun for halfe a acre		ij[d]
Item of John Warde for iiij acre		xvj[d]
Item of Feysand for ij acre		viij[d]
Item of Ric' Pecke for v acre		xx[d]
Item of H. Osburne for ij acre		viij[d]
	xxxviij[s]	v[d]

[p 12]

Item of Merweyder a acre		iiij[d]
Item of W. Bocher a acre		iiij[d]

The Est Meyde

Imprimis of Peyte for vij acres of meyd	ij[s]	iiij[d]
Item of the meller for halfe a acre		ij[d]

Item of Roger Quicke for iij acres		xij^{d}
Item of Bokyngam for iij acres and a rode		xiij^{d}
Item of Ric Samwell a acre and a halfe		vj^{d}
Item of John Warner for a acre		iiij^{d}
Item of Eyre for ij acres		viij^{d}

The Heymede

Imprimis rec' of W. Wuttun for parcell of meyde		xv^{d}
Item of Wyllm' Samwell a parcell of meyde		xx^{d}
Item of J. Osburne and Fynne for the tythe Barkarysmeyd	ij^{s}	
Item of Wypperles for the tythe of the Kow meyde		xij^{d}
Item J. Cowper for the tythe of the Ox home		xij^{d}
Item rec' of T. Pulter for the the [sic] of hys close	ij^{s}	
Item rec' for the tythe of the Clemeyd	ij^{s}	
	xvij^{s}	viij^{d}

[13]

Mogurhanger Meyd

Imprimis the dyche furlong	ix^{s}	
The Kowmeyd	ij^{s}	iiij^{d}
Item the longe Eyrydlond and Schorte	vj^{s}*	iiij^{d}
Item the Eymeyde	vj^{s}	
Item the Dammysend	vj^{s}	
Item Oxhyllys	ij^{s}	iiij^{d}
Item Wyppyngpole	ij^{s}	iiij^{d}
Item Trumpyngtun Hoke	iij^{s}	iiij^{d}
Item the Stykbeke and the Fenne	vij^{s}	
Item recevyd for a quarter of wyete peyse	iiij^{s}	
	xlviij^{s}	viij^{d}

[14]

The rec' for peyse

Imprimis rec' of Mastur Lucy for iij buschelles and a half			xxj^{d}
Item of W. Chessam for halfe a quart of peyse		ij^{s}	
Item of Thomas Pulter for iij quarter iij^{s} viij^{d} a quarter		xj^{s}	
Item J. Osburne a quarter the price		iij^{s}	viij^{d}
Item of rec' of Masteres Malyns for a buschell			vj^{d}
Item of Wyllm Pecke for xv quarter of pey iiij^{s} a quarter	iij^{li}		
Item rec of Ranold for halfe buschell			iij^{d}
Item rec' of the man of the Hartys Horne for a buschell			vj^{d}
Item sende to the Wrast by W. Tomas the xxix day of Apryll iij buschelles			
Item by the same man the x day of Jule iij bushcelles			
Item to Mastur Doctur ij buschelles			
Item when they fachyd Rye a busch and a halfe			
Item spende on the horses in lent (r^{c}) a busche a halfe			
	iij^{li}	xix^{s}	viij^{d}

[15]

The receytes for barle and malte

Imprimis of Mastur Lucy for ij quarterys of barle	vj^{s}	viij^{d}
Item Thomas Pulter for iij quarter of barle	xj^{s}	

Item rec of J. Osburne for a quarter of barle	iij^{s}	viij^{d}
Item rec of Annes Quicke for a quarter of malt	iiij^{s}	
Item of J. Warde and H. Gullyn for a quarter of malte	iiij^{s}	
Item delyveryd to the churche a quarter		
Item brued at Blonham in lent a quater		
Item delyveryd Curtes of Elstow of malt viij schore and x quarterys		
Item for the watur	vj^{s}	
Item for the Eylond	vj^{s}	
Recept	xl^{s}	xvj^{d}
Summa Totalis xxiij^{li} x^{s} j^{d} ob		

[16]

The payments for the parsonage of Blonham begyng at Sent Micaelis day the yere of the rane of owr soferand Lorde King Henry the viij the xxx yere [1538]

Imprimis payd to Mereweyder odde money for pygkys		j^{d} ob
Item payd the v day of october for wyne		ij^{d}
Item the same day for oyle		j^{d} ob
Item payd to Cleytun for thakyng ij days and a half v^{d} a day		xij^{d} ob
Item payd the xix day of October for wyne		ij^{d}
Item payd for takyng of ij swanys at Temysford		j^{d}
Item for W. Tomas dyner and hys felow when they fachyd rye		ij^{d}
Item payd Wypperley for makyng the oxstall		vj^{d}
Item payd to W Cowper odde money for pykys		j^{d}
Item payd to H. Lonysdale odde money for pygkys		j^{d} ob
Item payd the ij day of November for wyne		ij^{d}
Item payd to Owmfrey od mone for pygkys		j^{d}
Item pay for frankynsens		ij^{d}
Item payd (for the ^{c}) xvj day of november for wyne		ij^{d}
Item payd for heyrethred to sow the heyre		j^{d}
Item payd for ij seckys	ij^{s}	
Item payd the last day of November for wyne		ij^{d}
Item payd to Henr' Samwell for iij dosen and halfe of larkys		xiiij^{d}
Item payd to Verdew for ij ropys for W. Tomas		vj^{d}
Item payd for a cord for Wakefyld anodyr for Boge		ij^{d}
Item payd for makyng of the new buschell		iiij^{d}
Item payd the xiiij day of december for wyne		ij^{d}
	vij^{s}	ix^{d}

[17]

The paymentes begynyng a Cristumas

Imprimis for the clarkys brekfast the same day		viij^{d}
Item payd for ij C of syngyng brede		ij^{d}
Item pay for W. Tomas drynkde ij tymys		ij^{d}
Item to Mary Hylles od mone for pygkes		j ob
Item to T. Pecke for careyng of vi lodys of wood	ij^{s}	
Item payd to Fynne od mone for pygkes		j^{d} ob
Item payd for ij lynys for a tramell		viij^{d}
Item payd for a heyrynlyne for the dragke		x^{d}

Item payd for mendyng of the trunke		j^{d}
Item payd for mendyng of the dragk		ij^{d}
Item payd for packethrede to mend the nett		ij^{d}
Item payd to Turner the fallyng of a rode of wood		xvj^{d}
Item payd for lampoyle		ij^{d}
Item payd for makyng the pascall and ij tapurs		j^{d}
Item for W. Tomas and hys felow when they fachyd weyte		ij^{d}
Item to Robert Tomas for ij dosen larkys		viij^{d}
Item for C nayle to mende the bott		iiij^{d}
Item payd for a stene of pyche		x^{d}
Item pay for wyne to serve the church thys quarter		xij^{d}
Item payd to Wypperley for mendyng the botte		v^{d}
Item to the same man for leyyng a syl yn the kechyn and a dog-pece in the entre of the kechyn		vj^{d}
	x^{s}	viij^{d}

[18]

The paymets begyng' at Sent Mareday

Imprimis to Masteres Malyns for the half swan bredyng on hyr grownde		xvj^{d}
Item payd to Mathow (of^{c}) odmoney for a cawfe		j^{d}
Item payd to Turner for fallyng of half a rode of wood		viij^{d}
Item payd for iiij galans of wyne for Estur x a galan	iij^{s}	iiij^{d}
Item payd for iij C howsyllyng brede		iij^{d}
Item pay for oyle and creme		iiij^{d}
Item payd for frankynsens		ij^{d}
Item for W. Tomas when fachyd rye		j^{d}
Item for bred and drynke when we waschyd the auterys		viij^{d}
Item payd to R. Samwell odmoy for pygkys		j^{d}
Item for master Henry servandes for the logyng at Fynnys		iij^{d}
Item payd for Artur when he fat the oxen		j^{d} ob
Item to Turner for fallyng of a rode of wood		xvj^{d}
Item payd to J. Tomas for fallyng of xxx pole of wood		xij^{d}
Items for reymovyng the weyt yn the barne		j^{d}
Item for W. Tomas and his felow when they fat Weyte and Rye		ij^{d}
Item payd for wyne to serve the churche that quarter		xij^{d}
	x^{s}	xj^{d} ob

[19]

Item payde to Verdew for a peyre of bode trases and iij peyre of lasche trasys and iij half ropys and vj penne halterys	v^{s}	ij^{d}
Item payd to the same man for a heyryn rope		iiij^{d}
Item payd for wyne to serve the churche a quarter of the yere		xij^{d}
Item at the chosyng of the clarke of the convocacion to make certyficat at Northehamtun		viij^{d}
Item payd to T. Pecke for careyng of vij lowdes of wood	ij^{s}	iiij^{d}
Item to Wakefeld for makyng xlvj bays abowte the parsonag	iij^{s}	iiij^{d}
Item payd for dygyng of xij lowd of cley		vj^{d}
Item for careyng the same cley		xij^{d}
Item to Wakefeld for makyng the heyg' betwene Wutun		xij^{d}

Item for makyng of the heyg to Hyllys ward		vj^{d}
Item payd to Wakefeld for kepyng of the oxen begynyg on Sent Nicolas day contenoyng unto Low Sunday conteynyg xviij wekys xvj^{d} a weke the summe	xxiiij^{s}	
	xxxix^{s}	x^{d}

[20]

The peymentes begynnyg at Mydsomer

Imprimis for Ric. Pecke for ij days (f^{c}) thackyng fyndyng hymself		xij^{d}
Item to Wakefell to fynd hymselfe to serve hym		viij^{d}
Item drawyng to thacke		iiij^{d}
Item for W. Tomas dyner and his felow when they fat the last weyte		ij^{d}
Item payd to Robert Fyschar odmoney for pygkys		j^{d}
Item payd to Owmfrey odmoney for pygkes		j^{d}
Item payd to Warner odmoney for pygkes		j^{d} ob
Item for drawyng of thake for the walle		iij^{d}
Item for thackyng of the walle		v^{d}
Item for servyng of the thacker		iij^{d}
Item payd for a man to mowe wyell Wakefeld went with the swanherd ij days		viij^{d}
Item payd to Mager' Hylles odmoney for pygkys		j^{d} ob
Item to Bokyngam for careyng ij lowdys of hey		viij^{d}
Item to J. Osburne for careyng of ij lowdys of hey		viij^{d}
Item to H. Osburne for careyng a lowd of hey owt of the Pertre close		iij^{d}
Item to Gefferey for careyng a lowd of hey		iiij^{d}
Item for makyng of v lowd of hey iij^{d} a lowde		xv^{d}
Item for a lowd yn the closys		ij^{d} ob
	vij^{s}	vj^{d} ob

TURVEY CHURCHWARDENS' ACCOUNTS 1551-1552

Because of the rarity and importance of early churchwardens' accounts, the surviving Bedfordshire material was published by the Society in 1953. *Elizabethan Churchwardens' Accounts* edited by the Rev. J.E. Farmiloe and Rosita Nixseaman (BHRS Vol. 33) included full transcripts of the accounts for three parishes in the east of the County, namely Clifton 1543, 1589-1608, Northill 1561-1612, and Shillington 1571-1604. The volume also included an analytical introduction.

When these accounts were published in 1953 the existence of the Turvey accounts for 1551-2 was unknown. They survive among the Stopford-Sackville manuscripts at the Northamptonshire Record Office (ref: SS 1808), and consist of three pages torn from an account book. The pages are 12 inches high and were originally about 4½ inches wide. The inclusion of the accounts in this volume completes the publication of the Bedfordshire material of the period before 1600.

Editorial method

The entries are dated 1551-1552 and are written partly in English and partly in Latin, all in a difficult hand. The Latin passages, which have been translated into modern English, are shown in italics. They usually deal with formal matters such as meetings and statements of accounts. The original spelling has been retained for the passages in English, although contracted forms of Christian names have been replaced by the full names in modern spelling.

The accounts

Although they cover an unsettled period in English religious history, these accounts contain little to indicate the prevailing climate of uncertainty and change. There are, however, clues. In addition to the name of Richard Woodford, the Rector, and his churchwardens, the accounts also mention the 'collectors of the towne rentes' suggesting that the church was well endowed with property, and in 1551 there is a reference to the 'wardens of the sepulcre lyght'.

In 1552 there is a payment of two shillings and ten pence 'in harnyst [earnest] at Bedfforde a Fore the Kinges Jstys [Justice] ffor . . . chorche goodes the exspenses' — undoubtedly a reference to the compilation of the Edwardian Inventories of church goods in that year. Sadly the actual return for Turvey has not survived.

In general, however, the accounts deal largely with routine matters such as Visitation expenses, minor repairs to the church, work on the bells, washing the surplice, and purchase of bread and wine for the communion. More interesting are the references to a May Ale in 1552 and to work on the roof and windows of the church by the plumber and glazier of Elstow, while the reference to the clock is the earliest mention of a church clock in the County.

Chris Pickford

[S.S.1808(a)r]

Turvey
Thexamynacon' of thaccomptes of Wylliam Ball & Wylliam Nycolles wardens of the sepulcre lyght, Robert Batson & Thomas Stevynson church wardens and Thomas Stevyns & Edward Faxton wardens & collectors of the towne rentes accordynge as they be wrytten with t'hand of Edward Wall Gent. auditor to the lord Mordaunt, the vijth day of June *in the fifth year of the reign of King Edward VI [1551]*

Videlicet In the account of the aforesaid William Ball & William Nycolles at the end of the same account it appears that they owe 62s 11½d — *62s 11½d*

From which is charged:
Richard Woodford rector of the church of Turvey 20s
The accountants themselves for their own arrears 42s 11½d

In the account of the aforesaid Robert Batson & Thomas Stevynson wardens of the church, at the end of the same account it appears that they owe 66s 8d — *66s 8d*

From which is charged:
Richard Woodford rector of the church of Turvey 5s 6d
The accountants themselves for their own arrears 61s 2d

In the account of the aforesaid Thomas Stevyns & Edward Faxton wardens & collectors of the town rents, at the end of the same account it appears that they owe £4 5s 2d — *£4 5s 2d*

From which is charged:
William Skevyngton — *5s*
The accountants themselves . . . — *£4 2d*

Sum Total of the aforesaid three debts £10 14s 9½d

Examination by Richard Woodforde William Lyon Thomas Stevyns William Adams William Skevyngton William Ball William Nycolles Richard Asshton John Hilles Richard Lylliott Thomas Lawton Robert Batson Thomas Stevynson William Longworth John Boys and others gathered in the rectory of Turvey on the day and year above mentioned.

[S.S.1808(a)v]

On the day & year written below:
Stephen Osmonte William Purrior elected churchwardens for the following year
Robert Batson & Thomas Stevynson the old churchwardens delivered into the hands of the new wardens aforesaid — *£3 14d*

William Ball & William Nycolles delivered into the hands of William Adams with the agreement of the parishioners 42s 11½d, which sum of money the aforesaid William Adams redelivered into the hands of William Purrior one of the church wardens in the presence of Thomas Stevyns bailiff of Turvey on the [?]15th (quinto[c]) (xv[to i]) day of June in the fifth year of the reign of King Edward VI [1551]
42s 11½d

[signed] by me Thomas Stevynes

Payments

Item:	for leyng outt the sayd day that I Recevede the chursse - - - [?revenue]	xiiij - - -	
Item:	for a boke at the Vissytassyon		vj[d]
Item:	the exspenses at the Vyssythass'	j[s]	v[d]
	Sum jv[s] ij[d] paid before the fall of money		
Item:	for the church gate	xj[s]	j[d]
Item:	for the Vyssytassyon' off Synmychyell		xj[d]
Item:	for wythess' for the baudryk off the belles and for maykynge off them		xxj[d]
Item:	to Robertte Norman' For mendyng' off the churche dorre		ij[d]

[S.S.1808(b)r]

Item:	to Jhon Smythe for mendyng off the locke off the churche dorre		x[d]
	& for a chaye [key] & a locke mendyng to the steppyll doore		vj[d]
Item:	to Ellyn' Stox for mendyng off the sorplys		iiij[d]
Item:	To the plomer of Elnestowe for 4 days of himself & his boy mendynge the leads about the churche, le day for himself & his boy xj[d]	iij[s]	viij[d]
Item:	to Kateryn' Batson, for their borde the same 4 days	iiij[s]	
Item:	to the same plomer' for xxix li. of soder, le li ix[d] in toto	xxj[s]	ix[d]
Item:	for nayles to the same plomer'		xij[d]

Paid by the churchwardens in the month of March in the 6th year of Edward VI [1552]

Item:	Paid to the glasiar of Elnestowe for glasyng the wyndoes in dyvers places about the churche, beynge hired to mende the same and fyndynge glasse by grete [at a fixed rate] paid by bothe the churche-wardens in Aprill *in the 6th year of the aforesaid reign.*	x[s]	
And to Robert Norman for mendyng the grete bell whele			ij[d]
And to Lane of Carleton for mendyng the bauderykes of the belles, paid *in the month of April in the year aforesaid*			ij[d]

[S.S.1808(b)v]

Item: the viij day of May, expenses at the Wysetassyon at Bedfforde xx^{d}
A geyn Wyssentyed [Whitsuntide] I bawte too belle rowppes ij^{s} iiij^{d}
& in harnyst [earnest] at Bedfforde a Fore the Kinges Jstys [Justice] ffor - - - chorche goodes the exspenses ij^{s} x^{d}
& off Mykyellmas geven at Bedfforde for the Wyssytassyon the exspenses xxij^{d}
Item: layid out for the bowl of - - - communion - - - - - -
Item: peyid to Elyn Stokkes for wahssyng the churche clothes ij^{s}
Item: peyid to Wylliam Smythe for 2 mattes in the chancell xxj^{d}
Item: for breyd and wyne to the communion x^{d}
Sum paid sinze the latter fall of money iij^{li} xiv^{s} v^{d}
Sum of all payments as above appears *£4[?] 18s 7d*

[S.S.1808(c)r]

Thaccompt of Stevyn Osmont & William Purrior the churche wardens made before the parysshe on Christemas day *in the sixth year of the reign of Edward VI [1552]*

The charge of the said churche wardens:

First: the money that they receyvdd at their entrance iij^{li} xiiij^{d}
Item: they received of Wylliam Adams xlij^{s} xj^{d} ob
Item: they receyved of the parysshe at the May Ale with x.s. for my lordes rewards, *this sixth year of the aforesaid King* lvi^{s} viij^{d}

Sum total of their charges viij^{li} ix^{d} ob
From which the said churche Wardens paide as apperith in the leaf before and before the fall of the money iv^{s} ij^{d}
The said churche Wardens paid alsoe since the latter fall of the money as apperith before iij^{li} xiiij^{s} v^{d}
Sum of all payments as well before and sinz the fall of money iij^{li} xviij^{s} vij^{d}
And there is owed *£4 2s 2½d*
the same churche Wardens had in their handes at both the falls of the money xlvj^{s} vij^{d} ob
which by the falles was but xxiij^{s} iij^{d} ob qr

(And they had lend out to Wylliam Freysbe before the Fall liij^{s} iiij^{d} *deleted*)

Thus there is owed *58s 10¾d*
On William Freysbeas parcell 53s 4d to the same William Adams given before the fall by the foresaid William Purrior with the consent of the said William *21s 4d*
And above the aforesaid accounts *37s 6¾d*

[S.S.1808(c)v]

The whiche issue of xxxvij^{s} vj^{d} ob qr was delyvered the said Christemas daye to Thomas Lambert & Wylliam Sprott then chosen for the new Wardens for the yere folowyng.

Item:	peyid to John Osmond smyth for mendyng of the clokk	xx[d]
Item:	payid for wyne 2 quartes	xij[d]
Item:	At another tyme for wyne	ij[d]
Item:	for breydd to the communion	vij[d]
Item:	payed to Lane of Carleton for mendyng the bell baudryxe	iij[d]
Item:	for mendyng of the forbel and makyn a claspe to the same	. . .
Item:	payed to George Andrew for skouryng the ledes	ij[d]
Item:	to Robert Norman for mendyng the greyt bell wele and mendyng of formes	iiij[d]
Item:	payd for a wyne bottle	iiij[d]
	Sum total	*4s 11d*
	paid by Thomas Lambert	

[S.S.1808(a, b, & c)]

List of personal names in the manuscript

Page references give the page: a, b, or c, and the side recto or verso.

Adams, William	ar, av, cr	Mordaunt, the lord	ar
Andrew, George	cv	Norman, Robert	av, cv
Asshton, Richard	ar	Nycolles, William	ar, cv
Ball, William	ar, av	Osmond, John	cv
Batson, Robert	ar, av	Osmont(e), Stephen	av, cr
Batson, Keterin	br	Purrior, William	ax, cr
Boys, John	ar	Skevington, William	ar, av
Faxton, Edward	ar	Smythe, John	br
Freysbe, William	cr	Smythe, William	bv
Hilles, John	ar	Sprott, William	cv
Lambert, Thomas	cv	Stevyns, Thomas	ar, av
Lane of Carleton	br, cv	Stevynson, Thomas	ar, av
Lawton, Thomas	ar	Stockes (Stoxe), Elyn	br, bv
Longworth, William	ar	Wall, Edward	ar
Lylliot, Richard	ar	Woodford, Richard	ar
Lyon, William	ar		

Names of church officials

Rector:	Richard Woodford	
Churchwardens:	Robert Batson Thomas Stevynson	'old' June 1551
	Stephen Osmont William Purrior	'new' June 1551
	Thomas Lambert William Sprott	'new' December 1552
Wardens of the Sepulchre light:	William Ball William Nycolles	'old' June 1551
Collectors of the town rents:	Thomas Stevyns Edward Faxton	'old' June 1551

Bedfordshire Archidiaconal Visitations for 1578

Among the records of the Bedford Archdeaconry deposited at the Bedfordshire County Record Office is a volume (cat. no. ABC 3) containing court proceedings for the archdeaconry in 1578. It contains also on pp. 3-13 and 206-215 the presentments of churchwardens at the archidiaconal visitations in April and October 1578, which are transcribed below.

[p 3]

Detecta in Visitatione domini Archidiaconi Bedd'
8 et 9 Aprilis anno 1578

Felmersham Richard Leache, Robert Rotham, and Thomas Leache have not receaved the Communion at Easter last. William Burye, Thomas Hodsone, Robert Otwaye & his wife for the lyke offence.

Bedford Cutbertes Carent multis necessarijs, vide billam.

Farandiche The chancell & parsonage are in decaye by the parson's defalt. They have but one sermon this year.

Wooton The chancell is in decaye at the Quene's defalte. William Borne of Marston detayneth a legacye of iij^{s} iiij^{d} by the yeare for the poore of Wotton. He is behinde for xx yeares.

Turvey Adre Cooper was gotten with childe in Turvey by Thomas Parkins of Hygham.

Patnam [Pavenham] Our chansell is in decaye & redye to faule downe, at the defaute of Trynitye College in Cambridge.

Bletsoo We present our parson for cuttinge tymber of all the parsonage grownds. Our chancell is a little oute of repayre.

Bidnam We doe present that we had no Communion but once this yeare, and that our last churchwardens dyd not make there accompte for the yere, Thomas Wryghte, Bartholomewe Brytten.

[p 4]

Chellington Our chancell is in decaye at the parson's defalte, but the parson hathe begone to mende hit. Our churche wyndowes want glasinge. Our parson hathe ij benefycyes.

Carelton Our cancell is in decaye at our parson's defalte. Henrye Bytheraye & his wyfe doe lyve asunder, & that our parson hathe ij benefycyes & he is not resydent with us.

Kempstone Joanes A Hewe is suspected to lyve incontynentlye with a wydowe, she is called by the name of Williamsonne's daughter, as the common fame goeth within the parish.

Bedford Sancti Petri **[sic]** There is no pulpitte in the littel churche. The x commandments are not on the walles. The chancell & churche are not paved in some places.

Bedford Peters **[sic]** Rafe Wylson kepte Davys Buckham his wyfe in his howse, he hathe had warninge to put hir awaye & wyll not.

Milton Harnes There is a suspicion of whoredom betweene William Swyngland & John Fletchers wyfe. The vicar hathe cut downe trees in the churche yarde & not employed them upon the cancell nor mansion howse.
[interleaved ABC 3a
[r]
Exco' ultimo Aprilis anno 1578 apud Amptill
[v]

This may certify your worship that our vicar hathe solde fyve ashe trees which did growe in the churchyard of Milton Ernes, and hath converted money thereof into other tymber more necessarye for the reparing of his house being in decay, in witnes wherof we the churchwardens have set to our handes.

X Thomas Jackson mark
X John Church his mark]

Bedford Sancti Johannis Theyre churche is in decaye & other thinges besydes, but they wyll reforme them withoute anye further authorytye. Item that the mynister weareth not his surples at the Communion. Item the chancell is in decaye by the falte of Mr Linford. Item Elizabeth Jussoppe is with childe.

[p 5]

Item. Amys Glover dothe not come to the churche upon the Saboth daye. Item Davye Price cometh not to the churche to be catekysed nor to the dyvyne service. Item Robert Groves cometh not oftentymes to the churche upon the Saboth daye.

Coople Alice Churche is with child by Nicholas Gawnte. The vicar Mr Rosen is not resydent.

Woodill [Odell] John Felpe of Harrolde dothe not keepe his parishe churche on the saboth daye, but goeth commonlye from towne to towne & selleth meate on the Sondayes.

Bedford Sancte Maries Mistres Gostwicke cometh not to the churche to heare dyvyne servyce.

Eton [deanery]

Eaton ij women went awaye from John Godyn of Eaton at Michaelmas or there aboutes with childe as the common fame is.

Thurlye We present one wyndowe broken of late, we truste to crave your goodness in that case for hit shalbe made in all haste.

Roxton Cancellus ruinosus culpa collegij Trinitatis in Cantabrigia. Thomas Bayes of Tempsford & Elizabeth Newman of Roxton do lyve incontynentlye as the common fame goeth.

Stoughton parva The parsonage is downe by the defaute of the parson & that Henrye Marborough is farmer of that parsonage.

[p 6]

Colmorth Nicholas Dicons receaved not these ij yeres. Thomas Judde dyd not receave last yere. John Blye dyd not receave at Easter, neyther William Quarrell, Margaret Quarell, Thomas Kinge, Anne Moosley, (Thomas Watson[c]). Item Thomas Watson suspected with Agnes Mascole the wyfe of Raphe Maschole for evell lyvinge.

Wyldon Alice Wylshere was absent one daye from churche, but she is contente to paye xij[d].

Ravensden An evill hedge of the churche yerde, thoroughe Thomas Cappman his defalte.

Risleye John Malte is suspected to lyve incontynentlye with Elizabeth Lystlowe, as the common fame goeth in the parishe. Agnes Jonson is a common sower of discorde & a slanderer of hir neyghbors.

Shefford et Dunstable [deaneries]

Blunham Anne Trouton hathe had ij children at one byrthe by Francis Bearde hir brother by the mothers syde.

Olde Warden Anne Wood came to our towne from London & there delyvered of a child, the father we knowe not.

Sondey Thomas Browne dyd receave into his howse his wyfes sister beinge with child, & beinge forbidden by the churchewardens sayd she shoulde putte the towne to no charge, & she went awaye unchurched.

[p 7]

Milton Brian Agnes Aires alias Stephen, gotten with child at Luton by John Egleton alias Cobbe dwellinge with W. Bruce of Luton. Item Lewes Iffens [?] of Milton because he wyll not paye his dewe unto the clerke for a howse called Sandrege for iiij yeres & a halfe.

Streatlye The vicar hathe ij benefyces.

Shitlington Certayne pales belonginge to Holwelberye of our Churche yarde are owte of repration which were latlye in the handes of Thomas Snagg & nowe beinge in the handes of Mr John Sancte Jones.

Barton Thouroughe certayne controversyes betweene the parson & his parishioners, certeyne have not receaved, as John Prior th'elder, Thomas Prior th'elder, Nicholas Denton, Thomas Lawrence, with others. Item Samuell Fuller our parson withholdeth from the parishe a bushell of malte & a pecke of wheate dewe by custome to us at Hocktyde, a bushell of wheate & a bushell of malte dewe by custome at Whitsontyde also. Item wee have no homelyes reade. Item wee have no other sermons than he maketh hyme selfe.

Stotfold William Crouche withholdeth certayne money from the towne dewe unto the towne.

[p 8]

Langford Our cancell wyndowes are in decaye broken & the roofe thereof lyke to falle, theroughe Mr Wynche his defalte.

Camelton cum Shefford Agnes Spratte for keepinge hir daughter Alice Spratte beinge begotten with childe at Shefford as we thinke.

Tylsworth We have had but one sermone since Michaelmas, which was the Sondaye after New yers daye.

Southill Tratters wyfe is not yet absolved. Item Mr Marboroughe beinge parson dothe not repayre our cancell beinge in decaye. Item Thomas Tylcocke wold have had his pleasure of Laussey his wife.

Arleseye The fence of the churche yarde is lette forthe to be mended & not yet done.

Carrington John Robertes serveth under our vicar & wee knowe not whether he be lycensed so to do or no.

Henloo Thomas Underwood the younger is suspected to lyve incontynentlye with the wyfe of Thomas Fare, as the commom fame goeth in the parishe.

[p 9]

Toternhoo We present the servant of James Cossontene for goynge awaye in Lent & we knowe not whether she hathe receaved the communion or not at Easter, but she is come agayne.

Hockley We present John West for fellinge of certayne trees in the churche yarde, and hathe solde them but hathe made no accompte for them. He was presented the last visytation by Richard Skame, John Groome, & Robert Dolte.

Houghton Regis We present that one Barbara Dicons is with child gotten by one John Stringer, as the reporte is, who is deade, beinge not maryd lawfullye.

Over Gravenhurste Item wee present that our churche fence is owte of repayre thoroughe the defalt of the towne, but the tymber is provided redye to make hit.

[p 10]

Flyghte [deanery]

Marston We present John Theede in absentynge hymselfe from the churche for the most parte of this whole yere last past, and as yet hathe not receaved the communion syns Easter was xij monthes.

Item in the howse of the sayd Theede are nowe susteyned and mayntayned dyvers women, that is to saye one olde woman havinge ij daughters, th'one nowe of late gone awaye & th'other nowe beinge there who was before Michaelmas last suspected to be with child and went hir waye oute of the towne, and after she was delyvered come agayne & nowe remayneth there & is conducted from place to place by one William Humberstone late of Amptill, nowe come to be a dweller in Theede his house, which Humberstone hathe not receaved the communion in lyke maner. Mr Snag bound Theede in v li. to put them aweaye, he hathe not.

Eversholt Thomas Hamton gent hathe not receaved the communion this yeare. Item Edouard Boodyll hathe (begotten[c]) reported that he hathe had carnall knowlege of Marrye Nitingale. Item Margaret Alee is delyvered of a child, but who is father we knowe not.

[p 11]

Cranfeyld Our churche mowndes are in decaye. Item William Purryer hathe withholden a legacye geven to the poore of our parish thes ij yeres, the which is iij^{s} iiij^{d} a yere, but nowe the sayd William is wyllinge to paye the sayd legacye. Item Francis Fuller cometh not to the churche upon the Sabothe daye as he owte to doe.

Milbrooke The wyfe of Francis Stouton is a slanderer of hir neyghbors.

Tingryfe William Fenson dyd begette Margarette Soulde with child before they were maryed & nowe they are maryed. Item they have not receaved this Easter. Item William Welles is suspected to lyve incontinentlye with Julian Knighte, as the common fame goeth within the parishe. Item our parson is not resydent. Item Thomas White hewed wod on our Ladye Daye.

Pulloxhill Item that Robert Barber & Thomas Barber doe lette the chancell in decaye.

Fletweeke We present Elizabeth Sondon to be broughte in child bed in Flygthtweeke, the father wee knowe not, the brute [rumour] is that the father is John Beele of Malden.

[p 12]

Westoninge Marye Stevens hathe had a child by Enocke Smithe.

Ridgemont Thomas Rowbyns begotte his wyfe with child before he maryed hir.

Lytlington The churche yarde is in decaye, but that we wyll repayre hit agayne.

Malden Vide billam de Flyghtweeke hinc compar'. John Cherye of Pulloxhill hathe separated hyme selfe from his wyfe at Malden, and hathe not come to his parishe churche there, nor receaved but once this ij yere.

Flytton Our mynister hathe not lycence to serve & that he serveth ij cures.

Harlington Our vicar hathe ij benefyces. Item Thomas Bowsered hathe not receaved the communion this yeare. Item Richard Kyllingworth of Flighte dothe owe unto the poore of our parishe v^{s} for iij yeres rent of a cowe.

[p 13]

Clophill We present William Spellinge the 23 of Marche beinge then called Palme Sondaye in the churche & tyme of eveninge prayer, before suche maydes as then had receaved the communion, dyd in theyre seate lye upon his backe verye unreverentlye tyll the'ende of the fyrste lesson, and also other tymes dothe seem to forgette to yeilde dewe reverence in the tyme of dyvyne service. Item Edouard Fysher gentleman hathe not receaved the communion sence Easter nowe ij yeres past in our parishe, but he hathe promised to prepare hymselfe thereunto on Sondaye nexte. Item Agnes the wyfe of Michaele Tylcocke hathe byne complayned of for hir incontynencye & hathe not done penance accordinglye, but suche as she thought good.

[p 206]

Presentata in visitatione domini archidiaconi Bed' apud Bedford et Wooburne, 1 et 2 Octobris anno 1578

Shefford et Dunstable [deaneries]

Tuddington John Menard, William Smithes man, dyd gette Margaret, his masters mayde, with childe. She is gone. Item John Fuller refuseth to paye the moneye he was levyed at by the whole parishe towardes the reparations of our churche.

Langford Our chancell is owte of repayre in tymber & wyndowes, at the parsons defaute. Our churche wyndowes are in decaye by reason of fowle that cometh in at the chancell wyndowes which hathe broken them.

Campton cum Shefford Elizabeth Grinston is a common scole & an eavesdropper. Item William, Mr Thomas man, dyd mowe corne on the Sabothe daye. Item Robert Pror & Alice Hewes are suspected of incontynencye, & the sayd Robert suer to others. Item Michaele Izaac wyll not come to the churche on the Saboth daye.

Houghton Regis Presentant John Welles of the Heathe & Reache upon talke dothe resort to one Brownes wyfe whom they thinke lyveth incontynentlye with hir & so is it commonlye reported. Item W. Haukens th'elder dyd not receave the communion sence Christmas.

[p 207]

Stotfold Presentant Richard Freeman for getting with childe Anne Ares beinge not maryed to hir. Item Edouard Hoggas the like offender with Jo. Harradowne. Cate Wrighte hathe not receaved sence the tyme of hir offence, neyther done hir penance.

Over Gravenhurste Mistress Poore dyd mend hir parte of the churche yarde & pulled hit uppe agayne.

Studham The chancell is oute of repayre by the defalte of the Quene & hir servers, whose names are William Hallse other we knowe not.

Chalgrave Luke Heade in the parishe of Chalgrave hathe gotten with childe Margerye Shellye, who upon Michaelmas daye last was maryed at Hockley.

Eyghton [Eaton Bray] John Buckmaster dyd mysuse the scholemaster in the churche for beatinge of the children of the sayd John. Item Robert Ashewell for not lyvinge with his wyfe. He cometh not to his parishe churche.

Shitlington Creeke the scholemaster kepeth a suspected person in his house who is with childe. Item Pearse cometh not the churche on the Sabothe deye.

[p 208]

Cadington Per vicarium: Harrye Chambers & his wyfe, William Braye & his wyfe, Umpherye Waterton & his wife, Oliver Slater & his wyfe have not receaved the communion accordinge to the Quenes Iniunctions.

Barton Nicholas Denton & William Crawley have not receaved the communion. They have offered themselves but the parson will not receave them. Item John Prior & Thomas Mathewe for not paying the clarkes wages.

Sandey Present one sir Owen the curat of Sandey because he dyd marrye a yonge woman, but wee know not hir name and she was with child before she was maryed to hyme.

Tempsford Presentant Edouard Nookes theyre curat for that they knowe not whether he hathe taken orders or no.

Blunham Presentant Jone Richardson hathe maryed with her husbandes brothers sonne, also Thomas Bysley for that he hathe betrothed hymselfe unto Margaret Samuell abowte ij yeres sence & nowe denyeth to marrye with hir.

[209]

Barford Cancelli sunt ruinosi culpa collegij Trinitatis in Cantabrigia.

Southill The cancell is in decaye at Mr Marboroughe his defalt. Item there is a woman with child & is at Thomas Walers house.

Flyghte decanatus

Fletweek John Atwood for sowinge of discorde amonge his neyghbors.

Amptill We present Jone Bates which lyveth in Amptill & hir husbande in Hardfordsheere, & we knowe not the cause of theyre separation. Item we suspecte one Laurence Wryghtes wyfe of Amptill to leade an incontynent lyfe in the house of Henry Crouche of Amptill. Item there were certayne blowes geven in the churche yarde betwene Thomas Inones & Laurence Wryghte.

Marston John Theede dothe neyther receave the communion or come to our churche.

Lytlington William Butler & Francis Vauce for not payinge the levye which was made by the parishe for the repayringe of the churche.

Husband Crawley The glasse wyndowes are in decaye but they crave a daye to amende the same. Ad reparandum citra natalem Domini et ad certificandum die instans' proxime post.

[p 210]

Flitton William Fare & Magdalene Wadson receaved not the communion these xij monthes.

Hawnes John Ampes hathe not receaved this yere.

Malden Presentant Mr Kychyner the parson of the Nether Graven' [hurst] he preached the xjth daye of Maye & we knowe not whether he had a licence. Item Thomas West, gent, for not cominge to churche & hathe not receaved this yere, & the same Thomas a common swearer. Item Wylliam Brotherton cometh seldome to the churche & hathe not receaved this yere. Item William Carter cometh seldome to churche. Item William Carrington cometh seldome to churche, & is a drunkard. Item John Berton keepeth a woman in his house called Elizabeth Sanders, beinge suspected to have gotten hir with childe. Item Umphrey Savage is suspected with one Marye Saverse the wyfe of John Severse of Malden, & the same John for not cominge to churche.

Mylbrooke We present Richard Mylward dwellinge in Malden, he dothe owe v^{s} to the towne of Milbrooke & wyll not paye hit for the defalt apoynted by youe.

[p 211]

Wooburne Edouard Ireland hathe gotten with childe a wydowe one Catheryne Shelton, as she sayeth. Item John Martyne lyveth unorderlye from his wyfe & is a common drunkard. Item the wyfe of Robert Groves hathe not receaved this yere.

Cranfeyld Our cancell wyndowes are in decaye thorough Mr Whetstons defalt.

Holcotte Presentata pro rectorem vide billam.

Clophill Present: Symon Brewer dyd receave & kepe in his house a woman greate with childe, & hathe so kepte hir and divers tymes answered that he wyll do hit in spite of our tethe, thes wordes he hathe spoken to Giles Mathewe. Item Harrye Worsley dyd keepe in his house in the yere 1577 a woman greate with childe which we suspected, but sythens she hathe byne conveyed from us. Item this yere 1578 the same Henrye Worsley hathe kepte an other woman which we suspecte for that she dyd change hir name & is nowe conveyed from us. Item William Spyllinge hathe not receaved the holy communion sence Easter anno domini 1577. Item Richard Oxenbowe hathe dealte with Alice Huckell by carnal knowledge but sence is toward maryage with hir, so that we desyre respecte that they be not called before maryage, leaste he forsake hir.

[p 212]

Bedford et Clapham [deaneries]

Bedford Sancti Petri [blank]

Fensam [Felmersham] Richard Alcocke is reported by his daughter to have ij wyfes, & sence she hathe reported she spake these wordes upon ill wyll & is nowe gone upon the same.

Cutburth [Bedford St Cuthbert] We have not our service on the Saboth dayes as we ought.

Bedford Sancti Johan' We present Henrye Cartwryghte the churche warden, absent at this visitation. Item the churche so farr in decaye that the parishe is not able to fynishe that they have begone therein. Item Robert Grove negligent in cominge to churche. Item Henry Cartwryghte absent sundrye tymes. Item Marye his wyfe seldome at churche. Item Robert Turvey payeth not his dewtye for the pervision of the communion.

Bedford Marie Robert Sutton is suspected to have gotten Margaret Wolfe beinge his mayde with childe in the yere of our Lord 1577. Item Mistres Gostweeke cometh not to churche.

Houghton Conqueste There is one Margaret in the house of Anthonye Benet hathe a childe, the father we knowe not.

[p 213]

Stevington One father Glover dothe kepe a strumpette in his howse whose name we knowe not. Ad reparandum ecclesiam citra natalitias et ad certificand' die iu' proxime post.

Goldington Roger Everton dyd gette Alice Feld with chyld.

Carlton Our cancell is in decaye bothe of glasse & stone at our parsons defaute.

Wotton There is a woman delyvered of a childe at Abates house, hir name or father of the childe we knowe not.

Harrold Alice Dase is with childe & the father gone, as the talke goeth. Item the cancell wyndowes are in decaye by the defaute of Mr Farrar. Gardiani susceperunt inst' emendare citra duas septimanas.

Wylthamstead Elizabeth Jonys hathe had a childe but we knowe not the father of hit.

Bedford Pauli William Capere is suspected of naughtye companye with John Drawseworthes wyfe.

Bidnam Jone Bawdwyne is with childe, who is the father we knowe not.

[p 214]

Eaton [deanery]

Wylden John Wylsher the younger dothe absent hymeselfe from the parishe churche & William Alnwike lykewyse, they have missed ij Sondayes together.

Roxton Cancellus indiget reparationes culpa collegij Trinitatis in Cantabr'.

Stoughton parva Our parsonage is [in] greate decaye.

Colmworth We have had no service on the weeke dayes not from Maye daye last tyll September & no service on Sancte Peters Eve nor Sancte Bartholomewe Eve nor Michaelmas daye at nyghte & they had iiij children christened iiij wayes, & he woold not let the parishe see his licence & one syr Brian Hayward dyd in the like case. Item Harrye Newman, John Newman, & Francis Newman doe absent themselves from the churche & the sayd Francis dothe not use hymmeselfe reverentlye in the churche. Item Thomas Deane & Francis Iates wyll not paye anyethinge to the reparations of the churche.

[p 215]

Item William Moore doth withholde certayne legacyes from the poore of Colmworth which his father had geven amonge them. Item Umphrey Austyne churche warden last yere wold not present the lead that was myssinge oute of the steeple. Item Nicholas Dicons, Thomas Jud, William Quarrell & his wyfe have not receaved this xij monthes. Item the Quenes Iniunctions or the bisshoppes were not made thes iij yeres nor the catechisme taughte.

EGGINGTON COURT ROLLS (1297-1572)

INTRODUCTION

(J. S. Thompson and K. T. Ward)

Provenance

This collection of records of proceedings of the court of the manor of Eggington was deposited at Bedfordshire Record Office in November 1963 by Messrs. Lovel Smeathman & Son of Hemel Hempstead who had acted as stewards for the manor. It comprises sixteen parchment membranes numbered X310/1/1-16 and containing a record of 32 courts dated from 1297 to 1572. The membranes have been numbered 1 to 16 and stitched together at the head, but this has been done since their deposit at Bedford. In addition, four paper documents numbered X310/2-6, which are draft records of the court proceedings entered on the membranes numbered 12, 14, 15 and 16, have been used in connection with the translation and interpretation of the records of the relevant courts.

At one time the collection was definitely associated with papers forming part of the collection of the solicitors Messrs. E. T. Ray of Leighton Buzzard (RY at the Bedfordshire Record Office). The Ray papers (RY 2-99), which include some 17th century extracts made from the rolls, constitute a corpus of material relating largely to the title and administration of the Eggington manorial land, *inter alia,* in the 17th and 18th centuries. A schedule in the collection lists Court Rolls of the manor of 'Egginton' up to 1728 but no 'roll' later than 1630 exists in the Ray papers and those brief court records extant from 1578 to 1630 consist of seven small parchment documents forming part of an original file of steward's papers. Paper drafts of 19 courts held up until 1860, however, exist in the Lovel Smeathman deposit (being catalogued as X310/2-23) along with a sizeable set of rentals of quit rents from 1540/1 up to 1859 (X310/26-48). It may be, on the basis of the evidence of the rolls written up from the paper drafts discussed below, that fair copies were never written up from the drafts after 1572.

Eggington is a small village in the south-west corner of Bedfordshire, near Leighton Buzzard and the Buckinghamshire border. Formerly a hamlet in the ancient parish of Leighton its population in 1801 was 206 and an estimated figure for the late 17th century, based on the Hearth Tax returns, is 115. The earliest reference to the history of the manor of Eggington in the Victoria County History (V.C.H.) dates back only to 1518 when it is recorded as having been in the possession of William Man, which agrees with court 14a in this collection. The V.C.H. also refers to 'John de Ekendon' as a joint owner of one hide of land at Milton Grange (3 miles north of Eggington) in 1247, but this was 50 years earlier than the first of these documents.

Dating of the courts

The following list gives particulars of the 32 courts recorded in these 16 documents. Each court is identified by the number of the membrane, followed by an editorial suffix (a, b, c . . . *etc*) when the membrane includes more than one court. These numbers are given in square brackets at the beginning of each court in the text.

Court	Date		Regnal year	Court of
1 a	27 June	1297	25 Edward I	Henry Chyld of Ekendon
b	20 Nov	1301	30 Edward I	Henry Child of Hekendon
c	23 Apr	1304	32 Edward I	Henry Child of Ekendon
2 a	10 Nov	1298	26 Edward I	Henry Child of Ekendon
b	[no date]			[no name]
3 a	2 Dec	1305	34 Edward I	Henry Child, held at Ekendon
b	16 July	1306	34 Edward I	Henry Child of Hecundon
c	6 May	1308	1 Edward II	Henry Child of Ekundone
d	1 Jan	1308	1 Edward II	Henry Child
e	[3 July	1312]	5 Edward [II]	Henry Child
f	[?]		[?] Edward [II]	John Child
4 a	26 Sep	1314	8 Edward II	John de Ekyndone
b	18 July	1334	8 Edward III	John Child of Ekendon
5 a	21 Feb	1348	22 Edward III	John Chylde
b	7 Feb	1359	33 Edward III	[no name]
c	11 May	1367	41 Edward III	John Chyld son of John Chyld
d	10 Jan	1370	43 Edward III	John Child & Margery his wife
6	25 June	1377	51 Edward III	William Styn & Margery his wife
7	25 June	1377	1 Richard II	William Styn
8	18 Dec	1413	1 Henry V	Joan Chyld
9	11 June	1425	3 Henry VI	William Child
10	9 Dec	1428	7 Henry VI	[no name]
11 a	9 Feb	1433	1 Henry VI	Christiana, formerly wife of Roger Man
b	19 July	1435	13 Henry VI	Christiana, formerly wife of Roger Man
12 a	26 Oct	1500	16 Henry VII	William Man [court baron]
b	29 July	1501	16 Henry VII	William Mann [court baron]
13	12 Nov	1506	22 Henry VII	William Manne, lord of the aforesaid manor [Ekyndon]
14 a	13 June	1514	6 Henry VIII	William Man
b	2 June	1529	21 Henry VIII	"in the name of" William Man
c	2 Aug	1531	23 Henry VIII	[no name, court baron]
15	28 Mar	1560	2 Elizabeth I	John Man [court baron]
16	19 Apr	1572	14 Elizabeth I	John Man [court baron]

The above list of courts follows the order in which the membranes have been numbered and stitched together at the head, probably about 1963. It is clear that they were intended to be in chronological order, but a difficulty arises in the case of membranes 1 and 2, where the date of court 2a is between those of courts 1a and 1b. This is surprising, but since we do not know how or why several courts came to be recorded on the same small membranes, no further comment can be made.

Other difficulties arise in courts 3e and 3f, where the courts are not in chronological order. For court 3e the text gives the regnal year as 5 Edward I but this would make the date of the court 1277, about 60 years earlier than courts 3a to 3d. It seems unlikely that this was the true date, and it is possible that the clerk has made a mistake, and has written "King Edward", i.e. Edward I, instead of "Edward son of King Edward", which is the usual designation of Edward II. This correction would give the date tentatively entered in brackets: 3 July 1312.

In court 3f the date is again uncertain, because the text ends abruptly with "King Edward f'". The "f" could be the first letter of the word "filius" (son), and this may indicate that the scribe was intending to write "Edward son of King Edward" followed by the regnal year. The name "Edward II" has therefore been entered in brackets but there is no other clue to the actual date.

There are further difficulties in courts 6 and 7, which both appear to have been held on the same day: 25 June 1377. This was only four days after Richard II succeeded Edward III and it is not surprising that the scribes should refer to different regnal years. It may be that two courts were in fact held on the same day but we have no way of finding out what actually happened. It could be explained if the business of the court was written up, probably from draft notes, in two stages; one a day or two after the court and the other on a later occasion, when the scribe responsible had become aware of the change of monarch, but this can only be speculation. The subject matter of these two documents is quite different; 6 deals with fealty and acknowledgements while 7 records the size and rent of tenants' holdings. Also the membranes themselves are different; 6 is large, clear, and legible whilst 7 is small and faded, with the left hand edge indented, as if it had been previously used for some other purpose.

The draft documents (X310/2-6)

For some of the documents we have the rough drafts from which the final versions were presumably copied. A list of these is given below:

Numbers of documents and courts

Final version	Draft version
X310/1/12 a	X310/2 i
12 b	2 ii
X310/1/14 a	X310/3
14 b	X310/4 i
14 c	4 ii
X310/1/15	X310/5
X310/1/16	X310/6

These drafts are written on paper and are not in very good condition. Most of them are fairly legible, however, except in a few cases where there have been extensive alterations or deletions in the text which make them difficult to read.

In general there is good agreement between the paper drafts and the final versions copied on to the parchment membranes. Sometimes the drafts give useful additional information, such as identifying the particular feast of St Peter in the date of court 12b, which the copyist has chosen to ignore. Elsewhere the writer of the final version seems clearly to have misread or misunderstood abbreviations in the draft. In one court (14b), part of the draft text is almost illegible, and the copyist has literally not been able to make sense of it.

In all cases, the final version has been taken as standard in preparing the translation, but when it differs significantly from the draft this is pointed out in an editorial note.

It is quite rare for draft records of manorial courts to survive. Indeed some court rolls afford evidence of having been written out entry by entry whilst the court was actually in progress and this may be the case as far as most or all of the other Eggington rolls are concerned. We are therefore very fortunate to have drafts for all the surviving records of courts held between 1500 and 1572 except the court of 1506. It is clear from the differing palaeographical styles and the discrepancies between drafts and final fair copies (as a result of simple misreading and miscomprehension rendering one or two sentences unintelligible gibberish as written), that different scribes were responsible for each. It is likely that the rolls concerned, all executed in the same hand, were written up at the same time in the late 16th century by a scribe struggling to cope with the legibility of the drafts and the language generally. Credence is lent to this suggestion by the fact that the copyist has conspicuously treated quite differently each of the vernacular place-names recorded in the seven courts. The existence of the oddities of wording in the final record of the 1529 court and, to lesser degree, the other courts involved would certainly have remained a complete mystery had the drafts not survived. Indeed it has given the editors some satisfaction to have read the drafts with more success than the copyist! One wonders how often palaeographers have been baffled by like difficulties where an imperfect fair copy is the only record. The omission of details such as essoins from the final version, as recorded by editorial notes in the text, give more cause for concern in our interpretation of Court Rolls *per se* as a complete record.

COMMENTARY ON THE TEXT

(K. T. Ward)

This collection of documents spans a considerable period and constitutes a valuable series of court records for a small manor. The individual membranes probably do not form an unbroken series. There is one gap of 65 years between courts 11b and 12a, for instance, and there are two other gaps in excess of 25 years. Three membranes actually contain a range of courts spanning more than 15 years in each case. Nevertheless, within the overall span from 1297 up to 1572 there are identifiable runs of courts of a particular lord or lady of the manor which probably each amount to a full record of the time. The reason for the larger gaps, possibly indicative of vicissitudes in the manor's history or a reflection of variable concern for record keeping, is not known. It is likely, however, despite the employment in the text of the ancient formula that suitors were bound to attend every three weeks, that the court did only meet on the few occasions demonstrated by the records covering an identifiable run of courts. The population of the manor was probably sufficiently small to allow infrequent if not irregular meetings and the nature of its principal business by far, acknowledgements of tenure, and the form it took, would permit this.

The first specific titling of the court occurs in 1500 when it is referred to as a Court Baron. It is clear from the content of the records that it always functioned very much as a small private seigneurial court administering the tenure of those holding land in the manor. The lord of the manor certainly never exercised any form of franchised leet jurisdiction or prescriptive view of frankpledge. In short, the court was almost exclusively concerned with the transfer of land, either by conveyance or inheritance, and its attendant obligations and incidents. A rental survey of 1589 in the Ray collection (ref. RY54) records that the manor consisted then of about 160 acres of land held by undertenants, paying quit rents, and 80 acres of demesne.

There is nothing amounting to evidence of the court functioning as a court customary for villein tenants, even in the sixteenth century. The very occasional and flimsy references to custom do not constitute enough to alter the overwhelming impression of a Court Baron. It may be, however, that in the main period spanned by these records any distinction between customary or unfree and free contractual tenure was blurred. Whether or not this is the case, difficulty of interpretation of these records often lies with the paucity of background detail given on particular transactions or 'acquisitions' (the verb 'to acquire' is often vaguely employed), almost all of which took place extra-curially. The writer feels nevertheless that customary tenure was probably not significant in this manor (although customary land at Eggington did form part of the manor of Leighton Buzzard alias Grovebury as is evident from the Ray papers). There are no statements of manorial custom and, with one exception involving John the reeve in 1298, no evidence of judgement being sought in personal actions such as debt and trespass. Litigation of interpersonal or civil disputes is simply not part of the court's business. This serves again to stress the limited range of the activities of this small court.

It is never entirely clear whether the Lord or Lady of the Manor is presiding over the court in person but this is likely in the absence of a named steward or similar official in the heading to each court. A bailiff is referred to from 1413 (during which court the only reference to a seneschal or steward occurs) and is regularly ordered to distrain and seize for heriots and payment of reliefs and also, in 1506, to summon heirs and other people to make fealty. At that court defaulters who owed suit of court were pardoned because they had not been summoned. The only other court officials are affeerors (two in number) referred to and named in 1367, 1435 and 1500. As is usual these are named at the end of the record of each particular court's business. By 1514, however, and again in 1529 affeerment was "by the whole homage" and in 1572 the roll records simply "Affeerors: none".

A homage is first specifically referred to as such in 1428, the first year in which it is recorded as making collective presentments. Before that date there are presentments by the 'suitors' of the court (1370 and 1377) and general employment of the third person plural of the verb *presentare* leaving the subject as the personal pronoun 'they' only. This leaves it unclear as to whether presentments are being made by those generally bound to provide suit of court or the, presumably, constituted homage. An indication of numbers of those obliged to provide suit, incidentally, is provided by an endorsement on membrane 10 which names 16 men and 1 woman as "the tenants and suitors of court". The first indication of the size of the homage occurs in 1500, the same date at which an entry for essoins first appears in the form of the courts, when 5 jurors are named. The size of the jury appears, on the evidence of the rolls, to have fluctuated thereafter: 1501 (8), 1506 (8), 1514 (6), 1529 (5), 1531 (5), 1560 (3) and 1572 (5). In all these courts bar two (1506 and 1560) nil returns are recorded for essoins, but doubt is cast on the accuracy of the record of the homage given in the rolls by the draft for the 1572 court which records 4 homagers, 2 essoins and 2 jurors as dead. Inexplicably the fair copy for that court gives a list of 5 named jurors and ignores the essoins and those *mortuus*. Pledging, incidentally, which it is generally accepted disappeared in the late 14th or early 15th centuries, is last recorded at this court in 1413. Examples of self-pledging are to be found in the mid 14th century.

A small percentage of the court's business was brought by presentment. The majority of recorded business originated from appearances (possibly after summons) of those involved in transfers of land to register and record them in the court by acknowledgement of tenure. The presentments found are almost exclusively concerned with defaults in respect of appearances to acknowledge by what right tenants hold particular land or are concerned with transgressions of feudal obligations attached to tenure such as suit of court and payment of rent or other dues such as heriot. Defaulters were usually distrained or amerced. Distraints, which the bailiff was often ordered to carry out and probably took the form of seizure of property, were extensively employed as a penalty for compliance, those distrained being under obligation to appear in the court, to show evidence of title or do or perform a certain service. Amercements, small penal payments whose amounts were probably fixed by the affeerors, were less consistently used.

Attendance to make fealty and acknowledge tenure undoubtedly accounts for the vast majority of recorded business. Transfer of land in court occurs only twice. Enfeoffments before 'the full court' (presumably meaning the totality of suitors present) are recorded in 1297, transmission in each case clearly being effected in court, and in 1301 a surrender and acknowledgement of the tenure of a new tenant is recorded. In every other instance, transfer (referred to as alienation, surrender, gift and feoffment, and even 'demise by charter') or conveyance *inter vivos* has by implication taken place outside before the date of the court, by charter (in fee; i.e. deed of gift), *inter partes,* perhaps privately before the lord (who is cited as the donor in some instances) although evidence for this being the usual form is slight. There is some evidence in the 14th century courts that 'licence' was required to enter the fee of the lord. In 1312 John Huberd was presented for alienating a tenement sans licence "neither showing the charter or justifying himself" (presumably at the court) and Walter Randolf found pledges for a similar 'trespass'.

Each new tenant made fealty and acknowledged his tenure of land in the fee of the Lord of the Manor of the same and the fixed incidents and services (see below) which accompanied that tenure. In some entries the tenant is then described as having been 'admitted' (see the 1433 and 1506 courts for instance) or as having entered the fee of the lord. Thus at the court in 1348 Thomas le Taillour entered the fee of the lord by acquiring a cottage from John Huwet in fee. On some occasions tenants are described as having been seised by the lord such as in 1301 when Henry Child, the Lord of the Manor, seised Roger Basele and his heirs of a tenement surrendered to him by William Wodeward and his wife. This procedural activity and the business of dealing with defaulters or those in some way in breach of acknowledgement or performance of due services such as fealty and attendance (i.e. common suit of court) begins to be the staple matter of the court from 1312.

The only specific reference to a particular type of tenure, although feudal incidents attached to tenure are recorded in detail almost throughout, is a single mention of knight's service in 1297. Interpretation of the varied technical language used to refer to conveyance of land and define tenure is not straightforward. Yet, despite the variety of terminology, it is most likely that the rolls are at all times concerned with free socage tenants. Charters are only occasionally mentioned in acknowledgements but references to a tenant holding land freely are common. In 1298 a tenant acquires a tenement to have and to hold for himself and his heirs for ever (subject to tenurial incidents), just as his charter from the Lord of the Manor shows, one of only three expressly cited *habendum* clauses in the text (the others being in 1308 and 1514), and in court 3f two tenants acquired land in perpetuity (*perpetuo* being the verb employed). At the same court two tenants made fealty for land acquired by gift and feoffment, the employment of the past tense here again emphasising the past nature of the actual transaction. Reference to those making acknowledgement holding freely occurs with regularity after 1433, the absence of the adverb both before and after perhaps being no indication of anything other than free tenure.

So what of copyhold and its emergence as a distinct tenure? Only two references are made to the word 'copy'. The first (1413) is not entirely clear but may be a reference to seizure of land held by copyhold tenure. The second mention, however, in 1572 occurs in the course of describing the abuttals of a deceased tenant's holding of land freely by charter but would seem to be evidence of copyhold tenure within the manor. The dearth of such reference in the extant rolls however must support the conclusion that almost all the land in the fee of the lord which was not demesne was held by free tenure.

There is some evidence of sub-letting, often a difficult practice to identify in manorial court records. In 1334 John Morel makes fealty and acknowledgement for 5½ acres "which are in the hands of other tenants" whose names he is to present at the next court. Secondly, in the 1377 courts the payment and agreement respectively to apportion lands are likely to amount to licences to allot land to sub-tenants. These references should serve as a reminder to what has been called the 'unreconstitutable majority' or the 'undermanni', the large numbers of people resident in the manor who go unrecorded in the court record.

The other principal mode of transmission of land which occurs at the court is inheritance *post mortem.* Several lengthier entries are concerned with the details of establishing the right to inherit and be admitted to land in the manor. Typically, they take the form of brief obituaries reporting the death of a tenant, describing the land which he held and the terms and obligations of that tenure, and identifying the lawful heir. The latter was undertaken with some precision and involved judgement of the court. Thus in 1334 John son of John le Reve, whose wardship and marriage were demised by the lord according to the 1314 court (the guardians being specifically ordered to maintain the heir's property until he comes of age), was found by inquest to be aged 21 years and 43 weeks. The heir's age is recorded in a number of entries including those where wardship had to be established for the minority of the heir. Commission of custody of two wards is specified in some detail in 1560, one of the consequences being postponement of fealty; in all cases of inheritance the new tenant or, in the case of wardship, the guardian or custodian was liable to payment of a relief, an incident or exaction upon succession which varied considerably in monetary terms.

The only reference to a life estate occurs in connection with inheritance. In 1298 Joan, relict of Michael Est, said in full court that she had two acres by gift from her husband and gave the Lord of the Manor 12d as an entry fine "that she might hold [the land] . . . for the term of her life". One suspects, however, that absence of further reference is no indication of the likely incidence of such an estate.

A little more should be said as to the participation of women in the recorded business of the court. They were actively involved in all transactions involving land although much less frequently than the men in the manor. Enfeoffment of heirs of two daughters jointly in 1297 and inheritance *post mortem* by the relict of the deceased tenant, by showing a charter "from which it is clear enough that Joan herself should be jointly enfeoffed with the said Edmund for them and their heirs for ever", in 1514, indicate the partibility of land and the involvement of women. There is, incidentally, one specific reference to dowry in 1314. Women were usually the preferred committees in cases of custody of wards entailing the important preservation of an heir's estate. An entry in 1312 overtly recognises the pecuniary significance of this responsibility as does the valuation (by the suitors) and penalty involved in the guardianship of John Morell's estate, committed to two men, after his mother's death, which was presented at the 1413 court by which time her land had been occupied by someone without title. Interestingly Letitia, wife of John le Reve, was one of the only three people accused of trespass in the complete series of records, her offence being depasturing without licence, and women appear to have been liable to the same tenurial obligations as men upon seisin of land in the manor as several entries bear witness.

Tenure in the manor whether inherited *post mortem* or acquired by gift or charter *inter vivos* usually involved several of the following incidents or services: fealty, rent (a fixed annual payment), feudal aid, boonworks, marriage and wardship, heriot (-service), relief, (common) suit of court and fines for entry and custody. Most of these incidents appear to have been as important in the 16th century as in the 14th century on the basis of these rolls. The sole exception to this remark is payment for annual feudal aid which occurs only occasionally from 1308 to 1367.

The boonworks or labour service were light and usually consisted of reaping ('corn' is sometimes specified) with one man in harvest for one day annually with a meal provided by the lord once in the day. On one occasion (court 3f), the text records "with bread provided by the lord during the same time" as the service but in most cases the words 'food' or 'meal' are employed. Boonwork of one half day and two days are also recorded along with, in 1314, more complex arrangements such as a tenant required to reap in every third year and in another entry a proxy being specified to reap on behalf of a tenant in every third year.

Payment in kind appears to have been accepted for rent since John Stratle discharged part of his payment by giving a capon to the lord although this is the only evidence of such defrayal. Heriot, however, appears to have been sought in kind, there being no evidence of commutation of the liability, and is specifically referred to on two occasions: a horse in 1348 (value: 10s.) and, after presentment of a death, a horse in 1413 (value: 6s. 8d.). In 1506 the bailiff was ordered to distrain three heriots for three tenements and appurtenances owned by a recently deceased tenant and at the same court two heriots fell due to the lord by alienations indicating at least two occasions on which it was sought. This incident was also remitted on occasion (e.g. 1572).

This commentary is intended primarily as a summary analysis of the technical content of the Eggington rolls and indeed it is hoped that the translation of the text will be a useful addition to the corpus of readily available material for the study of the history and development of manors and the structure of the rural community of the medieval period and its society, economy and demography. It hardly needs to be said that the text represents an excellent potential quarry for the local historian replete, as it is, with local place names (in excess of sixty in number indexed after the translation) and personal names for the medieval period. The editors sincerely hope that the translation is of value to all those who use it.

EDITORIAL CONVENTIONS USED IN THE TEXT

Square brackets [ ] contain editorial notes; and within these brackets *double inverted commas* " " are used to indicate translated quotations from the manuscript. In some cases the note consists of a word or words added simply for the sake of clarity, as in "to this [court] John Smith came", or when the modern version is given of the date of a court. In other cases the notes refer to marginalia, interlineations, &c.

Round brackets ( ) indicate that the amount of a fine, for instance, is written as superscript in the manuscript.

Single inverted commas ' ' are occasionally used when the reading of the manuscript is clear but the language employed is English rather than Latin or the meaning is uncertain or untranslatable. A single inverted comma at the end or in the middle of a word (particularly a proper name) indicates a contraction of some kind.

A line of dots . . . . . indicates that a word or letters are illegible.

Numerals have been converted from roman to arabic (except after the names of kings), but when numbers have been expressed in words, then words are generally used in the translations. For amounts of money, *ob(olus)* has been rendered as ½d and *q(uarta)* as ¼d; while *s(olidus)* and *d(enarius)* are used for shillings and pence.

Punctuation is practically non-existent in these documents and has been added by the editors for clarity but as sparingly as possible.

Gaps sometimes appear in the manuscript presumably when the scribe was uncertain of a name or intended to add it later. In such cases '[blank]' is inserted in the text.

Marginal notes are found on the left hand side of some of the membranes. When these merely reproduce information already in the manuscript record of a particular court these have not been included in the text. Others have clearly been added at a later date (one entry refers to 1633) and are evidence of some of the documents perhaps being used as the basis for a later terrier or similar record. These have all been added to the text in the form of editorial notes at the end of each appropriate paragraph. Occasionally such annotations, particularly about changes of tenancy, are written immediately above the paragraph concerned rather than in the margin. These are given at the end of the paragraph.

Personal names. Modern English spelling has been used for Christian names, and surnames have been copied as written. An exception is made when the second name is spelt without a capital and represents an occupation: thus "John prep[ositus]" is translated as 'John the reeve', while "John Sutor" is copied as written, not translated as 'John Tailor'.

TRANSLATION

(J. S. Thompson and K. T. Ward)

[1 recto]

Court [1a] of Henry Chyld of Ekendon held in the same vill on the Thursday next after the feast of the nativity of St John the Baptist in the 25th year of the reign of King Edward [I] [27 June 1297].

Still judgement was given previously by the court that the tenement of Henry Tristram and the tenement of Hugh Ordwy should be distrained until the aforesaid Henry and Hugh come to make good their defaults.

Henry son of John Morel gives to the lord for relief ["of"; sic, i.e. for] that tenement, and for default of knight's service [*lourica; "lour"* in MS], which he had by inheritance from his father John Est in the vill of Ekendon [on the] pleas [of] Geoffrey Radenoch and William Sired; and the said Henry made fealty to the lord to pay the rent and services pertaining to the said tenement. [Note in margin: "relief 4s".]

John Leritus and his wife Agnes came in [i.e. before the] full court and enfeoffed Alice and Hilcont, daughters of the said Agnes, in one plot with 2 acres of land with its appurtenances, and their heirs, rendering annually to the lord the rent and services pertaining to the said plot.

Roger Mirad in full court enfeoffed William Mirad in half of his tenement, situated next to the tenement of Henry Chyld, and he made fealty to the lord, [rendering] services and rent annually, that is 6d.

William Reve made fealty to the lord &c.

The said Roger Mirat came in full court and enfeoffed Robert son of Gilbert Peytewyn and his son Cecil [in] the other half of his tenement next to the tenement of Henry Chyld, and Gilbert Peytewyn made fealty to the lord in the names of the said R. and Cecil to pay annually the rent and services pertaining to the said tenement.

Hugh Reve made fealty to the lord for a certain tenement which fell to him after the death of his brother Thomas, rendering to the lord annually the rent and services pertaining to the said tenement.

Roger Phelipp made fealty to the lord for a certain plot and two acres of land which was from Henry, son of Roger, rendering in respect thereof annually to the lord the rent and services pertaining.

Geoffrey Radenoch acknowledged that he holds from the lord one messuage which was his sister Juliana's and he made fealty to the lord &c.

William Wodeward made default and is to be distrained to make good the default.

[1 dorso]

Court [1b] of Henry Child of Hekendon held on the Monday next after the feast of St Hugh in the 30th year of the reign of King Edward [20 November 1301].

It is still ordered to distrain the tenement of Henry Tristram as before until . . ["etc."?]

["Likewise"?/"They say"?] . . . that ["the aforesaid"?] Hugh Hord ["wy"?] . . . made default.

William Wodeward and his wife Matilda surrender into the hands of Henry Child one tenement which lies between a tenement of John and a tenement of William the reeve. On the same day the aforesaid Henry seised Roger Basele and his heirs of the aforesaid tenement to perform the services due and accustomed. And the said Roger made fealty and acknowledged [rent of ?] 9d and [service of] a day in harvest with food provided by the lord, and suit of court.

Court [lc] of Henry Child of Ekendon held on the Thursday next after the feast of Hokeday [2nd Tuesday after Easter] in the thirty second year of the reign of King Edward [I] [23 April 1304].

It is still ordered to distrain Henry Tristram as before.

It is still ordered to distrain Hugh Ordwy for default.

[2 recto; Note: part of this document has been cut off and lost leaving a fragment eight inches long with incomplete texts on both sides. On the recto the text starts four inches below the top of the fragment and ends at the line of the cut at the bottom; on the dorso the text starts at the line of the cut at the top of the fragment and ends about two inches before the bottom. The two texts are in different hands, and presumably refer to different courts; it is not certain which is the earlier.]

Court [2a] of Henry Child of Ekendon held in the same vill on the Monday next after the feast of St Leonard in the 26th year of the reign of King Edward [I] [10 November 1298].

It is still ordered to distrain the tenement of Henry Tristram and the tenement of Hugh Hordny as before.

Ralph Astel, plaintiff, sets himself against John the reeve, and the aforesaid John, being present, seeks *'prece partium'* [assent of both parties] until the next court in this form, that both are to come to the next court without essoin; and at this [court] were found pledges John Lyne and John Roger, and Ralph Astel found pledges Richard le Wite [and] Gilbert Peytenin.

Richard le Wyte made fealty and acknowledged that he holds from the lord . . . [The bottom of the membrane has been cut off here]

[2 dorso; The top of the membrane has been cut off here]

[Court 2b. Note: the courts on the recto and dorso of this membrane have been designated 'a' and 'b' as they occur on the front and back as the membranes have been stitched together. 2b is possibly earlier in date, however, because the usual practice is for the first court to start at the top of the membrane which is more likely in this case (although the cut means that the evidence is missing) rather than halfway down the skin as is the case with 2a.]

Walter Silvester is in mercy for default [at the] last court; pledges Richard of Urgendon [and] Geoffrey de Radenethe, fine [?] 3d.

Roger son of John Philipp the younger, namely Roger next Loke, and Herbert Reve [are ordered] to produce Henry son of Roger at the next court to make good his default [at the] previous court.

Also, still, judgement was given by the court that the tenement that was Henry Tristram's and the tenement of John Est with [that] of Hugh Ordwy be distrained until the said Henry, John, and Hugh come to make good their defaults.

Also on the same day Roger Sired was seised in full court with one messuage and made fealty to Henry Child, to have and to hold for himself and his heirs for ever by rent [of] 12d a year and one day in harvest and suit of court for all claims and demands just as his charter, which he had from Henry Child, shows.

Also it is ordered to distrain Joan, relict of Michael Est, that she should come to the next court to show by what right she holds the tenement which was her husband Michael's. And the said Joan came in full court and said that she had two acres of land by a gift from her husband Michael, to [be] shown ["etc"?]; and she gives Henry Child 12d that she might hold the said two acres of land for the term of her life; pledges, Roger Ordwey [and] Herbert Reve.

Court [3a] of Henry Child held at Ekendon on the Thursday next after the feast of St Andrew the Apostle in the 34th year of the reign of King Edward [I] [2 December 1305].

William Philepe came in full court and made fealty and acknowledged that he holds from the lord two acres of land with one messuage; and he found pledges Richard de . . . [and] John le Reve to find Henry Child or his heirs [struck through: "for the term of his life"] one good price of 8s or 8s [*?* sic] as the fine of the aforesaid William in the name of his heirs.

It is ordered to distrain the tenement of Henry Tristram for several defaults.

It is ordered to distrain Hugh Ordwy for several defaults.

John Laurence of Tulesworpe made fealty and acknowledged that he holds from the lord one messuage with appurtenances, rendering to the lord 12d a year, and he will make suit according to custom.

Court [3b] of Henry Child of Hecundon held on the Saturday before the feast of St Margaret the virgin in the 34th year of the reign of King Edward [I] [16 July 1306].

It is ordered to distrain the tenant of land and tenements Henry Tristram [for] defaults as before.

It is ordered to distrain Hugh Ordwy as before for several defaults and for rents and services for tenements.

Concerning Matilda Souht for a fine for one acre of land and for custody of one acre, 3s by the pledge of William Phelip.

Concerning Alice, relict of John Colop; for having custody of Christian, heir of John Colop, until the full age of the said Christian, she will give 20d a year in all.

Concerning Amabilia, relict of Roger Blecke, who made fealty and acknowledged that she holds from the lord four acres of land which she had from the gift of her husband Roger, saving every right.

Concerning John Ordwy, executor of Roger Basely, who should have sold the effects owed to the lord by the pledge of John Lyne; amercement, 6d.

Concerning John Lyne, who is executor for the same by the pledge of John Ordwy; amercement, 3d.

Court [3c] of Henry Child of Ekundone held on the [feast] day of "St John before the Latin Gate" in the first year of the reign of King Edward [II] son of King Edward [6 May 1308].

Reygner Est was received as next heir of his brother John Colope by the judgement of the court, and he gives 2s 6d to the lord for having entry and acknowledged that he would make fealty to the lord, rendering faithfully the customary services.

Concerning Robert, son of Gilbert Peytenin, who should hold one messuage which his sister Cecilia surrendered to him; and he gives 12d to the lord for having seisin, rendering to the lord the rent and customary services.

Still, [it is] ordered to distrain the tenement of Henry Tristram as before until &c.

Still, it is ordered to distrain Hugh Ordwy for several defaults.

John Laurence of Tulesworpe [is] in default for not coming to court.

Still, it is ordered to distrain Richard Blount for several defaults.

Court [3d] of Henry Child held on the Monday next after the feast of St Thomas the martyr in the first year of the reign of King Edward [II] son of King Edward [1 January 1308].

Still, Richard Blund is [to be] distrained as before.

Concerning John Child, who should hold one messuage with a curtilage which messuage Reygner Est surrendered to him; to have and to hold the aforesaid messuage for him and his heirs for ever by the services due and accustomed in respect thereof.

Court [3e] of Henry Child held on the Monday next after the feast of the Apostles Peter and Paul in the fifth year of the reign of King Edward [II?] [3 July 1312; see introduction].

Still, it is ordered to distrain the tenement of Henry Tristram as before for several defaults.

Still, it is ordered to distrain Hugh Hordny for several defaults.

William Ateg'ne made fealty to the lord and acknowledged upon his fealty that he holds from the lord one messuage [and] 2 acres of land, rendering 4½d a year, and a day in harvest in the third year, and suit of court every three weeks, [and] 1¼d a year for feudal aid, by inheritance of his wife Alice. And he gives 12d to the lord for entry. [Note in margin, "fine 12d".]

Walter Randolf has found pledges to make amends for the trespass of entering the fee of the lord without licence; [namely] William Philip [and] John Hordny. [Note in margin, "amercement, 4d".]

Walter Randolf made fealty and acknowledged that he holds from the lord four acres of land by service, 18d a year and suit of court. And he gives 12d for entry by pledges William Philip and John Hordny. [Note in margin, "fine, 12d".]

Richard de Brikendon, because he did not come; in mercy, 4d.

Letitia, who was the wife of John le Reve, is accused of depasturing without licence a pasture which was in the lord's possession, and she has found pledges to make amends for the trespass; namely, William Philip [and] John Hordny. [Note in margin, "amercement, 4d".]

It is presented that John Huberd has alienated a certain tenement into the hands of his wife Alice without licence, neither showing the charter nor justifying himself. Therefore it is ordered that the tenement be taken into the lord's hands until &c, and he is in mercy for contempt. [Note in margin, "amercement, 6d".]

Letitia who was the wife of John le Reve gives 2s to the lord and has found pledges to save wardship, marriage, principals, houses, and all other things, for the use of the lord, because profitable, until they are delivered; [namely] William Philip and John Hordny. [Note in margin, "fine, 2s".]

[Two notes are stitched to the bottom of the membrane here, in almost exactly the same words: "On this day the lord has pledges for wardship and marriage of the heir de Reve ["for relief" in the one note rather than "de Reve"] for lands now Thomas Dogget's."]

[3 dorso]

Pledges. John Clerek for the Commission for the Peace, with his daughter Alice have found pledges Richard Blount and William Phelip'.

Concerning Alice for the same, [she] has found pledges, John Ordwy and J. Lyne.

Court [3f] of John Child held on the Monday next after the feast of the Purification of St Mary in the [blank] year of the reign of King Edward [see introduction].

John Lauwe acquired in perpetuity half an acre of land from William Gilberd from the fee of the lord, and he has a day to show the charter at the next [court] and to do that which is needful; pledges, John Ordwy and William le Reve.

Richard Huhet acquired in perpetuity from William Lin one messuage from the fee of the lord by statute service [*"per formam statua"* in MS], as appears by suit which he proffered, and he made fealty and acknowledged that he holds from the lord the said messuage just as William Lin formerly held it.

Roger son of Richard D . . . ud came and sought his inheritance which his father Richard held, which Roger is of full age and the next heir, and acknowledged that he holds one messuage which contains one acre of land and 6 acres of land from the lord by charter for 2s at Michaelmas and 3½d at the feast of St Othye [Osyth?] the Blessed and by one reaping in harvest with bread provided by the lord during the same time and by heriot. He does not [yet] have certain acknowledgement but seeks a day to acknowledge and has a day for agreement lasting until the morrow and he made fealty &c.

Richard, son of Roger Bylecke, and his heir entered [into] those four acres of land which his mother Amabilla held, and made fealty and acknowledged them to be [his] inheritance by service, 18d a year and suit of court and by relief, that is 18d. He found pledges William le Reve and John Ordwy.

Roger Radenheh, because he has not Henry Morel, for whom he went bail at the last court, to do that which is needful; pledge, Richard Huet; and it is ordered to distrain the aforesaid Henry Morel to do the services owed.

John Huberd is in mercy because he sealed a certain charter in the name of John Child, as acknowledged in court; pledges, William le Reve and William Reynfrey.

Robert son of Gilbert acquired in perpetuity from Roger Radenh' half an acre of land from the fee of the lord.

Henry Derdyngton came in full court and remedied default and afterwards made fealty for land and tenements which he had by the gift and feoffment of Richard Wyte and he is excused default.

John Spakeman made fealty for lands and tenements which he had by the gift and feoffment of John Berde.

Robert Peytonin gives [?] . . . for entry [into] one half [acre?] which he had by the gift of Roger de Radeneth and for half an acre of land which he acquired from Roger Geffrey, and for half an acre of meadow land acquired from Hugh son of Herbert, and he made fealty; pledges, William Reynfrey and Roger Radeneth.

William le Reve holds from the lord one messuage, 1½ acres and one rood of land, ["by making"?] fealty, by service, [and] 8½d to be paid at Michaelmas, suit of court [and] . . .

. . . that . . . tenement that Henry Tristram held . . . and again made default.

[4 recto]

Court [4a] of John de Ekyndone held there on the Thursday next after the feast of St Matthew the Apostle in the eighth year of the reign of King Edward [II] son of King Edward [26 September 1314].

William Reynfrey made fealty to the lord and acknowledged that he holds a third part of one virgate of land with appurtenances which John Reve formerly held by charter from the lord by reason of the dowry of his wife Joan, formerly wife of John, and he pays 17¼d a year and 17½d at Michaelmas in every third year. And he renders to the lord annually feudal aid on the feast of St Osyth the virgin [7 October]. For which whole tenement he makes suit of court every three weeks and heriot when it falls due.

The same William and his wife Letitia have, by demise of the lord, wardship and marriage of John, son and heir of John Reve in Ekynd[on], and safely to maintain and sustain the houses and all the said tenements and buildings sufficiently and well until the full and legal age of the said heir, and then to award [?] [the same] to the said heir, when he shall have come of age, according to his written charters and documents. He has found pledges, that is, John Lyne and J. Ordwy. And meanwhile he will make to the lord annually the services due and accustomed, that is, two parts [?], 4s and 4d and [also] annual feudal aid.

[Two marginal notes stitched on here. One reads: "He was seised by wardship [and] relief for the lands now Thomas Dogget's." The other is much the same; the subject is named but half the name is torn off, and the words "for the lands" are preceded by the surname "Reve".]

John Ordewey made fealty to the lord and acknowledged on his oath that he holds one messuage and half a virgate of land with, moreover, a certain small piece of land of the said messuage, and 2 acres which John the clerk holds, [and] he renders 2s 1½d a year at Michaelmas, and he owes suit of court as the aforesaid William, and he reaps for one day in harvest with one man with food provided by the lord once in the day; in [every] third year extra because William a[tt]e Grene [struck through: "John the clerk aforesaid"] will do that day in the third year on his behalf. And he gives to the lord [for] annual feudal aid in respect thereof, 3¼d at the feast of St Osyth the virgin, and heriot when it falls due. [Note in margin: "Walter Butte".]

Hugh the reeve made fealty to the lord and acknowledged on his oath that he holds from the lord one messuage with a croft and meadow-land adjoining with appurtenances and three acres of land, and he renders six pence a year at Michaelmas, and suit of court as above written, and he will do one day with one man reaping with food provided by the lord once in the day, and heriot when it falls due. [Note in margin: "T. Sinsten".]

John Lauwerence made fealty to the lord and acknowledged that he holds one messuage with appurtenances and he renders 12d a year at Michaelmas and owes suit of court and heriot just as the others above-written. [Note in margin: "Churche Place".]

William ate Grene made fealty to the lord and acknowledged that he holds one messuage and two acres of land with appurtenances by charter [and] he renders 4½d a year at Michaelmas and reaps for one day in every third year as aforesaid and will make suit of court and heriot as aforesaid and annual feudal aid, that is 1¼d at the term above written. [Note in margin: "Alson Morel".]

John son of William Line made fealty to the lord and acknowledged that he holds from the lord by charter one messuage with appurtenances and he renders 18d a year at Michaelmas, and he will make suit and heriot and reaps as aforesaid. [Note in margin: "W. Gurney".]

Richard of . . . made fealty to the lord and acknowledged that he holds one messuage and six acres of land with appurtenances by charter and he renders 2s a year at Michaelmas and will make suit and heriot, and reaps as aforesaid and gives annual feudal aid on the feast of St Osithe the virgin, that is 2½d. [Note in margin: "It is being enquired who holds at the next [court] . . ."]

Walter Randulf made fealty to the lord and acknowledged that he holds from the lord 4 acres of land for 18d a year at Michaelmas and suit of court as aforesaid. [Note in margin: "Edmond Wodley".]

Henry Morel made fealty to the lord and acknowledged that he holds from the lord by charter one messuage and six and a half acres of land with appurtenances, [and] he renders 17d a year at Michaelmas, and he owes suit of court and heriot and reaps for one day as aforesaid. [Note in margin: "Note that this H. had Tuesday in Easter week to enquire concerning the yearly rent of the aforesaid Roger Radenhaft."]

Walter Gileberd made fealty to the lord and acknowledged on his oath that he holds from the lord by charter one messuage and two roods of land with appurtenances, [and] he renders 7d a year at Michaelmas, and he owes suit and heriot as the others aforesaid and reaps for one half day. [Note in margin: "the same".]

John Huberd made fealty to the lord and acknowledged that he holds from the lord, by demise of the same by charter, one messuage with appurtenances, [and] he renders 12d a year at the aforesaid term, and he owes suit [and] heriot and reaps for one day as aforesaid, and he has a day before the next court to show the charter; pledges, John Ordewy [and] Hugh the reeve.

Roger Radenheth made fealty to the lord and acknowledged that he holds by charter one message and 2 acres and 1 rood of land with appurtenances, and renders 14d a year at Michaelmas and he owes suit of court and heriot and reaps for one day as aforesaid.

Roger Peytenyn made fealty to the lord and acknowledged that he holds from the lord by charter one message, and he renders six pence a year at Michaelmas, and he owes suit of court and heriot and reaps for a day.

All the above-written tenants present that Henry de Herdingtone, [struck through: "John Berde"], William Reve, Hugh Hordewy, and tenant Henry Tristram made default, and it is ordered to distrain them all individually.

Also they present that John Berd entered two parts of that tenement which William Felyp once held from the fee of the lord without licence and therefore they give judgement that he be distrained.

Afterwards John Berde came and made fealty and acknowledged that he holds, as a gift from the lord by charter, one message with appurtenances, [and] he renders 22d a year at Michaelmas, suit of court and heriot as aforesaid; of which tenement, however, he acquired two parts from a certain Felicia, wife of Henry de Tonne, and Mary, sister of the said Felicia; and he entered and gives to the lord for having entry, 16d; pledge, John Lyne.

[4 dorso]

Court [4b] of John Child of Ekendon held on the Monday next after the feast of St Kenelm, king and martyr, in the 8th year of the reign of King Edward III after the Conquest [18 July 1334].

Hugh Derd'gton made fealty and acknowledged that he holds from the lord one message [and one] virgate of land with appurtenances in Ekendon by fealty, 3s 6d at Michaelmas, and he owes reaping for one day in harvest with one man with one meal provided by the lord, and he owes suit of court every three weeks, and heriot at the time of the death of John Hewet. [Interpolated here: "John Hewet now holds by ["service"?]."]

Hugh Ordwy made fealty and acknowledged that he holds from the lord one message and half a virgate of meadow-land on Villamnmede, next a meadow of John Ordwy, by fealty, 2s 6d a year, and other services as Hugh Derd'gton. [Added in a later hand: "John Fowler".]

John Sutor and his wife Alice made fealty and acknowledged that they hold from the lord one message and two acres of land, by right of Alice herself as heir after the death of William le Reve, by fealty, 7½d a year and other services as above.

John Hugwet made fealty and acknowledged that he holds from the lord one message by fealty, 18d a year, and other services as above.

William Ordwy made fealty and acknowledged that he holds from the lord one message by fealty, 12d a year, and other services as above.

John Gilbart made fealty and acknowledged that he holds from the lord one message by fealty, 7d a year, and half a day in harvest, suit of court, and heriot.

John Morel made fealty and acknowledged that he holds from the lord one message and 6½ acres of land by fealty and 17d a year, both for that part and for 5½ acres which are in the hands of other tenants, whose names he should present at the next court, and other services as above.

John Jeffre made fealty and acknowledged that he holds from the lord one messuage and two acres and 1 rood of land by fealty, 13d, and other services as above.

John son of Hugh le Reve made fealty and acknowledged that he holds from the lord one messuage and half an acre of land by fealty, 2½d, suit of court, and heriot.

The presenters say that John Spakeman made default to Roger de Brikendon. And [?sic; ?for] a tenement that was late Henry Tristram's [sic?].

Also they present that Lord Richard Ordwy, chaplain, acquired one acre of land from Christian West.

Also John son of John Ordwy acquired one half acre from his father John Ordwy. [Note in margin: "Ordered to distrain all these to show and do etc. at the next [court]".]

And that they have no knowledge of other things to [be] present[ed].

John son of John le Reve came in full court saying that he is of full age, seeking his inheritance, and placed himself before the [jurors serving on] inquest of the court, and it was found that the same John's age is 21 years and 43 weeks.

[5 recto]

Ekendon: Court [5a] of John Chylde held there on Thursday the eve of St Peter in Cathedra in the 22nd year of King Edward III after the Conquest [21 February 1348].

It is ordered to distrain John son of John Ordwy to show at the next [court] by what right he entered into one half acre of land which he acquired from his father John Ordwy after he had been presented at the last court.

John, a tenant of the lord, has lately died [and] after his death there comes to the lord by heriot, one horse, price 10s. And afterwards came Roger, son and heir of the said John, and sought admission to his inheritance, that is one messuage and half a virgate of land with appurtenances of which the same John, his father, died seised. And he made fealty, [and] he renders 2s 6d to the lord for the same at Michaelmas, and 4½d for feudal aid at the feast of Pentecost, and he reaps the lord's corn with one man for one day with one meal, and heriot on vacancy of the said tenements, and suit of court every three weeks. And he gives to the lord for relief, 2s 10½d.

Thomas le Taillour entered the fee of the lord by acquiring one cottage from John Huwet in fee. And he made fealty, and renders 9d a year in respect thereof [to be] paid at Michaelmas, and he reaps the lord's corn in harvest for half a day with one meal from the lord once in the day, and heriot on vacancy and suit of court as other tenants. And he gives 10d to the lord for entry pledging the same himself.

Walter Geffrey entered the fee of the lord [for] one acre acquired from John Hugweth in fee. And he made fealty, and renders 9d a year in respect thereof [to be] paid as above, and he reaps the lord's corn for half a day in harvest with one meal from the lord once in the day, and heriot on vacancy of the same, and suit of court as other tenants. And he gives 10d to the lord for having entry pledging the same himself. [Entry in margin: "Henry Hutt".]

Richard Hankyns of Bylyngdon entered the fee of the lord by acquiring one toft and two selions of land in Clypston next William South's tenement on the south side, and for it he showed a charter in fee from John Spakeman junior, and he made fealty to the lord and he renders 20d a year in respect thereof [to be] paid at Michaelmas, and he reaps the lord's corn in harvest for one day with one man with one meal from the lord once in the day, and heriot on vacancy of the same, and suit of court as other tenants. And he gives for entry [end of sentence].

Equendon: Court [5b] held there on the Thursday next after the Purification of the Blessed Mary in the 33rd year of the reign of King Edward III after the Conquest [7 February 1359].

They present that Henry Angetil (3d), John Holendon (3d), Peter Brystwyk (3d), Henry Hobbes (3d), made default; therefore [they are] in mercy.

And that Nicholas Barbor (2d), John Emmesson (2d), priests, made default; therefore [they are] in mercy.

And that William Hoggeson (2d) made default; therefore [he is] in mercy.

And that Ralph Smyth (2d) of Eyton, John Bolehast (2d) [and] John Ketering (2d), made default; therefore [they are] in mercy.

And that John Morel holds and occupies half an acre of land, formerly John Reve's, and it is ordered to seize the said land into the lord's hands, saving all rights.

And that the same John Morel occupies one messuage and half a virgate of land which Roger Ordwy and Matilda, wife of John Morel, lately held and sold to Alice Morel, daughter of the said Matilda. And the aforesaid Alice is of age to hold; therefore it is ordered to seize the said messuage and land with appurtenances into the lord's hands until &c.

It is ordered to distrain Nicholas Barbour, John Emmesson, priests, William Hoggesson, John Bolehafft, John Ketering, John Clerk [and] Isabel Helewys to make fealty to the lord and to acknowledge by what service[s] they hold their land and tenements from the lord. And also Robert [interpolation: "Ralph"] Smyth of Eyton to show &c.

It is ordered to distrain Peter Bristwyk to show by what right he has entered into one half-acre of land, which John Ordwy son of his father John Ordwy formerly held, at the next [court].

And that John Morel (9d) ["has been"?; "*fr*" in MS] attached for harvest-service and other trespasses on three occasions; therefore he is in mercy by pledge etc.

Total for that court: 2s 9d.

Ekendon: Court [5c] of John Chyld, son of John Chyld, held there on Tuesday the feast of St Fremund in the 41st year of the reign of King Edward III after the Conquest [11 May 1367].

John Fouler made fealty and acknowledged that he holds from the lord one messuage and half a virgate of land, formerly Roger Ordwy's, as by the right of his wife Alice, [and] he renders 2s 6d a year [i.e. rent] and 4½d for feudal aid at the feast of Pentecost, and he owes reaping for one day with one man in harvest with a meal provided by the lord once in the day, marriage, and heriot when it falls due, and suit of court every three weeks.

John Coleman made fealty and acknowledged that he holds from the lord one messuage formerly Hugh Ordwy's, [and] he renders 2s 6d a year and 4½d for feudal aid at the feast of Pentecost, and he owes reaping for one day with one man in harvest with a meal provided by the lord once in the day, heriot, marriage and wardship when it falls due, and suit of court every three weeks.

Isabel Helewys made fealty and acknowledged that she holds from the lord one parcel and messuage formerly John Lyne's [and] she renders 9d a year and she reaps in harvest for half a day with one man with food provided by the lord once in the day, [and owes] marriage and wardship when it falls due, and suit of court as aforesaid.

Margery, formerly wife of the aforesaid Bristwyk, made fealty and acknowledged that she holds from the lord one messuage and one acre and one rood of land formerly William Hoggeson's, [and] she renders 12d a year, and she reaps as above for one day, [and owes] heriot, marriage and wardship when it falls due, and suit of court as above.

[Dots below indicate where one corner of the bottom of the membrane is missing]

John Huet made fealty and acknowledged that he holds from the lord one . . .
Richard Sweyn and a parcel of one virgate of land but by inquest . . .
therefore he has a day at the next court to acknowledge in full . . .
[interpolated: "[roods?] 4"]
The suitors of the court present that John Morel . . .
[interpolated: "John Jur[d]en"]
John Godfrey, Parsones, Ralph Smyth, St[even] . . .
All being present, the heirs of John Dogat, Will . . .
of John Bolehaft, Richard Blake, John . . .
Keterynge, have entered into the fee of the lord . . .
Lucas Est made fealty and acknowledged . . .
4 bovates of land adjoining, opposite . . .
by quantity of service[s] still unknown . . .
acknowledging John Hue[t] . . .
Augustus, son of William Waryn . . .
a messuage lately William Waryn . . .
M . . .

[5 dorso]

John Blekke made fealty and acknowledged that he holds from the lord four acres.

Richard Blekke, who held from the lord four acres of land by service [and] 18d a year, closed his last day after the last [court], after whose death came John, son and heir of the said Richard, and sought admission to the said land and it was granted to him because it was found by the whole court that he is ["next"?] heir. And he gives 18d to the lord for relief; pledge, John Reve.

Also it is presented by the jury that Richard Sweyn made default; therefore he is in mercy.

John Reve made fealty and acknowledged that he holds from the lord one acre of land formerly William Bourcotte's [and] he renders 2d a year which is part of 5s 6d [?].

John Stratle made fealty and acknowledged that he holds from the lord one messuage and two acres of land and one rood of land, with appurtenances, [and] he renders 14d a year, and he reaps for one day, and [makes] suit of court as the aforesaid free tenants. And he gives one capon to the lord to discharge part of the rent by apportionment.

Still, as before, it is ordered to give back into the lord's hands half an acre of land, formerly John Reve's, saving the rights of anyone until etc.

Affeerors: John Stile
John Wadelowe

Total for this court: 21d and 1 capon, which were paid.

Ekyndon: Court [5d] of John Child and his wife Margery held there on the Thursday next after the feast of the Epiphany of the Lord in the 43rd year of the reign of King E[dward] III after the Conquest [10 January 1370].

John Bolehaft came to this [court] and made fealty to the lord and acknowledged that he holds two acres of land lying in the field of Sheldon, by what service he does not know; therefore he is given a day [up] to the next [court] to acknowledge &c, and where the said land lies &c.

John Keteryng made fealty to the lord and acknowledged that he holds three and a half acres of land; of which one acre lies 'into' Blakkesmede next Henry Agas' land, half an acre there lies next John Nead's land, [and] one and a half acres [lie] on Aldefeld next John Sobbury's land; by service [and] rent [of] 7d a year. And other services he does not know; therefore a day is given [up] to the next [court].

William Chamberleyn made fealty to the lord and he has a day [up] to the next [court] to acknowledge what land and tenements he holds and by what service he holds from the lord &c.

The suitors present that John Pye, Geoffrey Prentys, John Morteyn, knight, Roger atte Persones, John Jurdon of Stanbrug, John Godfrey, Ralph Smyth of Eyton, Stephen Adam, the heir of John Doget, Richard Sweyn, John Hankynes of Tillesworth, William Wylde [and] John Dyne have made default; therefore it is ordered to distrain them that they should be at the next [court] to make fealty to the lord and to acknowledge what lands and tenements they hold from the lord and by what service &c.

Also they present that William Agas has entered into the fee of the lord [by] acquiring three acres of land from Richard Sweyn for a tenement formerly John Reve's. Therefore it is ordered to distrain him that he should be at the next [court] to make fealty to the lord and to acknowledge by what service he holds the aforesaid land &c.

John Fouler finds a pledge, namely John Morel, to satisfy the lord before the next [court] for one penny rent given for half an acre of land which lies at le Throp, which rent is in arrears from the first plague [up] to now &c; total [due], 21d.

John Michel, clerk, made fealty to the lord and acknowledged that he holds one messuage formerly Robert Peytenyn's and a certain part of one messuage formerly John Lyne's by service [and] rent [of] 6d at Michaelmas for the said messuage and 1d for the said part, and suit of court every three weeks; and he reaps &c.

John Hewet, John Reve, John Stratle, John Morel, John Fouler, John Wadelowe [and] John Blekke made fealty to the lord and acknowledged that they hold all the other lands and tenements for which they earlier made fealty to the lord as appears in the preceding courts.

[Note: The remaining 17 lines of the dorso side of this document are barely legible for several reasons. A large stain obscures the left hand end of lines 1 to

5; the bottom left hand corner of the document is missing for lines 9 to 17; and lines 9 to 11 have been over-written by a later endorsement identifying the document (see introduction). Such parts as are legible have been translated below. The layout of the text below from line 9 onwards shows the approximate line of the tear at the corner.]

W[illiam] . . . ["made fealty"] to the lord and ["acknowledged"] that he holds from the lord one toft
. . . to acknowledge at the next [court]
. . . ["acknowledged"] that he holds from the lord one acre of land
. . . service, rent [of] 2d a year . . . at Michaelmas
. . .
. . . agon made fealty to the lord and acknowledged acknowledged [sic] that he holds one acre and
. . . roods of land by ["service"?], rent [of] 2½d a year at Michaelmas
. . . [just as]
Roger W . . . Joan . . . , John made default
next
["of"/"by"] the lord one acre
which . . . is 9 ["years"?] &c
acre["s"?] of land ["lately of"?] Lucas Est
is 8 years &c. And
["of the aforesaid Alice"?]
. . .
["annually 4 days"?]

[6 recto]

Ekyndon: Court [6] of William Styn and [his] wife Margery held there on the Thursday next after the feast of the Nativity of St John the Baptist in the 51st year of the reign of Edward III after the Conquest [25 June 1377, but see introduction].

John Hewet came and made fealty; and he has a day [up] to the next [court] to acknowledge what lands and tenements he holds from the lord and by what service.

John Stretle came and made fealty, and acknowledged that he holds from the lord one toft, and he does not know what land; therefore he has [up] to the next [court] to acknowledge &c. And afterwards he came and acknowledged 2 acres of land & 1 rood by service, rent for the whole 14d, and suit of court, and he reaps for one day in harvest with one man.

John Reve came and made fealty and acknowledged that he holds from the lord one messuage and 20 acres of arable land lying in fields & closes by service, 5s 6d a year and suit of court.

John Morel came and made fealty and acknowledged that he holds one messuage with appurtenances by service, 17d a year and suit of court and heriot when it falls due, and he reaps with one man in harvest for one day. [Note in margin: "Peter[?] Boners".]

William Baron came and made fealty to the lord and acknowledged that he holds one and a half acres and one rood of arable land by service, 3½d [a year] and suit of court.

John Blecke made fealty to the lord and acknowledged that he holds 4 acres of arable land with appurtenances by service, 18d a year and suit of court.

Richard Perkyns made fealty to the lord and acknowledged that he holds one messuage, which he acquired from Margery Brystwyk, by service, 9d a year and one day in harvest and suit of court. [Note in margin: "Henry Hutt".]

Isabel Helewys [interpolated: "John Hutte"] made fealty and acknowledged that she holds half of one messuage, formerly John Lyne's, by service, 9d [a year], and she reaps with one man in harvest for half a day with food provided by the lord once in the day, and suit of court. [Note in margin: "now Henry Hutt's".]

Christian Monte [superscript in later hand: "[occupier] not known"] made fealty and acknowledged that he holds one acre and one rood of arable land and half a rood of meadow by service, 3½d [a year] and suit of court.

John Clerk [interpolated: "Hun[t?] . . . e"] made fealty to the lord and acknowledged that he holds from the lord two cottages, formerly Isabel Helewys', by service, 6d [a year], and half a day in harvest as other tenants do, and suit of court.

John Fougler made fealty and acknowledged that he holds from the lord one messuage and half a virgate of land, formerly Roger Ordewy's, by service, 2s 10½d a year, and he reaps for one day, and [is liable to] heriot when it falls due, and suit of court. [Note in margin: "Edmund Wodlow".]

John Waddelowe made fealty and acknowledged that he holds one messuage [struck through: "& one acre of land"] with appurtenances by service, 2s 10½d a year, and he reaps for one day as the aforesaid John Fougler, and [is liable to] heriot when it falls due, and suit of court.

William F[le] . . . made fealty to the lord and acknowledged that he holds from the lord one toft and one acre of land with appurtenances by service, 3½d [a year], and one day in harvest, and heriot when it falls due, and suit of court.

John Bolehast came and made fealty to the lord and acknowledged that he holds two acres [later note: "enquire"] of arable land in the field[s] of Sheldon by service [and] 4d a year for all services. [Note in margin: "John Carpintere".]

William Doget made fealty and acknowledged that he holds half an acre of land, which he acquired from John Reve, by service [and] 1d a year and about suit of court he does not know; therefore he has a day [up] to the next [court].

William Agate made fealty to the lord. And he has a day [up] to the next [court] to show [by his] charter what lands and tenements he holds from the lord and by what service.

The suitors of the court present that William Wilde (by word of William Pere), Elizabeth Morteyn, John Dyne, John Hankyn (by word of [struck through: "Mylyt"]), William Lawe, William Treweman, Roger Parsones, John Godfrey, John Freman, Ralph Smyth (by word of John Hawe[k/l?]), John Jurdan, John Keteryng (by word of Rendyng), John London, William Chamberleyn (by word of Aga . . .) [and] John Pye (by word of Lane) have made default; therefore it is ordered to distrain [them] against the next [court] to make fealty to the lord and to acknowledge what lands and tenements they hold from the lord.

William Juet gives 6d to the lord to apportion land, formerly Roger Brykendon's, &c.

[7 recto]

Ekendon: Court [7] of William Styn held there on the Thursday next after the Nativity of St John the Baptist in the first year of the reign of King Richard II after the Conquest [25 June 1377, but see introduction].

William Inwyth made an agreement [*"fecit finem"* in MS] [with] the lord to apportion lands and tenements[?], rent and services, which were indeed Roger Brokeman's. And the said allotment was made by William Agase, John Morel, William Perkyn, and Richard Blake who say that William Oswath holds the chief messuage and one acre of land lying together and is charged at 7½d a year.

John . . . holds four and a half acres of arable land lying separately in the fields of Clipston and Ekynton and is charged at 9d a year.

John Wadelow holds one acre of land, of which one half acre lies below North[way] next John Hugweth's land and the other half acre lies at Thedwey next John Hugweth's land and is charged 2d a year.

William Styn holds one acre of land lying below le Northwey next John Stretle's land and is charged at 2d a year.

Richard Blake holds one acre of land lying at le Mullewey next John Morel's land and is charged 2d a year.

John Jueth holds one acre of land lying at Helyetonstale ["on the south"?] and is charged 2d a year.

Margery Brystwyk holds one half acre of land lying on le Overpende next Christian Mount's land and is charged 1d a year.

Christian Mount holds one half acre of land lying on le Overpende next Margery Brystwyk's land and is charged 1d a year.

Hubert Thouchard holds one rood on Heyetanstale next Clipstabur[g]'s land and is charged at 1½d a year.

William Styn holds one rood on le Overepende next the said William's land and is charged 1½d a year.

[8 recto]

[[Court 8]] of Joan Chyld held there on the Monday next before the feast of St Thomas the Apostle in the first year [of the reign] of Henry V after the Conquest [18 December 1413].

John Hewet came to this court and acknowledged that he holds from the lady one messuage and half an acre of land by service, 4s 6d a year, suit of court, and heriot when it falls due, and he reaps with one man in harvest for one day, and he made fealty. [Later note: "now William Morell's".]

John Chyld came and acknowledged that he holds one messuage with appurtenances by service, 5s 6d a year, suit of court, and heriot when it falls due, and he reaps for one day in harvest, and he made fealty.

William Baron acknowledged that he holds from the lady one acre and a half and one rood of land by service, 2½d a year, suit of court &c. And he made fealty.

John Blake holds one half acre of land by service [and] 1d a year &c. And he made fealty.

John Hutte holds half of one messuage, formerly John Lyne's, by service, 9d a year, suit of court, and heriot when it falls due, and he reaps for one half day with one man in harvest &c. And he made fealty.

The same John holds one cottage by service [and] 6d a year, and he reaps for one half day with one man in harvest &c. And it remains in the hands of the lady. [Note in margin: "Amercement because he did not pay heriot".]

John Fowler holds one message and half a virgate of land, formerly Roger Ordewy's, by service, 2s 10½d [a year], suit of court, and heriot, and he reaps for one day with one man in harvest. And he made fealty.

John Wadlowe acknowledged that he holds from the lord [sic] one messuage with appurtenances by service, 2s 10½d [a year], and he reaps for one day with one man in harvest [and is liable to] suit of court, and heriot &c. And he made fealty.

William Styn [later interpolation: "formerly Richard Brikyndon's"] holds one toft and 6 acres [later interpolation: "enquire about these 6 acres which he holds"] of land with appurtenances by service, 2s 3½d a year, suit of court, and heriot when it falls due, and he reaps for one day with one man in harvest &c. And he made fealty.

William Perys [later interpolation: "The same William holds one messuage with appurtenances by service [and] 9d a year, with one man for half a day in harvest, &c."] acknowledged that he holds from the lord half an acre of land by service, 1d [a year], suit of court &c. And he made fealty.

John Godefrey [interpolation(apparently in a contemporary hand): "William Taylor and John Brownchilde, formerly Godfrey"] holds one acre of meadow by service [and] 6d a year &c. And he made fealty.

Laurence Colyn [later interpolation: "and the aforesaid acre lies in the meadow of Stanbryg"] holds half an acre of land by service, 1d [a year] &c. And he made fealty.

Thomas Jurdan acknowledged that he holds half an acre of land by service, 1d [a year] &c. And he made fealty.

Julian Bocher holds two acres of land by service, 4d a year, suit of court &c. And he made fealty.

Thomas Bendyng' holds 2 acres of land by service, 4d [a year and] suit of court. And he made fealty.

John London holds 8 acres of land by service, 16d a year, suit of court &c. And he made fealty.

John Lane holds one message with appurtenances by service, 2s 3½d a year, suit of court, and heriot when it falls due, and he reaps for one day with one man in harvest &c. And he made fealty. [Note in margin: "Amercement because a piece of land sold".]

John Gay acknowledged that he holds from the lady one message with appurtenances by service, 6d a year, suit of court, and heriot when it falls due, and he reaps for one day in harvest with one man. And he made fealty.

William Brustewyk holds one message with appurtenances by service, 12d a year, suit of court, and heriot when it falls due, and he reaps for one day with one man in harvest. And he has a day to make fealty. [Note in margin: "amercement because sold".]

The suitors present that William Brustewyk (2d) made default; therefore he is in mercy.

Also they present that Joan Morell, who held from the lady one messuage and three and a half acres of land called Morell, one toft called Tanneres (12d) [and] one message with appurtenances called Streteleyes by service, 2s 2d a year, suit of court, and heriot when it falls due, reaping for two days with one man in harvest, died on the feast of the Purification of the Blessed Mary last past whence there fell due to the lord [sic] as heriot one horse, price 6s 8d, and so [it was] sold. And they say that John Morell, son of the same, is next heir and 17 years of age, which [lands] [it is] ordered be seized into the lady's hands because of the minor age of the same. And they say that the aforesaid messuage with its appurtenances in all its outgoings is worth finally, over and above all deductions, 4s a year. Also they say that John Bokyn occupied the said messuage with its appurtenances, from the day on which the aforesaid Joan died up to this day, without a title. And the bailiff is ordered on behalf of the lady to take possession of the messuage with the land aforesaid. And afterwards came John Hewet and William Brustewyk and delivered up the said heir into the hands of the lady and made a final agreement with the seneschal to have [charge of] the said heir until the full age of the said heir; and this was granted to them. And giving to the lady, for the messuage and land during the minor age of the same, 40s. And the said custody begins thereafter and ends at the full age of the heir. And they find pledges William Styn & John Janyns alias Bokyn [deleted: "under penalty of 40s".]

[Note in margin, stitched on: "This lord [sic] is seised of one heriot, a horse price six shillings & eight pence, and wardship and marriage portion of John Morrell, for the messuage called Streetlies formerly Brocas, now in [the occupation?] of Thomas Atwell alias Wells".]

[Contemporary note in margin: "Fine of 40s for wardship of John Morell".]

Thomas London holds 8 acres of land by service [and] 16d a year which it is ordered to distrain for fealty to be made to the lady.

Thomas Bendyng' holds 2 acres of land by service, 4d a year [and] suit of court.

William Bocher holds 1 acre of land by service, 2d a year [and] suit of court.

John Bocher holds 1 acre of land by service, 2d a year [and] suit of court.

John Smalard holds 8 acres of land by service, 16d [a year and] suit of court.

[struck through: "William Taylor"] and [interlined: "John Brunehyld hold[s]"] one parcel called Byllam by service, 6d a year [and] suit of court.

William Jolyffe [interpolated: "of Layghton"] holds 3 acres of land formerly John Morell's by service, 6d a year [and] suit of court.

William Doget [holds] half an acre of land formerly John Reve's by service, 1d a year [and] suit of court &c.

John Dyne acknowledges that he holds from the lord [sic] 1 acre of land by service, 2d a year [and] suit of court. And he made fealty.

It is ordered to distrain Laurence Colyn ["above" interlined] of Stanbrugge to make fealty for half an acre of land [held] by service [and] 1d a year.

It is ordered to distrain John Hawkyn to make fealty to the lord [sic] for 7½ acres [and] one rood of land [held] by service [and] 7½d [a year].

John Dyne junior holds one acre of land by service [and] 2d a year and it is ordered to distrain him for fealty to be made to the lord [sic].

[Footnote in later hand: "11 messuages in the hands of tenants and 1 in the hands of the lord".]

[8 dorso]

Distraint was made for the heir of William Chamberlein, lord of Stanbrig, to make fealty to the lord of Ekendon to acknowledge what lands and tenements he holds and by what service; [and] by what fealty John Child and Margery his wife were seised.

Distraint. William Anabl to acknowledge by what service he holds two acres of land in the field of Sheldon, which were formerly of John Bolehaft in the same court.

[gap of about three inches here]

It is ordered to seize one toft and 4 butts of land and 2 others on the opposite side of the said toft which John Dogat and a certain Lucas Est hold; copy in the court of John Child, son of John Child.

[9 recto. Note: marginal notes alongside each entry comprise, as appropriate in each case, the words "fealty", "rent" (with the sum recorded) and "work(s)" (with the number of days recorded)].

Ekyndon: Court [9] of William Child held there on Monday the feast of St Barnabas the Apostle in the third year of the reign of King Henry VI [11 June 1425].

To this [court] came John Blake and acknowledged that he holds from the lord one half acre of land acquired from William Baron senior lying on the north side of Astwyk next William Wadelowe's land; rendering to the lord in respect thereof, 1d a year at the usual terms and suit of court every three weeks; and he made fealty to the lord &c. [later note: "now [in the tenure] of Henry Fowler of Clypston."]

To this [court] came John Wadelowe & John Fowlere and acknowledged that they hold from the lord half of one messuage, formerly John Lyne's, by the demise of John Huete, and it is situated next the manor [house] of the lord; rendering to the lord in respect thereof, 9d a year at the usual terms and suit of court every three weeks, and heriot when it falls due; and they reap with the lord in harvest with one man for half a day; and they made fealty to the lord &c. [later note: "now [in the tenure] of the chapel there."]

To this [court] came John Fowlere and acknowledged that he holds from the lord one messuage and one half virgate of land, formerly Roger Ordewey's; rendering to the lord in respect thereof, 2s 10½d a year at the usual terms and suit of court every three weeks and heriot when it falls due; and he reaps with the lord in harvest with one man for one day; and he made fealty to the lord &c. [later note: "now [in the tenure] of the chapel there."]

To this [court] came John Wadelowe and acknowledged that he holds from the lord one messuage with appurtenances; rendering to the lord in respect thereof, 2s 10½d at the usual terms and suit of court every three weeks and heriot when it falls due; and he reaps with the lord with one man in harvest for one day; and he made fealty to the lord &c. [later note: "now in the tenure of Edward Wadlowe."]

To this [court] came John Daye and acknowledged that he holds from the lord one messuage with appurtenances; rendering to the lord in respect thereof, 6d a year at the usual terms and suit of court every three weeks, and heriot when it falls due; and he reaps with the lord with one man in harvest for one day; and he made fealty to the lord &c. [later note: "William Morell now holds [it]."]

To this [court] came John Astolt alias the said Taillour and acknowledged that he holds from the lord three acres and one rood of land, of which two acres and the aforesaid rood were acquired from William Agas and lie in le Estfeld of Ekyndon, and the other acre [was] acquired from William Dóget and lies separately in Benefurlong [interpolation: "enquire"]; rendering to the lord in respect thereof, 6½d a year and suit of court every three weeks; and he made fealty to the lord &c. [Later note: "William Morell holds one acre in le Estfelde & Henry Honer holds half an acre and a rood of land in the same field"; and note in margin: "heir of Honer, enquire".]

To this [court] came William Brustewyk and acknowledged that he holds from the lord one messuage with appurtenances; rendering to the lord in respect thereof, 12d a year and suit of court every three weeks, and heriot when it falls due; and he reaps with the lord for one day with one man in harvest; and he made fealty to the lord &c. [later note: "Now in the tenure of Thomas Lane."]

To this [court] came the same William and acknowledged that he holds from the lord one half acre and one rood of land, of which the half acre [interpolation: "enquire"] lies in a furlong called le Pende next John's land and John Blake's land [sic], and the aforesaid rood lies at Throp next John Mont's land; rendering to the lord in respect thereof, 1½d a year at the usual terms and suit of court as above; and he made fealty to the lord &c. [later note in margin: "now Coke."]

To this [court] came Joan Pyers [interpolation: "enquire"] and acknowledged that she holds from the lord two roods of land which were formerly John Reve's; rendering to the lord in respect thereof, 1d a year at the usual terms and suit of court every three weeks. And she made fealty to the lord &c.

To this [court] came John Child and acknowledged that he holds from the lord one messuage and one virgate of land with appurtenances in Ekyndon; rendering to the lord in respect thereof, 5s 6d a year and suit of court every three weeks, and heriot when it falls due; and he reaps with the lord in harvest for one day with one man; and he made fealty to the lord &c. [later note: "now [in the tenure] of the chapel there."]

To this [court] came John Morell and acknowledged that he holds from the lord one messuage, three and a half acres of land, one toft called Tanners, and another messuage called Stretleys; rendering in respect thereof to the lord, for the aforesaid messuage and for the aforesaid [three] acres and a half of land, 14d a year at the usual terms, and also rendering to the lord, for the aforesaid toft, 4d a year at the aforesaid terms, and, for the aforesaid messuage called Stretleys, rendering to the lord, 14d a year at the abovesaid terms and suit of court as above and heriot when it falls due; and he reaps with the lord in harvest for two days with one man; and he made fealty &c.

It is ordered to distrain John Billyngdon and William Agas to make fealty to the lord for lands and tenements acquired from John Huet.

It is ordered to distrain John Bocher of Leyghton to make fealty to the lord for land formerly Juliana Bocher's and also to make fealty to the lord for his own lands &c which he claims to hold from the lord &c.

[9 dorso]

Ekyndon
Total of rents overleaf, 16s 8d; and working days overleaf, 7½ days. [Note: The total of the rents in the text is in fact 17s, but the total given here is the sum of the rents given in the marginal notes from which John Morell's 4d rent was omitted.]

[10 recto]

Ekendon: Court [10] held there on the Thursday next after the feast of the Conception of the Blessed Mary in the seventh year of the reign of King Henry VI after the Conquest [9 December 1428].

Essoins: none
The homage present that John Doget (2d) & William Sandrus (2d) have made default; therefore they are in mercy and the bailiff is ordered to distrain them to acknowledge what lands and tenements they hold from the lord and to make fealty.

John Hewet made fealty to the lord and acknowledged that he holds from the lord three acres of land lying in the field of Stanbryge of which two acres lie together and shoot upon le Wer'dyge, half an acre lies on Gesfurlong next William Lawrence's land, and half an acre lies on Honyfurlong and half an acre lies into 'Salterius' Welle, and one parcel of meadow lies in Estlecke; rent, 4s 7d a year. [later note in margin: "Doget".]

John Wadlowe [struck through: "holds from the lord"] made fealty and acknowledged that he holds from the lord one messuage and a croft lying there next John Fowler's tenement, for which he gives 2s 10½d a year, and [is liable to] heriot when it falls due, and a day in harvest with one man.

John Fowler made fealty and acknowledged that he holds from the lord one tenement and a croft and ten acres of land adjoining, which tenement & croft lie next John Gylde's tenement, half an acre lies on Hedon Hill next John Morell's land, half an acre lies there next John Wadlowe's land, half an acre lies there next John Hewet's land, one rood lies there next the said John's land, half an acre lies in Edewey next the said John's land, one acre lies on Overtheforowe next John Fowler's land, one headland of land lies at le Scharpe next William Wadlowe's land, half an acre lies 'into' Lecke next John Hewet's land, two roods lie on Astewyke next the said John's land, half an acre lies next le Estbroke next John Perkins' land, half an acre lies at Donstallus Welle next John Blake's land, half an acre shoots 'into' Brokefurlong next Perkyns 'hedlond', half an acre lies on Kyllyng Well next John Hutte's land, half an acre lies into Blakepyt Wey next the lord's land, half an acre lies there next John Morell's land, half an acre lies at Blakepyt Welle, half an acre lies on 'Salterius' Welle next Thomas Amy's land, one rood [?lies/?shoots] 'into' Stonywey next Ralph Brestwyke's land, half an acre and one rood shoot 'into' Stonyweye, half an acre lies on Bedewall next Richard Roger's land [and] half an acre lies on Regwey next John Agas' land; for [all of] which he gives 2s 10½d a year and [is liable to] heriot when it falls due and a day in harvest with one man. [Note in margin: "In the tenure of the vill, 1633."]

John Blake made fealty and acknowledged that he holds from the lord one and a half acres of land of which one acre lies at Westmylleweye next John

Morell's land [and] half an acre lies on Astwyk next William Wadlowe's land; rent, 3d a year. [Later note: "now of Henry Fowler & William Taillor of Leighton."]

John Morell made fealty and acknowledged that he holds from the lord three tenements of which one lies next John Agas' tenement, for which he gives 10d a year to the lord, another tenement lies there which was formerly John Stretelle's next the lord's croft, for which he gives 14d a year, and another tenement lies there next Joan Agas' tenement, for which he gives the lord 17d a year. Also he holds from the lord one and a half acres and one rood of land of which one acre of land lies on Banlond next land [blank], half an acre lies on Smalweye next Joan Hewet's land, and one rood of land [lies] on Stonhyll; rent, 3½d a year. [marginal note: "Brocas".]

[10 dorso]

John Hunte made fealty and acknowledged that he holds from the lord one tenement lying next the lord's land, rendering 9d a year and a day in harvest with one man. Also he holds three acres of land of which half an acre lies on Hoghand[waie] next John Hewet's land, half an acre lies 'into' Estlecke next John Agas' land, half an acre [lies] on Regweye next John Hewet's land [and] half an acre [lies] below le Hedon next John Agas' land; rent, 5d a year.

Joan Agas made fealty and acknowledged that she holds from the lord half an acre of land on Wofurlong next John Hewet's land; rent, 1d a year.

Ralph Brystwyk made fealty and acknowledged that he holds from the lord half an acre and one rood of land of which half an acre lies in le Pende next John Mounte's land [and the] rood of land in fact lies 'at the' Thorpe next the said John Mounte's land; rent, 1½d a year.

John Mounte made fealty and acknowledged that he holds from the lord half an acre and one rood of land of which half an acre [?sic] lies on le Pende next Ralph Brestwyk's land [and the] rood of land in fact lies at le Thorpe next land [formerly?] John Fowler's; rent, 1½d a year.

[11 recto]

Ekendon: The first court [11a] of Christiana, formerly wife of Roger Man, held there on the Monday next after the feast of the Purification of the Blessed Virgin Mary in the eleventh year of the reign of King Henry VI after the Conquest [9 February 1433].

To this [court] came John Wadelow and made fealty and faithfully acknowledged that he holds freely from the lady one messuage with a croft adjoining with appurtenances and half an acre of land with appurtenances, [which] lies at Thedewey next John Huet's land, by service [and] 2s 11½d a year, and he makes common suit of court and [is liable to] heriot when it falls due and he reaps the lady's corn for one day with one man in harvest; [and] also acknowledged that he holds freely from the lady half an acre of land, [which lies] below Northwey by [sic] and abuts 'into' Reyner's croft and lies next John Hutte junior's land, by service [and] 1d a year, and he was admitted. [Notes in margin: "fealty" and, in later hands, "Now of Ed. Wadlowe" and "Now of Thomas Andrew".]

To this [court] came John Fouler and made fealty and faithfully acknowledged that he holds freely from the lady one tenement with a croft adjoining and ten and a half acres of land with their appurtenances by service [and] 2s 10½d a year, and he makes common suit of court there and [is liable to] heriot when it falls due, and reaps as above. [Notes in margin: "fealty" and, in a later hand, "land now in the custody of the vill there".]

To this [court] came William Blake and made fealty and faithfully acknowledged that he holds freely from the lady one acre of land with appurtenances by service [and] 2d a year and he was admitted. [Notes in margin, "fealty" and, in a later hand, "[Now of] William Andrew".]

To this [court] came Margery Blake and made fealty and faithfully acknowledged that she holds from the lady half an acre of land with appurtenances lying at Astwyk next William Wadelow's land by service [and] 1d a year, and she was admitted. [Note in margin, "fealty".]

To this [court] came John Morell and made fealty and faithfully acknowledged that he holds from the lady lands [and] tenements by service [and] 3s 5d a year and he makes common suit of court and [is liable to] heriot when it falls due, and he reaps the lady's corn for three days with one man in harvest. Also he acknowledged that he holds freely from the lady one and a half acres of land and one rood with appurtenances, of which one acre lies together on Banlond, next Roger Regelot's land, half an acre of land lies on Smalwey next John Huet's land, and one rood of land lies on Stonyhyll, by service [and] 3½d a year, and he was admitted. [Notes in margin: "fealty" and, in a later hand, "now of Bernard Brokas".]

To this [court] came John Doget and made fealty and faithfully acknowledged that he holds freely from the lady 2 acres of land with appurtenances, of which one acre of land lies together next the lady's land, half an acre of land lies on Leckefurlong next William Baron's land, and another half acre of land lies at Westlane end next John Agas' land, by service [and] 4d a year, and he was admitted. [Notes in margin: "fealty" and, in a later hand, "Now of Thomas Lane at Lekke".]

To this [court] came William Baron and made fealty and faithfully acknowledged that he holds freely from the lady one acre of land with appurtenances, of which half an acre of land lies at le Throp next to land formerly John Walsche's, and the other half acre of land lies on Heyelynchehoke next John Huet's land, by service [and] 2d a year, and he was admitted. [Notes in margin, "fealty" and, in a later hand, "now of William Gonthropp at Throp".]

To this court came John Hutte and made fealty and faithfully acknowledged that he holds freely from the lady one tenement with appurtenances by service [and] 9d a year, and he makes common suit of court there and [is liable to] heriot when it falls due, and reaps for half a day in harvest with one man. Also he acknowledged that he holds freely from the lady three acres of land with appurtenances by service [and] 6d a year, and he was admitted. [Notes in margin: "fealty" and, in a later hand, "now of the chapel there".]

William Wadelow holds freely from the lady one rood of land with appurtenances lying on Heyedunstall, next the lord's [sic] land, by service [and] ½d a year. [Notes in margin, "distrain for fealty" and above, in a later hand, "enquire".]

To this [court] came John Man and made fealty and faithfully acknowledged that he holds freely from the lady 8 acres of land by service [and] 16d a year, and he was admitted. [First note in margin illegible; second note written above, in a hand, "enquire".]

Ralph Brystewyke holds freely from the lady half an acre of land and one rood, and the aforesaid half acre of land lies in le Overpende next John Mounte's land, and the aforesaid rood of land lies at le Throp next John Mounte's land, by service [and] 1½d a year. [Notes in margin: "distrain for fealty" and above, in a later hand, "enquire".]

To this [court] came John Mounte and made fealty and faithfully acknowledged that he holds freely from the lady half an acre of land and one rood, the aforesaid half acre of land lies on le Overpende next Ralph Brystewyke's land, and the aforesaid rood of land lies at le Throp between John Fowler's land, by service [and] 1½d a year, and he was admitted. [Note in margin: "fealty" [?]]

To this [court] came John Astholt and made fealty and faithfully acknowledged that he holds freely from the lady one acre of land with [its] appurtenances lying severally on le Banlond, one half acre of land lying there next John Regelot's land, and another half acre of land lying there next William Parson's land, by service [and] 2d a year, and he was admitted. [Notes in margin: "fealty" and, in later hands, "now William Morell" and "now Dogget".]

To this [court] came Katherine Gylow and made fealty and faithfully acknowledged that she holds from the lady 6 selions of land, containing altogether 2 acres of land, lying together in a furlong called Bedewelfurlong next John Doget's land by service [and] 6d a year, and she was admitted. [Notes in margin, "fealty" and, in later hands, "now Thomas Austin" and "now John Andrew".]

To this [court] came John Chyld and made fealty and faithfully acknowledged that he holds freely from the lady one messuage and one virgate of land with appurtenances in Ekendon by service [and] 5s 6d a year, and he makes common suit of court there and [is liable to] heriot when it falls due, and reaps corn for one day with one man in harvest, and he was admitted. [Notes in margin: "fealty" and above, in a later hand, "now of the chapel there".]

To this [court] came John Huet and made fealty and faithfully acknowledged that he holds freely from the lady one messuage with a croft adjoining with appurtenances in Ekendon, situated between a tenement called Lynes and Joan Huet's tenement, and 4½ acres of land lying in the fields of Stanbrygge and Ekendon, [and] a certain parcel of meadow, of which [4½ acres of land] 2 acres lie together in the field of Stanbrygge next Joan Huet's land and abut 'into' Weredych, half an acre of land lies on Gosefurlong next William Laurens' land, another half acre of land lies on Honyfurlong next William Saundres' land, half an acre of land extends 'into' Salteryswell next William Chyld's land, and one acre of land lies together and extends 'into' Byllyngdon, next Thomas Amy's land, and the aforesaid parcel of meadow lies in le Estlecke next the lord's [sic] meadow of Grovebury, by service [and] 4s 8d a year, and he makes common suit of court there and [is liable to] heriot when it falls due, and he reaps the lady's corn for one day with one man in harvest with food provided by the lady, and he was admitted. [Notes in margin: "fealty" and, in later hands, "William Morell" and "T. Dogett".]

Turn over because more on the back

[11 dorso]

Still for the court overleaf

To this [court] came John Agas, John Huet, and John Chyld, and made fealty and faithfully acknowledged that they hold from the lady 2 acres of land and 2 roods which they hold from her freely [and] which were acquired from John Chyld, by service [and] 5d a year, of which one acre of land lies together below Northwey next the lord's [sic] land of Grovebury and the other acre of land lies there next John Huet's land and the aforesaid 2 roods of land lie in le Estfelde and abut 'into' Stonewey next John Fowler's land, and they were admitted. [Note in margin illegible.]

It is ordered to distrain before the next [court] Reginald Lucy, knight, William Deyer alias the said Palmer, Thomas Hawkyn, John Agas [and] John Bocher of Leyghton to make fealty to the lady and [render] other services due to her for land and tenements which they hold freely from her. [Note in margin: "distraint by the homage".]

The homage there present that all is well and that they have nothing to present about other matters. [Note in margin illegible.]

Total of this court: nil

Ekendon: Court [11b] of Christiana, formerly wife of Roger Man, held there on the Tuesday next before the feast of St Magdalen in the 13th year of the reign of King Henry VI after the Conquest [19 July 1435].

The homage there present that John Morell (2d) [and] John Fouler (2d), who owe suit, have made default; therefore they are in mercy; and that they [the homage] have nothing to present about other matters.

Still so, it is ordered to distrain before the next [court] Reginald Lucy, knight, William Deyer alias the said Palmer, William Wadelow, Ralph Brystewyke, Thomas Hawkyn, John Agas and John Bocher of Leyghton to make fealty to the lady and [render] other services due to her for land and tenements which they hold freely from her.

Affeerors: John Huet
John Chyld

Total of this court: 4d.

[12 recto]

Egington: Court Baron [12a] of William Man held there on 26 October in the sixteenth year of the reign of King Henry VII &c [26 October 1500].

Essoins: none for this day.

Homage:

William Morrell	Ed. Wadlowe	Thomas Brothers
William Bunser	John Honer	["John Carpenter" in draft only and struck through]

["jurors" or "sworn"] who say on oath [that] Bernard Brokas (4d), Thomas Lane (2d), the heir of John Snowe [struck through in draft] (4d) [and] Thomas Austin (2d) owe suit and have made default.

Fealty:

To this court came William Gunthrop and acknowledged that he holds from the lord one half acre of land lying on Thruppe Hill between William Morrell's land on the east side and William Gurney's land on the west side, and he renders 1d a year ["fealty" in draft only] and suit of court every three weeks; and he made fealty &c.

Also they present that various tenants hold certain lands for which they have not paid rent or any other payment, but they do not hold because they owe rent as appears in a court roll of 12th Henry VI; and similarly that some entered into the fee of the lord as appears there; therefore it is ordered to distrain them against the next court to show how and by what service they hold. And further, they do not know by [what] certain classes [or "articles"] they came to these [lands] as appears there; therefore a day is given to the homage to enquire better in respect thereof against the next court.

Affeerors: Ed. Wadlowe
John Honer sworn.

Ekendon: Court Baron [12b] of William Mann held there on the Thursday next before the feast of St Peter [draft has here "ad vincula"] in the sixteenth year of the reign of King Henry VII &c [29 July 1501].

Essoins: none.

Homage:

William Bunser	John Honer	William Gunthrop
Thomas Austin	Ed. Wadlowe	Henry Fowler
Thomas Brothers	John Carpenter	

["jurors" or "sworn"] who say on their oath that Bernard Brokas (4d), the heir of John Snowe (4d), Thomas Lane (2d), William Morell (2d), Richard Andrewe of Clipston (2d) [and] John Bunker of Potsgrave (2d) owe suit and have made default.

Also they present that John Bunker has entered into the fee of the lord, that is in one acre of land of which half an acre lies [in] Brookefurlong next a headland of John Fowler and the other half lies at Dunstable Well next Richard Andrewe's land, which [acre] he holds from the lord by service, 2d a year and suit of court, and which was lately John Hutt's as appears in the ["as above written in" copied incorrectly from the draft] court roll of 7th Henry VI. Therefore he is distrained against the next court to make fealty &c for the fealty of John Fowler.

Also they present that John Snowe entered into the fee of the lord, that is [in] one headland lying at le Sharp next Dagnall's Peece which he holds from the lord by service, 1d a year, fealty [and] suit of court. Therefore he is distrained against the next court to make fealty &c.

Also they present that William Morell has entered into the fee of the lord, that is [in] half an acre of land lying next East Brooke ["Estbroke" in draft] between the said William's land on the north side and John Fowler's land on the south side, which he holds from the lord by service, 1d a year ["fealty" in draft only] [and] suit of court. Therefore he is distrained against the next court to make fealty &c [for land] which was formerly ["Sir"? or "the son of"] John Hutt's and afterwards John Fowler's as appears in the roll of 7th Henry VI.

A day is given: to this court came Henry Fowler and sought licence from the lord to have a day up to the next court to make his fealty because he is in mercy for two acres lying on Astwick, and he was then allowed to discharge himself or to make fealty.

[The following passage, which appears at the top of the dorso side of the draft, was apparently overlooked in the final version; "It is ordered to distrain the tenants of the land of Ekendon Chapel to make fealty towards the next court &c.

Affeerors: Thomas Austyn
Thomas Brothers
[both] sworn".]

[13 recto]

Ekyndon: Court [13] of William Manne, lord of the aforesaid manor, held there on Thursday, that is the day after St Martin the bishop [St Martin of Tours] in the 22nd year of the reign of King Henry VII [12 November 1506].

Essoins: none.

Homage:

William Gurney	Thomas Dogett
William Andrewe	Thomas Brothers
William Waryn	Ed. Wadelowe
Thomas Austeyn	John Fowler

["jurors" or "sworn"] who say on their oath that Anne Brocas, Walter Butte of Hachynge & Henry Fouler owe suit on this day and have made default. Therefore they are in mercy and [were] afterwards pardoned by the lord for it because they were not summoned. And further they present that William Morell, who held freely from the lord certain lands and tenements with their appurtenances, has closed his last day; and they say that Elizabeth Dogett is his daughter and heir and of lawful age. And further they present that Thomas Dey, who held freely from the lord one messuage with its appurtenances, and ["has" makes more sense] alienated the aforesaid messuage with its appurtenances to William Gurney &c. Therefore the bailiff is ordered to seize two heriots into the lord's hands for the aforesaid two messuages and distrain for relief of the same &c.

[The word "acknowledgement" appears in the margin and precedes each of the following entries.]

To this court came William Gurney and acknowledged that he holds freely from the lord by charter one messuage with appurtenances, formerly John Dey's, by rent [of] 6d a year to the lord in respect thereof, suit of court every three weeks and heriot when it falls due, and he reaps with the lord for one day in harvest with one man with food provided by the lord once in the day, and other services &c. [Note in margin: "now Robert Jeffes'".]

To this court came the same William Gurney and acknowledged that he holds freely from the lord by charter another messuage with its appurtenances, lately John Dey's and before [that] Richard Boners' and formerly John Morell's, by rent [of] 17d a year to the lord in respect thereof, suit of court every three weeks, and heriot when it falls due; and he reaps with the lord for one day in harvest with one man with food provided by the lord once in the day, and other services due before in respect thereof by ancient use and custom. And he made fealty to the lord for the said two messuages. [Note in margin: "now Robert Jeffes'".]

To this court came the same William Gurney and acknowledged that he holds freely from the lord a half part of ten and a half acres of land lying severally within the fields of Ekyndon and Clipston as by the right of his wife Joan, daughter and sole heir of Henry Hutte now deceased, by rent [of] 10½d a year to the lord in respect thereof & suit of court & other services. And he made fealty. [Note in margin: "now Stephen Gurney's".]

To this court came Elizabeth Bunker of Pottesgrove, daughter and sole heir of Henry Hutte, and acknowledged that she holds freely from the lord a half part of ten and a half acres of land with appurtenances lying severally within the fields of Ekyndon & Clipston by rent [of] 10½d a year to the lord in respect thereof, suit of court, and other services. And she made fealty to the lord &c. [Note in margin: "now Thomas Andrew's".]

To this court came William Andrewe and acknowledged that he holds freely from the lord one acre of land lying at le Westmyllewey by rent [of] 2d a year to the lord in respect thereof, suit of court, and other services previously due in respect thereof and [due] by ancient custom. And he made fealty to the lord. And so he was then admitted [as] tenant &c. [Note in margin: "now Richard Andrew's".]

To this court came Thomas Dogett as by the right of his wife Elizabeth, daughter and heir of William Morell now deceased, and acknowledged that he holds freely from the lord one messuage with a croft adjoining situated in Ekyndon and four and a half acres of arable land by rent [of] 4s 8d a year to the lord in respect thereof, suit of court every three weeks and heriot when it falls due; and he reaps with the lord for one day in harvest with one man with food provided by the lord once [in the day], and other services. And he made fealty to the lord &c. [Notes in margin: "now Doggett" and, in a later hand in English, pinned to the margin, "How much and what land came to Doggett and how".]

To this court came Thomas Brothers and acknowledged that he holds freely from the lord one half acre of land lying at Westlane Ende abutting into Northewey by rent [of] 1d a year to the lord in respect thereof, suit of court every three weeks, and other services formerly due and accustomed in respect thereof. And he made fealty to the lord. And so he was admitted [as] tenant. [Note in margin: "now John Andrewe's".]

To this court came William Waryn and acknowledged that he holds freely from the lord as by the right of his wife Katherine one half acre of land lying in Clippstonfeld at Wattes Wyllys, that is between Edmund Wadlowe's land on either side, by rent [of] 1d a year to the lord in respect thereof, suit of court and other services. And he made fealty to the lord and so was admitted [as] tenant. [Note in margin: "now Richard Andrew senior's".]

To this court came Thomas Austeyn of Stanebrugge and acknowledged that he holds freely from the lord three acres of land, of which two acres lie together on Bedwellefurlonge between William Andrews' land on the north side and Walter Butte's land on the south side, and half an acre lies on Middelfurlonge in le Estfelde of Ekyndon between Thomas Brothers' land on the south side and the lord of Ekyndon's land on the north side, and half an acre of land lies in the same field in le Overfurlonge extending into Hokeleyfelde, that is, between land of Anne Brocas on either side, by rent [of] 6d a year to the lord in respect thereof, suit of court, and other services. And he made fealty to the lord. [Notes in margin: "2 acres whereof now Richard Andrew junior's" and "and one acre now Richard Gurney's".]

To this court came Ed. Wadlowe and acknowledged that he holds freely from the lord one messuage with a croft adjoining with their appurtenances and half an acre of land with its appurtenances, lying at Thedewey next land formerly John Huett's, by service, 2s 11½d a year & suit of court every three weeks, and heriot when it falls due, and he reaps corn with the lord for one day in harvest with one man with food provided by the lord once in the day, and other services &c. And also he acknowledged that he holds freely from the lord half an acre of land lying below Northewey and abutting next Reyner's croft and lying ["it lies" in MS] next land formerly John Hutte junior's by rent [of] 1d a year to the lord in respect thereof, suit of court & other services. And he made fealty to the lord. And so he was then admitted [as] tenant &c. [Note in margin: "now Thomas Andrewe's".]

[Note in margin: "Orders".]

The bailiff is ordered to distrain into the lord's hands three heriots which fell due to the lord by the death of John Morell, because on the day that he died he held from the lord three tenements with their appurtenances, and to distrain the land and tenements of the same John into the hands of the lord, remaining until &c; and to summon the heirs of the said John against the next [court] to make fealty and to answer to the lord about relief and for various rents and services in arrears, withheld ["*retract*'" in MS] from the lord of this manor &c.

The bailiff is ordered to seize into the lord's hands two heriots which fell due to the lord by the alienation of John Dey [i.e.] for two messuages which he lately alienated to William Gurney, and to distrain for the relief of the same.

Also the bailiff is ordered to seize into the lord's hands one heriot which fell due to the lord by the death of William Morell & to distrain [upon] the heir for relief &c.

Also the bailiff is ordered to distrain 10 and a half acres of land for a relief to be levied for the use of the lord; [land] formerly in the tenure of Henry Hutte &c.

Also the bailiff is ordered to distrain one acre of land, formerly Blake's, for a relief to be levied for the use of the lord &c.

Also the bailiff is ordered to distrain for a relief to be levied for the use of the lord for lands formerly William Morell's &c.

Also the bailiff is ordered to distrain land now Thomas Brothers' for a relief to be levied for the use of the lord &c.

Also the bailiff is ordered to distrain William Waryn's land for a relief to be levied for the use of the lord for lands which he holds from the lord as by the right of his wife Katherine &c.

Also the bailiff is ordered to distrain Thomas Austeyn's lands, which he holds from the lord, for a relief to be levied for the use of the lord &c.

Also the bailiff is ordered to distrain Ed. Wadlow for a relief to be levied for the use of the lord and to seize one heriot for one messuage and certain lands which he holds in chief from the lord &c.

Also the bailiff is ordered to summon the heirs of two acres of meadow lying in Stanebrigge mede, formerly William Morell's.

And also, Thomas Austeyn [is] to make fealty to the lord for one messuage, formerly Katherine Gylowe's, and to render to the lord for heriot and relief &c.

And [the bailiff is ordered?] to enquire about other lands now in the tenure of Thomas Dogett, for which he has not yet made fealty nor paid to the lord for his relief, and to summon the same Thomas towards the next [court] to make fealty to the lord &c.

And to summon William Butte towards the next [court] to make fealty to the lord for lands and tenements which he holds from the lord and to answer to the lord for his relief. And to levy that which is lawful to the lord &c.

[14 recto]

Ekindon: Court [14a] of William Man held there on the 13th day of June in the sixth year of the reign of King Henry the Eighth [13 June 1514].

Essoins: none

Homage:

Thomas Dogett	William Gurney
Thomas Brothers	William Warren
Thomas Austin	John Bunker

["jurors" or "sworn"] who say on their oath that Anne Brokas, widow (appeared), Joan Wadlowe, widow (appeared), Walter Butt (2d) [and] William Andrewe owe suit of court on this day ["of this court and made on this day" [sic] in draft] and have made default. Therefore each of them [is] in mercy of the lord as above written.

Acknowledgement of fealty:

To this court came Thomas Hewat of Stanbridge and acknowledged that he holds freely from the lord by charter 2½ acres of land lying separately in the fields of Ekendon by service, fealty, suit of court and 2d a year, and he made fealty &c.

Also they present that a certain Edmund Wadlowe, who held from the lord one messuage with a croft adjoining and half an acre of land lying at Theedwaie ["Thedway" in draft] next to lands formerly John Hewet's by service [and] 2s 10½d [draft has: "2s 11½d"] a year, and half an acre of land lying below Northwaie and abutting against Rayner's croft by service [and] 1d a year and heriot when it falls due, and reaping ["he reaps" in MS] corn with the lord for one day in harvest with one man with food provided by the lord once in the day, has closed his last day since the last court, after whose death Joan Wadlowe, relict of the said Edmund, came to this court and showed the charter in full court from which it is clear enough that Joan herself should be jointly enfeoffed with the said Edmund for them and their heirs for ever, and on this the aforesaid Joan made fealty and acknowledged that she holds the said messuage and land freely from the lord by the aforesaid service &c.

Affeered by the whole homage.

Egindon: Court Baron [14b] held there in the name of William Man, son and heir of William Man, deceased, held there on the Wednesday next after the feast of Corpus Christi in the twenty-first year of the reign of King Henry VIII &c [2 June 1529].

Essoins: none ["for this" in draft]

Homage:

Thomas Doket	John Wadlowe
William Andrewe	Richard Gurney
William Warren	[all] sworn

The jurors and everyone of them [*"et eorum quemlibet"* in MS; the draft reads "sworn and charged"] say on their oath that John Brokas, Henry Fowler, ["to be found[?]" above Fowler's name in the draft], William Taylor of Sulberie, John Hewat, John Bunker, [in the draft the rest of the sentence seems to be: "[are?] feoffees to uses of the charity of this vill [blank] to the use of the vill for things . . ."; the final version, which does not make sense, given some licence in translating that which is *prima facie* unintelligible, reads: "feoffees to uses of free land now in the tenure of the vill by ["life-"?] rents . . ." ["*virita*"/"*viritant*" in MSS]].

Joan Gurney, widow, [and] Elizabeth Brothers, widow, owe suit at this court and have made default. Therefore they are in mercy.

A day is given that Thomas Doget should show evidence at the next court why he has not paid heriot, after the death of William Morell, & 'lex right' ["*lex regr*" in draft] as appears in the roll of this court held in the time of 'elsper'[?] &c.

And ["likewise" in draft] the chapel warden is distrained for a complaint [about] occupation ["because he has occupied" is the likely meaning of the draft] of certain land and tenements within this lordship &c.

And likewise the heirs of William Gurney and Edmund Wadlowe are distrained for heriots after the death of the said William and Edmund for the same &c.

The bailiff is ordered to seize into the lord's hands one acre of land lying ["upon" then blank, then "late[?] in the tenure[?]" in draft] in a certain furlong [blank] and now in the occupation of William Taylor of Laighton Bussard. Therefore it is ordered &c.

To this court came William Andrewe and acknowledged that he holds freely from the lord 2 acres of land lying at Bidwell furlong extending [this word not in draft] towards one pightle now in the tenure of Thomas Doget ["Doket" in draft], lately purchased of Thomas Austin, lying 'east and west', [for a] rent [of] 4d a year, and he made fealty, rent [draft finishes here and reads: "fealty and . . . two years' rent", possibly "to deliver" (i.e. "he delivers . . . two years' rent") or "to owe" (i.e. "he owes two years' rent")] to the lord, other services &c.

And namely [sic; "likewise" in draft] Richard Gurney came and acknowledged that he holds one acre of land lying in the East Feilde ["rent per annum, 1d" inserted in draft here] lately in the tenure of Thomas Austin. Rent to the lord, 2d a year [draft reads "[and owes?] two years' rent, that is 2d" but the copyist has misread it], and he ["likewise" in draft] made fealty &c.

And namely [sic; "likewise" in draft] he acknowledged that ["he acknowledged that" not in draft] he holds freely two cottages now [sic; "lately" probably intended in draft] in the tenure of his father William Gurney, deceased, and he renders 23d a year and he renders to the lord other 'duties', ["other duties" not in draft; intended meaning of draft is "two years' rent" as a heading in the margin makes clear] and he made fealty &c.

Affeered by the whole homage.

Egyndon: Court Baron [14c] held there on the Wednesday next after the feast of St Peter [draft has "ad vincula" here] in the 23rd year of the reign of King Henry VIII &c [2 August 1531].

Essoins: none.

Homagers ["the homage there, that is" in draft]

Thomas Doget	William Andrewe
John Wadlowe	William Warren
Richard Gurney	[all "sworn" in draft]

["jurors" or "sworn"; draft reads "sworn and charged"] who say on their oath that ["the heir of[?]" or "Henry [blank]" in draft] John Brokas (4d), Henry Fowler (4d), William Taylor of Sulberie (2d), John Bunker (2d), Joan Gurney, widow, [and] Elizabeth Brothers owe suit of court ["to this court" in draft] on this day ["on this day" not in draft] and have made default. Therefore they are distrained [not in draft].

Affeered by the whole homage.

[15 recto]

Ekendon: Court Baron [15] of John Man held there on the 28th day of March in the second year of the reign of lady Elizabeth, by the grace of God Queen of England, France and Ireland, defender of the faith &c [28 March 1560].

Homage:

Richard Gurney
Richard Andrewe senior
Richard Andrewe junior [each "sworn" according to draft]

["jurors" or "sworn"] who say on their oath that Bernard Brocas, esquire (essoin), [and] Andrew Corbet, knight, made default &c. [No verb in draft but note in margin: "default".]

To this court came Richard Andrewe senior and acknowledged that he holds from the lord freely by charter two acres of land, formerly Thomas Austin's, lying together on Bidwell furlong, between the aforesaid Richard's land on the north side and land formerly Walter Butte's and now the same Richard's on the south side [draft has, struck through, here: "and an half acre of which lies upon Middelfurlong in le E[a]st feylde"], by rent [of] 4d a year, after the death of his father William Andrewe. And also he acknowledged that he holds from the lord freely by charter one acre of land lying at Westmillwaie by rent [of] 2d a year, lately William Andrewe's, father of the aforesaid Richard, whence there falls due to the lord by relief, 6d; he made fealty and was then admitted [as] tenant &c.

To this court came John Andrewe and acknowledged that he holds from the lord freely by charter one half acre of land lying at West lane ende abutting on Northwaie by rent [of] 1d a year, after the death of his grandfather Edmund Andrewe, whence there falls due to the lord by relief, 1d; and he made fealty and was then admitted [as] tenant &c.

To this court came Richard Andrewe junior and acknowledged that he holds freely from the lord by charter one half acre lying in Clipston feilde at Wates Willowe, that is between the land of William Johnson, gentleman, on either side, by rent [of] 1d a year, after the death of his father Edmund Warren, [interpolation: "lately purchased from William Warren"], whence there falls due to the lord by relief, 1d; and he made fealty and was then admitted [as] tenant &c.

The jurors present that William Jeffs, who held freely from the lord by charter two messuages with appurtenances, lately William Gurney's, by rent for one messuage, 6d, and for the other messuage, 17d a year, suit of court every three weeks, and heriot when it fell due and [reaping; "he reaps" in MS] with the lord for one day in harvest with one man with food provided by the lord once in the day, and other services ["and other services in respect thereof" is struck through in draft], closed his last day after the last court; and that Robert Jeffs is his son and next heir and nine years of age and more, whence there falls due to the lord for relief, 23d, and [because] the same Robert [is] under age, they therefore commit him to the custody of Joan Perrot, mother of the aforesaid Robert, until &c, and fealty is postponed &c.

A day is given to Bernard Brokas, esquire, and William Johnson, gentleman, until the next court to show ["their" in draft] evidence, and further to do then [and] there according to custom &c ["there as the court gives judgement" in draft].

To this court came Thomas Coke and acknowledged that he holds from the lord freely by charter one half acre and one rood of land of which the aforesaid half acre of land lies ["in" in draft; omitted in final version] le Overpende and the aforesaid rood of land lies ["at" in draft; omitted in final version] le Thrup next the lord's land on the south ["side" in draft; omitted in final version] by rent [of] 1½d a year, whence there falls due to the lord by relief, 1½d; and he made fealty and was then admitted [as] tenant &c.

Also they present that William Dogget, who held freely from the lord by charter one messuage with a croft adjoining situated in Ekendon and four [draft has here: "four and a half"] acres of land with appurtenances by rent [of] 4s 8d a year, suit of court every three weeks and heriot when it fell due and reaping ["he reaps" in MS] with the lord for one day in harvest with one man with food provided by the lord once in the day, and other service, closed his last day after the last court, whence heriot falls due to the lord [Note attached to margin here: *"nota bene"*]; and that Thomas Doget is his son and next heir, and twelve years of age and more, whence there falls due to the lord by relief, 4s 8d, and because the same ["Thomas" in draft; omitted in final version] is under age, therefore the custody of the land is committed to Sybil Doget, widow, mother of the aforesaid Thomas, until &c, and fealty is postponed &c.

It is ordered to distrain the custodian of the land of the vill of Ekendon to be at the next court and to show how he has entered into the fee of the lord.

It is ordered to distrain Andrew Corbet, knight, the heir of Walter Butt, the heir [blank] Bunker, and the heir of John Steevens &c.

Affeerors: none

[16 recto]

Manor of Ekendon: Court Baron [16] of John Man held there on the 19th day of April in the fourteenth year of the reign of Queen Elizabeth [19 April 1572].

Essoins: none.

Homage:

Richard Gurney	Richard Andrew senior	Robert Jeffes
Thomas Doget	John Andrewe	

["jurors" or "sworn"] [who] say on their oath that Andrew Corbet, knight, [and] Bernard Brokas, esquire (essoin), [are] custodians of the land of the vill and the chapel there &c. [the draft version gives the names of four more jurors, with reasons for their absence: "Ralph Shep'd (essoin), Richard Andrewe, who was senior, is dead, Thomas Coke is dead [and] Stephen Gurney (essoin)"].

At this court they ["the jurors" in the draft] present that Richard Andrewe senior who held freely from the lord by charter two acres of land, formerly Thomas Austin's, lying together [on] Bidwell furlong between ["the same" here in draft] Richard's land on the north side and land of the same Richard, formerly Walter Butte's, on the south side, abutting towards the east on land of the same Richard on le Sharpe and towards the west [on] Thomas Dogget's land called 'a pightle', by rent [of] 4d a year; and also held freely one acre of land lying together at West Millwaie between land [blank] on the north side and land [blank] on the south side, and abutting east on Millwaie ["le Mylwaye" in draft] and ["towards the" here in draft] west on a headland of land of William Brokas, from the lord by rent [of] 2d a year; [that he] died after the last court seised thereof and that Richard Andrewe junior is his son and next heir and of full age, that is thirty years, whence there falls due to the lord [for] relief, 6d [draft has note in margin, "relief paid to the lord, 7d"]; and he made fealty and was then admitted [as] tenant &c. [Interpolated in a later hand: "And also he holds one headland of land at le Sharpe next Dagnalls Peece, lately John Snowe's, [and] formerly Walter Butte's, by rent [of] 1d a year".] [Draft includes, after "Walter Butte", the words "and formerly Henry Fowler's".]

Also they present that Thomas Coke junior ["junior" is not in the draft version, and may have been a mis-reading] who held freely from the lord by charter one half acre and one rood of land, of which the aforesaid half acre of land lies in the piece of land called le Pende furlong, alias [blank] furlong, between land [blank] on the side [blank] and land [blank] on the side [blank] abutting towards [blank] on land [blank], and the aforesaid rood of land lies at le Throp between the lord's free land on the east side and land of the same lord, which he held by copy, on the west side, and abutting towards the south on a headland of John Andrewe's, by rent [of] 1½d a year; [that he] died after the last court, seised thereof and that Thomas Cooke is his son and next heir, and thirty years of age and more, whence there falls due to the lord by relief, 1½d; and he made fealty and was then admitted [as] tenant &c.

Also they present that William Andrewe junior ["junior" is not in the draft version, and may have been a mis-reading of *"qui"*] who held freely from the lord by charter five acres and a rood of land with appurtenances, lately Bunker's and formerly Henry Hutte's, by rent [of] 10½d a year, and also held freely one messuage with a croft adjoining with its appurtenances, and one half acre of land lying at Theedewaie alias Edewaie ["Thedeway als. Edewaye" in draft], next to land lately John Hewet's, by rent [of] 2s 11½d a year and one boonwork in harvest by [sic; meaning "with"] a man for one day, and heriot; and also held freely from the lord by charter half an acre of land lying below Northwaie and abutting next Reinars Croft alias [blank] and lying next land lately John Huet junior's by rent [of] 1d a year; [that he] closed his last day after the last court and that Thomas Andrewe is his son and next heir and twenty-six years of age, whence there falls due to the lord for relief, 3s 11d and [nothing] for heriot in this life because it was remitted; and he made fealty and was then admitted [as] tenant. [Note: the word "nothing" appears in the draft version but not in the final version apparently because an abbreviated *"nihil"* had been read as *"in"*.]

It is ordered to distrain Ralph Shephard and Stephen Gurney to be at the next court and to show how the same Ralph entered into the fee of the lord, that is in various lands called Hewates and [sic] late Wiardrawers ["Wyardrawers" struck through in draft], and how the aforesaid Stephen entered into the fee of the lord, that is in various lands formerly Henry Hutte's; to be at the next court and to pay relief ["rent" struck through in draft here] and make fealty, and to do further as the court there gives judgement.

Affeerors: none

Minor endorsements on the membranes

The following are transcriptions or translations of various notes made on the back of some of the membranes. Many of the membranes have several such notes made at different times, and these have been separated by starting each entry on a new line. When any correction is indicated in the list below, this has always been made in a different hand and presumably at a later date. These endorsements may provide some clue as to the collation of these documents by previous custodians; note, for instance, the references to named individuals in 13 and 14, and to 'my grandfather' in 15.

1 [none]
2 [none]
3 Olde Roles
4 [none]
5 Court Roles. Rent due at Michaelmas for Edward the first & Edward the second
6 [struck out: "Court roles in Edward the third, also Henry the fifth"]
Roles in Edward the 1, 2, & 3
Court Roles in Edward the first, second, and third
7 Olde deedes & Dogets land Terars [terriers]
Richard the Second
Edward the first
8 Henry the 5th & Edw' the 3rd 2 courts
9 7 courts in Henry sixth mencioning terra de villa
Ekyndon
Ekyndon
Total rent overleaf 16s 8d and working days overleaf 7½
10 These are the names of tenants and suitors of court: John Hewet, John Wadlowe, John Fowler, John Childe, John Morell, John Agas, John Blake, John Hunte, Ralph Brystwyk, John Mounte, Thomas London, William

Sandrus, John Doget, William Caron, John Dennyng, Thomas Est, Joan Agas.
11 [none]
12 Roles Henrie 8
and queene Elizabeth not Ingrossed
not much material
13 [struck through: "3"] Roles in Henry 7th the 6th & . . . & the 5th
Roles: about Wells and Dogets lands
Court Roles for 3 courts in Henry Seventh but do not mencion terra de villa
14 3 roles in Henrie the 8th of the amerciaments of Anne Brockas & John Brokas
15 3 roles of my grandfather in Queen Elizabeth's raign Elizabeth 2 to 28th: 3 roles
16 [struck through; "three"; replaced by "two"] roles for John Man in Elizabeth 2 and 14th

There are also two endorsements on the draft version X310/3 (of court 14a) which read:

3 court roles of Wm Man in Henry the eight
Ekundon

Alphabetical Index to place-names in the text

Hekendon – see Eggington.
Herdingtone (1314).
Heyedunstall (1433).
Heyelynchehoke (1433).
Heyetanstale (1377); Helyeturnstale (1377).
Hoghand[waie] (1428).
Hokeleyfelde (1506).
Honyfurlong (1428 and 1433).

Kyllyng well (1428).

Lecke (1428); Lekke (1433).
Leckefurlong (1433).
[Leighton Buzzard] Layghton (1413); Leighton (1428); Leyghton (1425, 1433 and 1435); and Laighton Bussard (1529).
Lynes [tenement] (1433).

Middelfurlong(e) (1506 and 1560).
[Mill Way] Millwaie (1572; le Mullewey (1377); Mylwaye (1572).
Morell [messuage and land] (1413).

[North Way] Northwaie (1514, 1560 and 1572); North[way] (1377); (le) North(e)wey (1377, 1433 and 1506).

le Over(e)pende (1377, 1433 and 1560).
le Overfurlonge (1506).
Overthebrowe (1428).

le Pende [furlong] (1425, 1428 and 1572).
[Potsgrove] Potsgrave (1501); Pottesgrove (1506).

Radeneth(e) (1298 and wurt 3f).
Rayner's Croft (1514); Reyner's Croft (1433 and 1506); Reinar's Croft (1572).
Regwey(e) (1428).

Salterius welle (1428); Salteryswell (1433).
le S(c)harp(e) (1428, 1501 and 1572).
Sheldon [field(s)] (1370, 1377 and 1413).
Smalwey(e) (1428 and 1433).
Stanbridge (1514); Stanbrig (1413); Stanebrigge mede (1506); Stan(e)brug(ge) (1370, 1413 and 1506); Stanbryg(g)(e) [feld/meadow] (1413, 1428 and 1433).
[Stone Way] Stonewey (1433); Stonywey(e) (1428).
Ston(y)hyll (1428 and 1433).
Streetlies [messuage] (1413); Streteleyes (1413); Stretleys (1425).
Sulberie (1529 and 1531).

Tanner(e)s [tuft] (1413 and 1425).
Thedewey – see Ede Way.
[Thorp] le [and "the"] Thorpe (1428); (le) Thrup (1425, 1433 and 1572); le Thrup (1560); Thruppe Hill (1500).
[Tilsworth] Tillesworth (1370); Tulesworpe (1305 and 1308).
Tonne (1314).

Urgendon – see Eggington.

Villamnmede (1334).

Wates willowe (1560).
Wattes wyllys (1506).
le Wer'dyge (1428).
Weredych (1433.
Westlane (End(e) (1433, 1506 and 1560).
Westmillware (1560 and 1572); (le) Westmyllewey(e) (1428 and 1506).
Wiardrawers/Wyardrawers [lords] (1572).
Wofurlong (1428).

INDEX OF PERSONAL NAMES

The published HUNDRED ROLLS are fully indexed, and therefore select names only are included here.

INDEX OF PLACES